THE INCREDIBLE HULKS

HEART OF THE MONSTER

WRITER: GREG PAK

PENCILS: PAUL PELLETIER

INKS: DANNY MIKI

COLORS: MORRY HOLLOWELL
WITH JESUS ABURTOV (ISSUES #631-632 & 634)

HULK OUT

PENCILS: TOM GRUMMETT

INKS: CORY HAMSCHER & SCOTT HANNA

COLORS: JESUS ABURTOV

LETTERS: SIMON BOWLAND

COVER ARTISTS: PAUL PELLETIER & DANNY MIKI
WITH CHRIS SOTOMAYOR (ISSUES #630), JIM CHARALAMPIDIS (ISSUES #631-634)
& VAL STAPLES (ISSUE #635)

ASSISTANT EDITOR: JAKE THOMAS • EDITOR: MARK PANICCIA

SPECIAL THANKS TO ALLEN MARTINEZ & CRIMELAB SYNDICATE

COLLECTION EDITOR: CORY LEVINE • EDITORIAL ASSISTANTS: JAMES EMMETT & JOE HOCHSTEIN
ASSISTANT EDITORS: ALEX STARBUCK & NELSON RIBEIRO
EDITORS, SPECIAL PROJECTS: JENNIFER GRÜNWALD & MARK D. BEAZLEY
SENIOR EDITOR, SPECIAL PROJECTS: JEFF YOUNGQUIST • SENIOR VICE PRESIDENT OF SALES: DAVID GABRIEL
SVP OF BRAND PLANNING & COMMUNICATIONS: MICHAEL PASCIULLO

EDITOR IN CHIEF: AXEL ALONSO • CHIEF CREATIVE OFFICER: JOE QUESADA
PUBLISHER: DAN BUCKLEY • EXECUTIVE PRODUCER: ALAN FINE

INCREDIBLE HULKS: HEART OF THE MONSTER. Contains material originally published in magazine form as INCREDIBLE HULKS #630-635. First printing 2011. ISBN# 978-0-7851-5631-4. Published by MARVEL WORLDWIDE, INC., a subsidiary of MARVEL ENTERTAINMENT, LLC. OFFICE OF PUBLICATION: 135 West 50th Street, New York, NY 10020. **Printed in the U.S.A.** ALAN FINE, EVP - Office of the President, Marvel Worldwide, Inc. and EVP & CMO Marvel Characters B.V.; DAN BUCKLEY, Publisher & President - Print, Animation & Digital Divisions; JOE QUESADA, Chief Creative Officer; JIM SOKOLOWSKI, Chief Operating Officer; DAVID BOGART, SVP of Business Affairs & Talent Management; TOM BREVOORT, SVP of Publishing; C.B. CEBULSKI, SVP of Creator & Content Development; DAVID GABRIEL, SVP of Publishing Sales & Circulation; MICHAEL PASCIULLO, SVP of Brand Planning & Communications; JIM O'KEEFE, VP of Operations & Logistics; DAN CARR, Executive Director of Publishing Technology; SUSAN CRESPI, Editorial Operations Manager; ALEX MORALES, Publishing Operations Manager; STAN LEE, Chairman Emeritus. For information regarding advertising in Marvel Comics or on Marvel.com, please contact John Dokes, SVP Integrated Sales and Marketing, at jdokes@marvel.com. For Marvel subscription inquiries, please call 800-217-9158. **Manufactured between 10/6/2011 and 10/25/2011 by QUAD/GRAPHICS, DUBUQUE, IA, USA.**

10 9 8 7 6 5 4 3 2 1

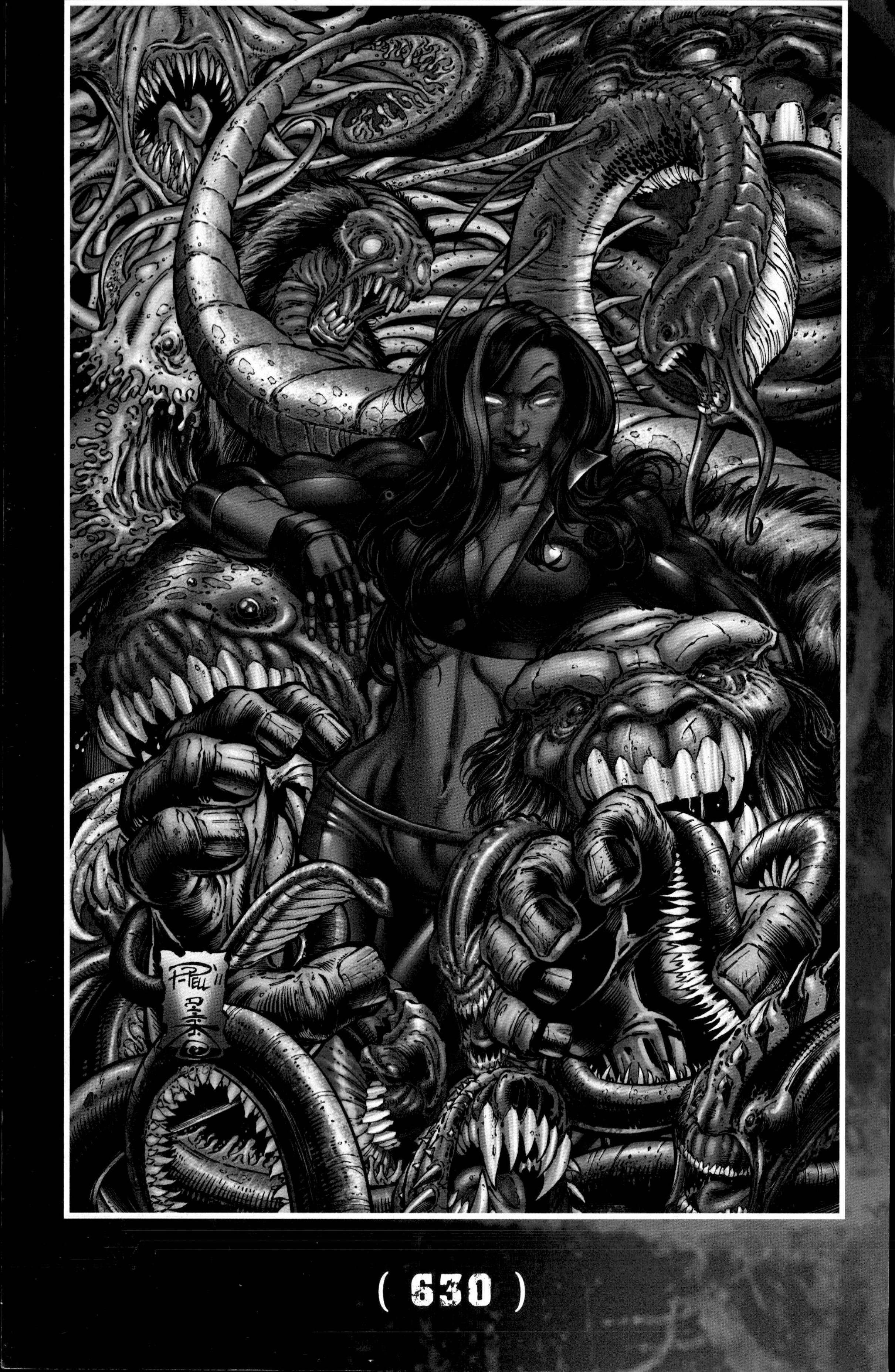

(630)

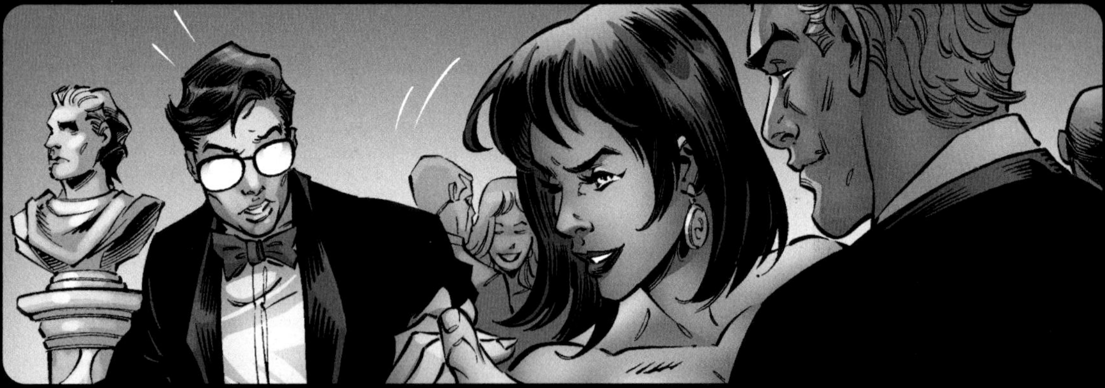

Bruce Banner [a.k.a **THE HULK**] was trying to rekindle the romance with his ex-wife Betty [a.k.a. **RED SHE-HULK**], but Betty, feeling boxed in and unsure, ran into the arms of Banner's nemesis, Tyrannus.

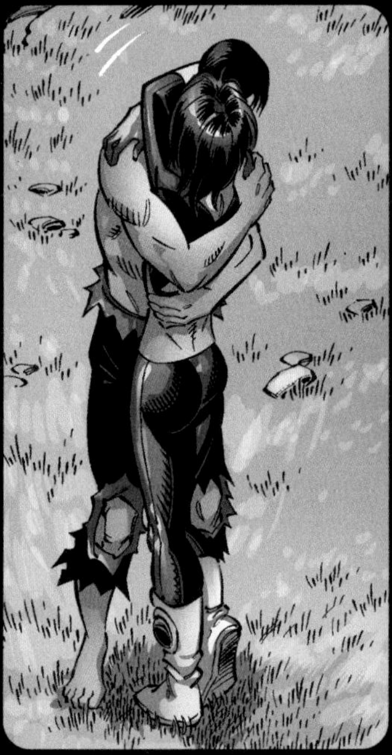

The two briefly came together while fighting the power-mad villain...

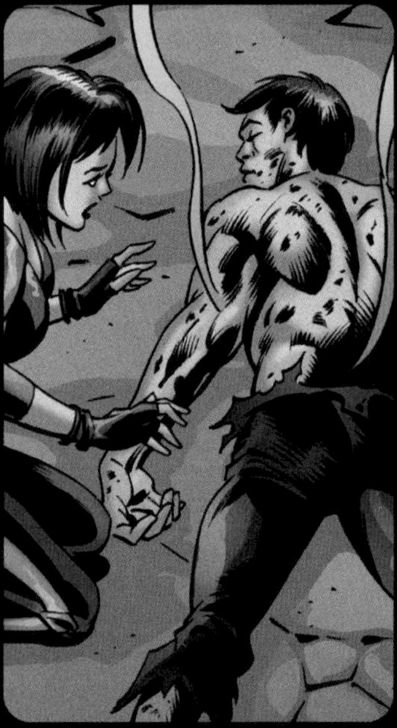

But after watching Bruce be beaten to within an inch of his life yet again, Betty decided she couldn't keep on like this...

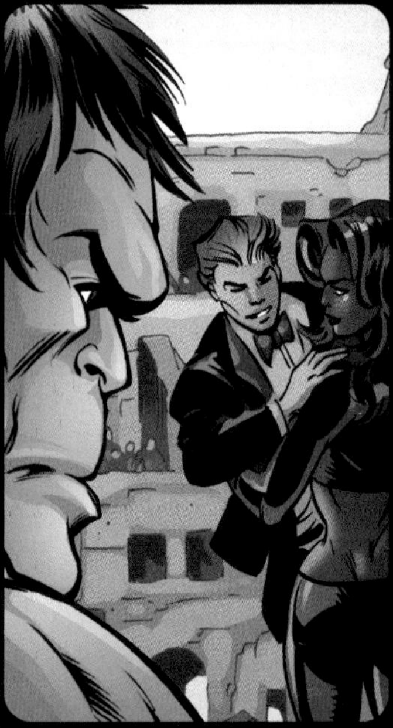

And gave herself over entirely to the brash, impulsive Red She-Hulk, who then ran off with Tyrannus.

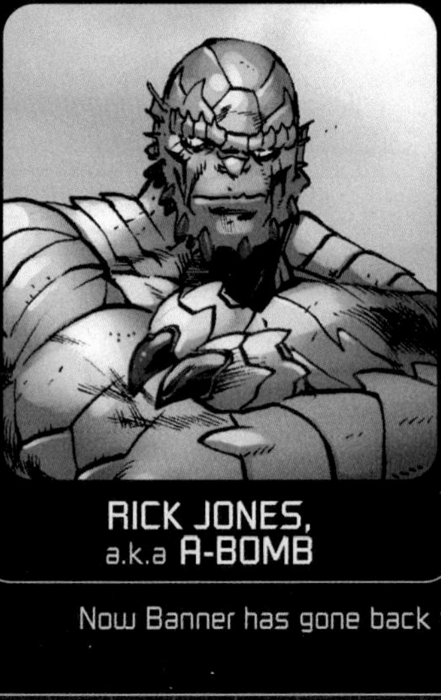

RICK JONES,
a.k.a **A-BOMB**

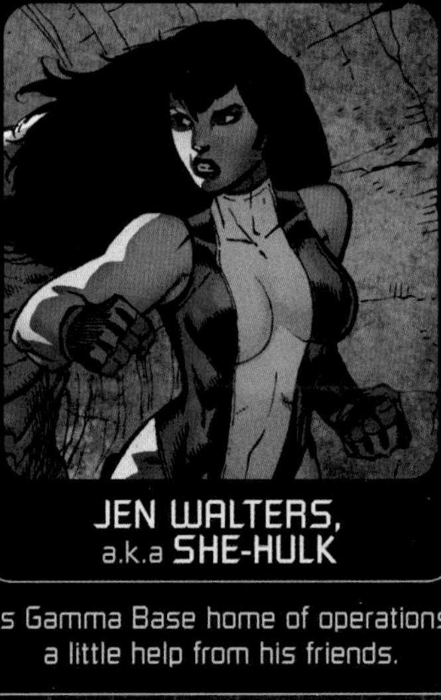

JEN WALTERS,
a.k.a **SHE-HULK**

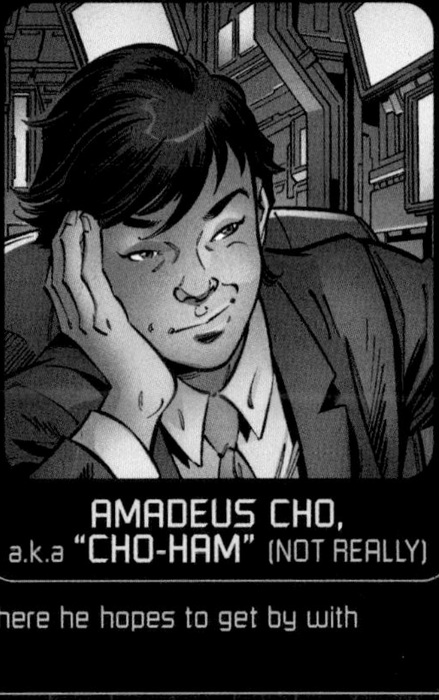

AMADEUS CHO,
a.k.a **"CHO-HAM"** (NOT REALLY)

Now Banner has gone back to his Gamma Base home of operations, where he hopes to get by with a little help from his friends.

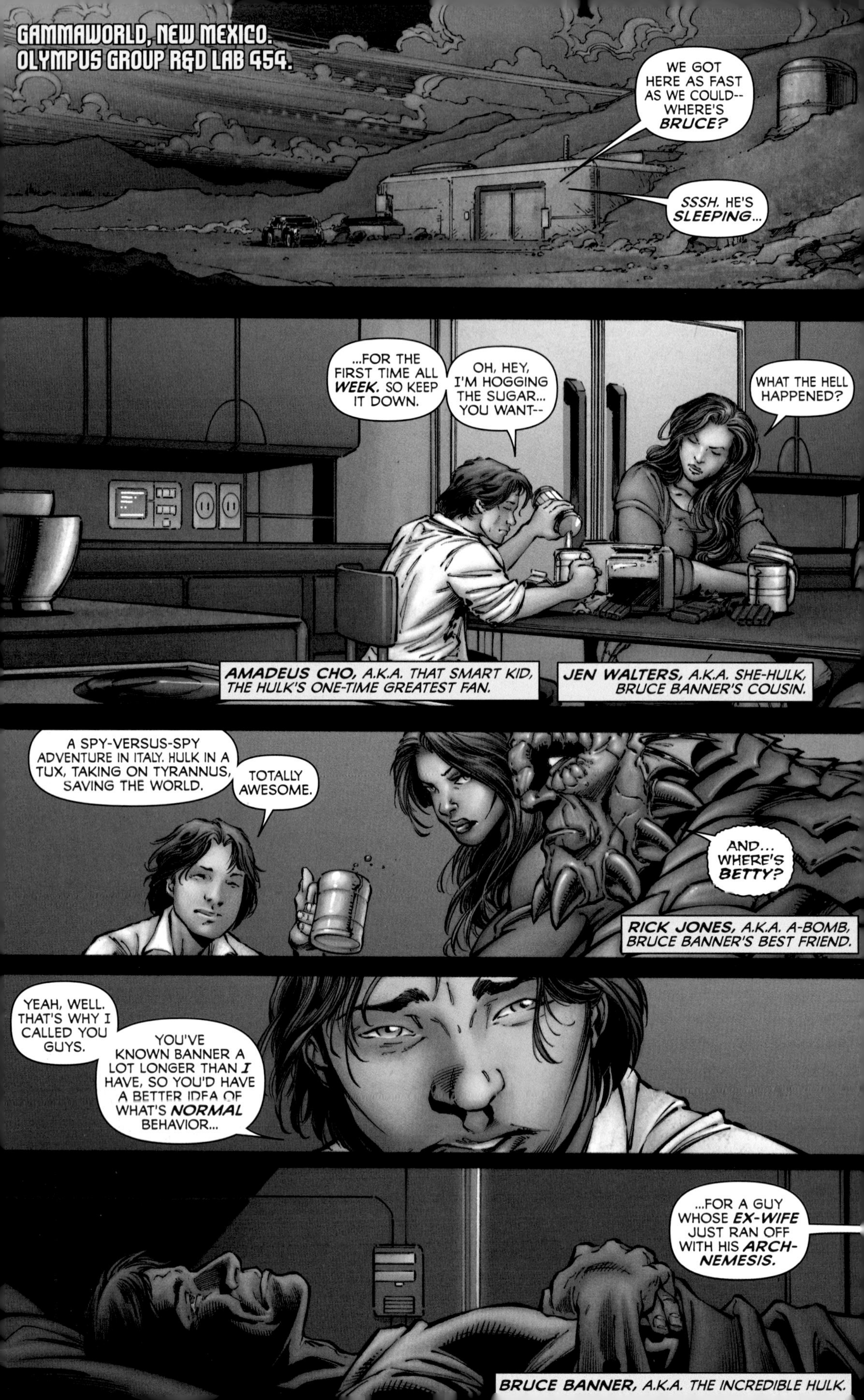
GAMMAWORLD, NEW MEXICO.
OLYMPUS GROUP R&D LAB 454.
WE GOT HERE AS FAST AS WE COULD-- WHERE'S BRUCE?
SSSH. HE'S SLEEPING...
...FOR THE FIRST TIME ALL WEEK. SO KEEP IT DOWN.
OH, HEY, I'M HOGGING THE SUGAR... YOU WANT--
WHAT THE HELL HAPPENED?
AMADEUS CHO, A.K.A. THAT SMART KID, THE HULK'S ONE-TIME GREATEST FAN.
JEN WALTERS, A.K.A. SHE-HULK, BRUCE BANNER'S COUSIN.
A SPY-VERSUS-SPY ADVENTURE IN ITALY. HULK IN A TUX, TAKING ON TYRANNUS, SAVING THE WORLD.
TOTALLY AWESOME.
AND... WHERE'S BETTY?
RICK JONES, A.K.A. A-BOMB, BRUCE BANNER'S BEST FRIEND.
YEAH, WELL. THAT'S WHY I CALLED YOU GUYS.
YOU'VE KNOWN BANNER A LOT LONGER THAN I HAVE, SO YOU'D HAVE A BETTER IDEA OF WHAT'S NORMAL BEHAVIOR...
...FOR A GUY WHOSE EX-WIFE JUST RAN OFF WITH HIS ARCH-NEMESIS.
BRUCE BANNER, A.K.A. THE INCREDIBLE HULK.

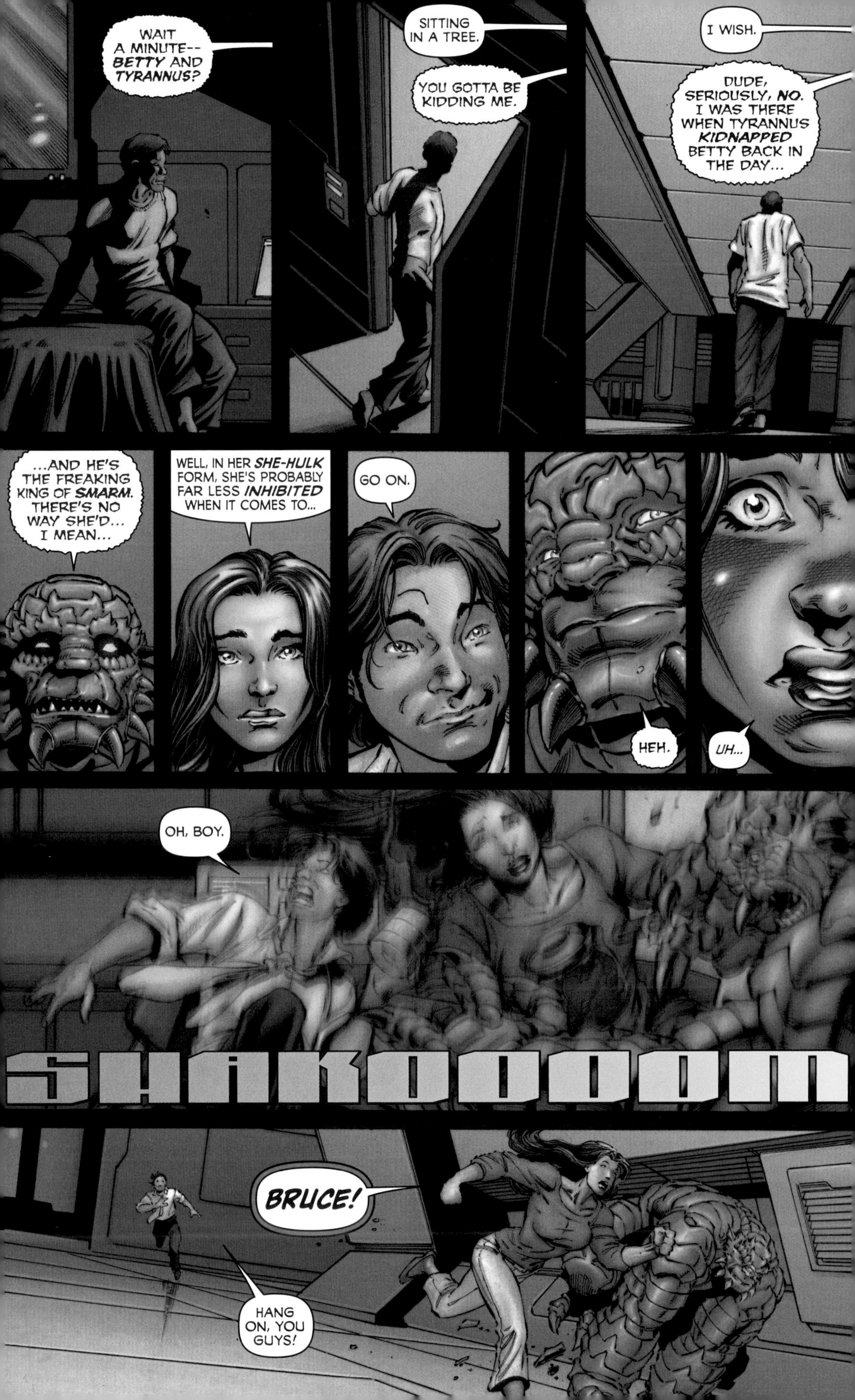
WAIT A MINUTE-- BETTY AND TYRANNUS?
SITTING IN A TREE.
YOU GOTTA BE KIDDING ME.
I WISH.
DUDE, SERIOUSLY, NO. I WAS THERE WHEN TYRANNUS KIDNAPPED BETTY BACK IN THE DAY...
...AND HE'S THE FREAKING KING OF SMARM. THERE'S NO WAY SHE'D... I MEAN...
WELL, IN HER SHE-HULK FORM, SHE'S PROBABLY FAR LESS INHIBITED WHEN IT COMES TO...
GO ON.
HEH.
UH...
OH, BOY.
SHAKOOOOM
BRUCE!
HANG ON, YOU GUYS!

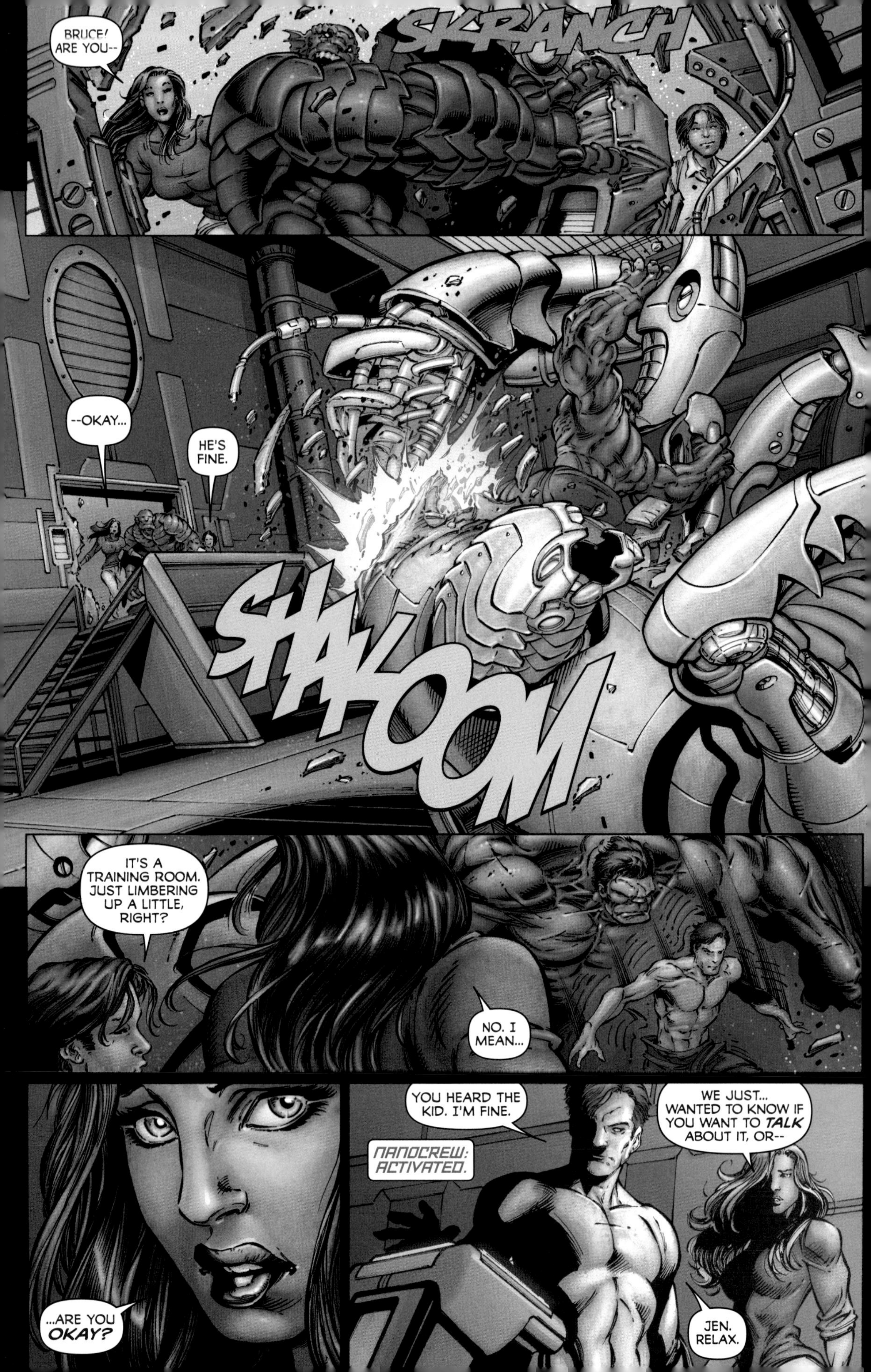
BRUCE! ARE YOU--
SKRANCH
--OKAY...
HE'S FINE.
SHAKOOM
IT'S A TRAINING ROOM. JUST LIMBERING UP A LITTLE, RIGHT?
NO. I MEAN...
...ARE YOU OKAY?
YOU HEARD THE KID. I'M FINE.
NANOCREW: ACTIVATED.
WE JUST... WANTED TO KNOW IF YOU WANT TO TALK ABOUT IT, OR--
JEN. RELAX.

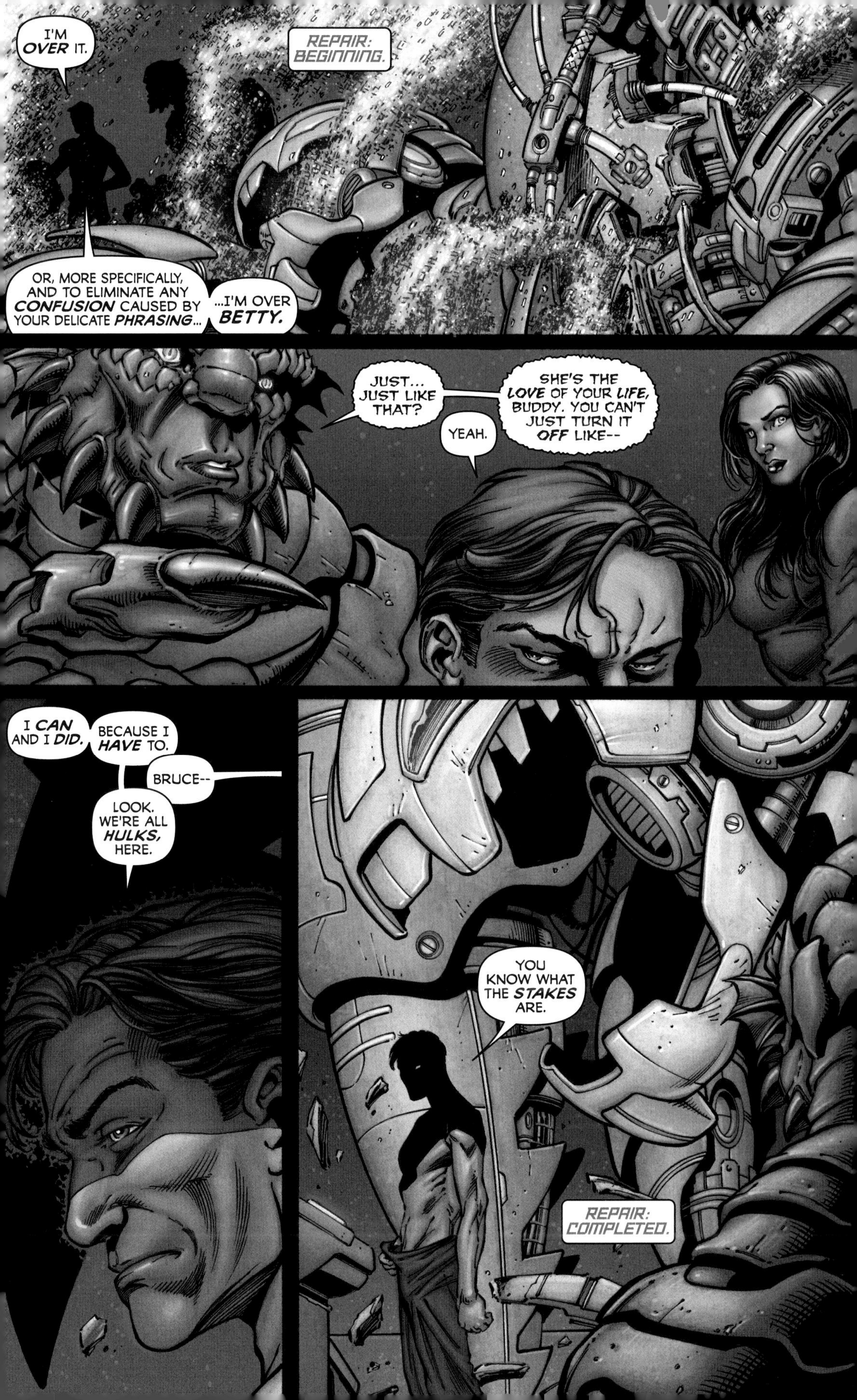
I'M OVER IT.
REPAIR: BEGINNING.
OR, MORE SPECIFICALLY, AND TO ELIMINATE ANY CONFUSION CAUSED BY YOUR DELICATE PHRASING...
...I'M OVER BETTY.
JUST... JUST LIKE THAT?
SHE'S THE LOVE OF YOUR LIFE, BUDDY. YOU CAN'T JUST TURN IT OFF LIKE--
YEAH.
I CAN AND I DID.
BECAUSE I HAVE TO.
BRUCE--
LOOK. WE'RE ALL HULKS, HERE.
YOU KNOW WHAT THE STAKES ARE.
REPAIR: COMPLETED.

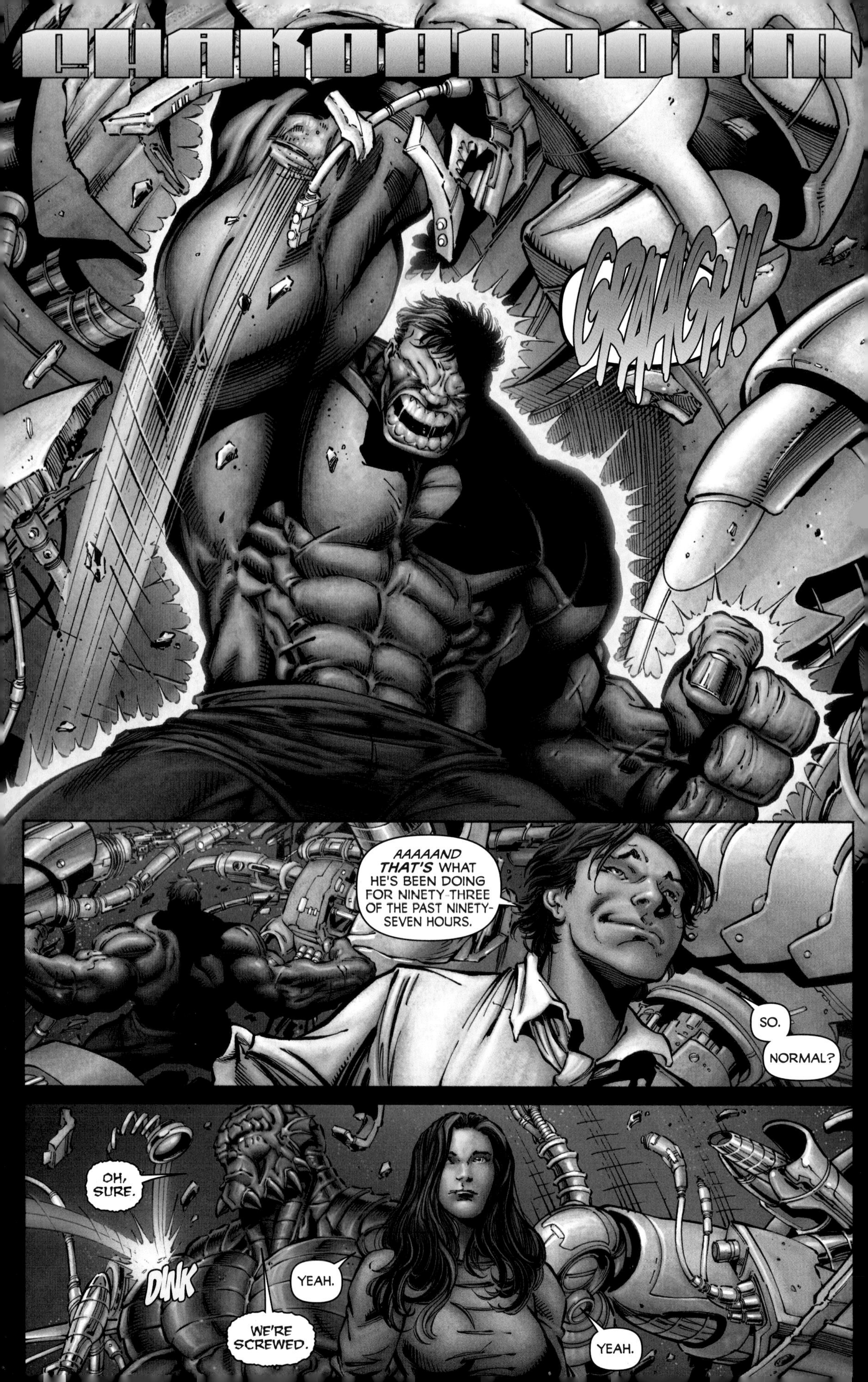
CHAKOOOOOOOM
GRAAGH!!
AAAAAND THAT'S WHAT HE'S BEEN DOING FOR NINETY-THREE OF THE PAST NINETY-SEVEN HOURS.
SO.
NORMAL?
OH, SURE.
DINK
YEAH.
WE'RE SCREWED.
YEAH.

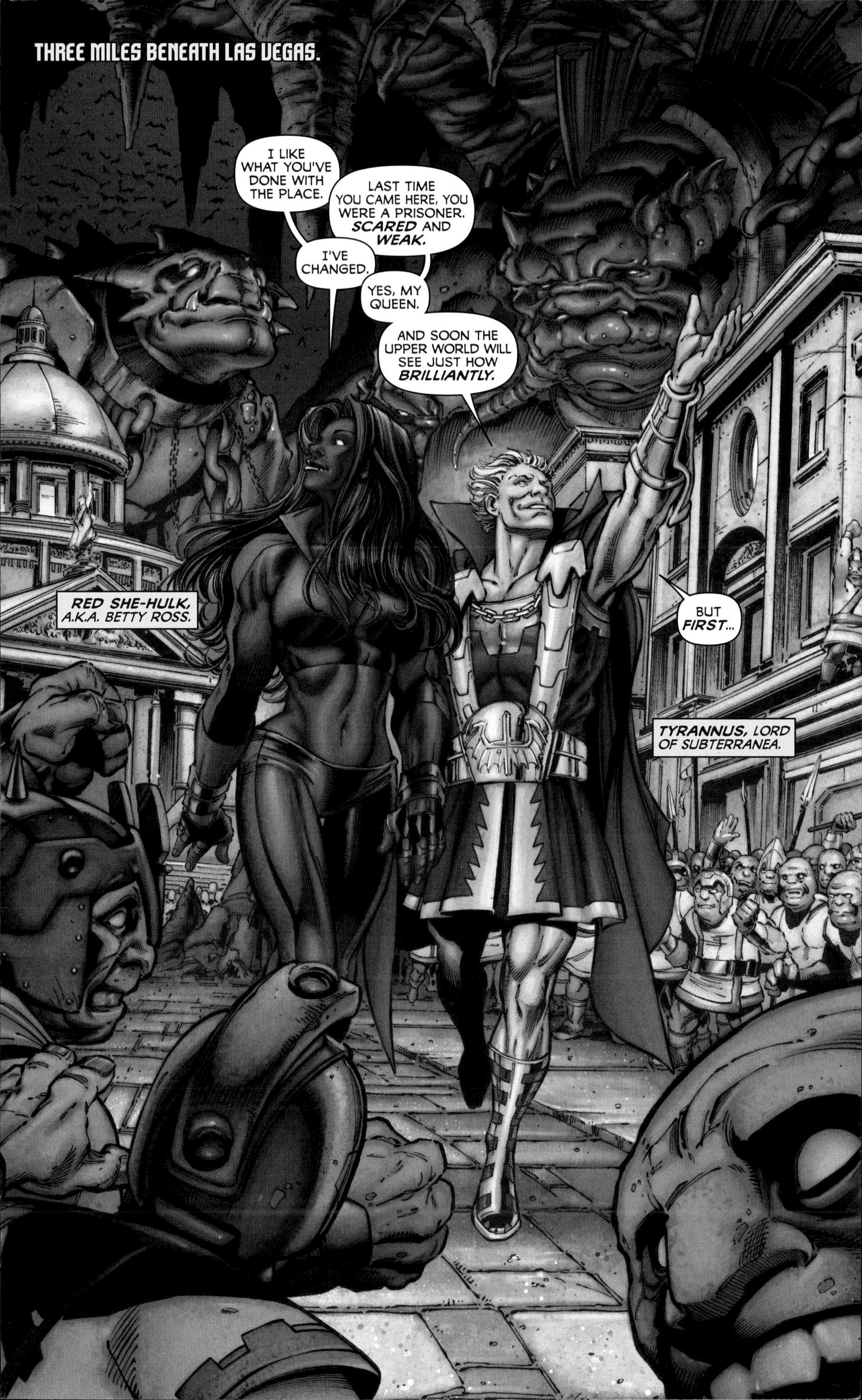
THREE MILES BENEATH LAS VEGAS.
I LIKE WHAT YOU'VE DONE WITH THE PLACE.
LAST TIME YOU CAME HERE, YOU WERE A PRISONER. SCARED AND WEAK.
I'VE CHANGED.
YES, MY QUEEN.
AND SOON THE UPPER WORLD WILL SEE JUST HOW BRILLIANTLY.
RED SHE-HULK, A.K.A. BETTY ROSS.
BUT FIRST...
TYRANNUS, LORD OF SUBTERRANEA.

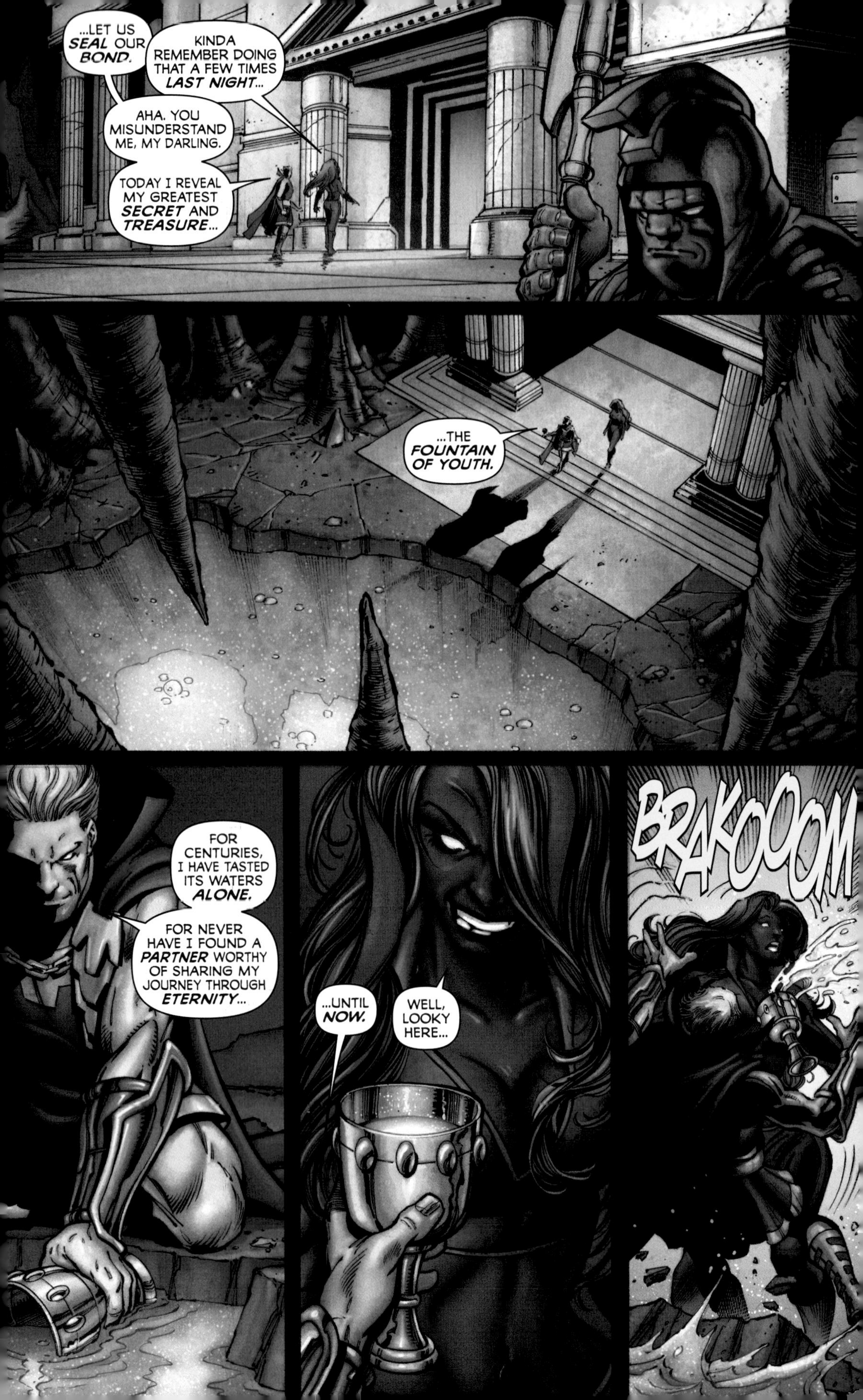
...LET US SEAL OUR BOND.
KINDA REMEMBER DOING THAT A FEW TIMES LAST NIGHT...
AHA. YOU MISUNDERSTAND ME, MY DARLING.
TODAY I REVEAL MY GREATEST SECRET AND TREASURE...
...THE FOUNTAIN OF YOUTH.
FOR CENTURIES, I HAVE TASTED ITS WATERS ALONE.
FOR NEVER HAVE I FOUND A PARTNER WORTHY OF SHARING MY JOURNEY THROUGH ETERNITY...
...UNTIL NOW.
WELL, LOOKY HERE...
BRAKOOOM

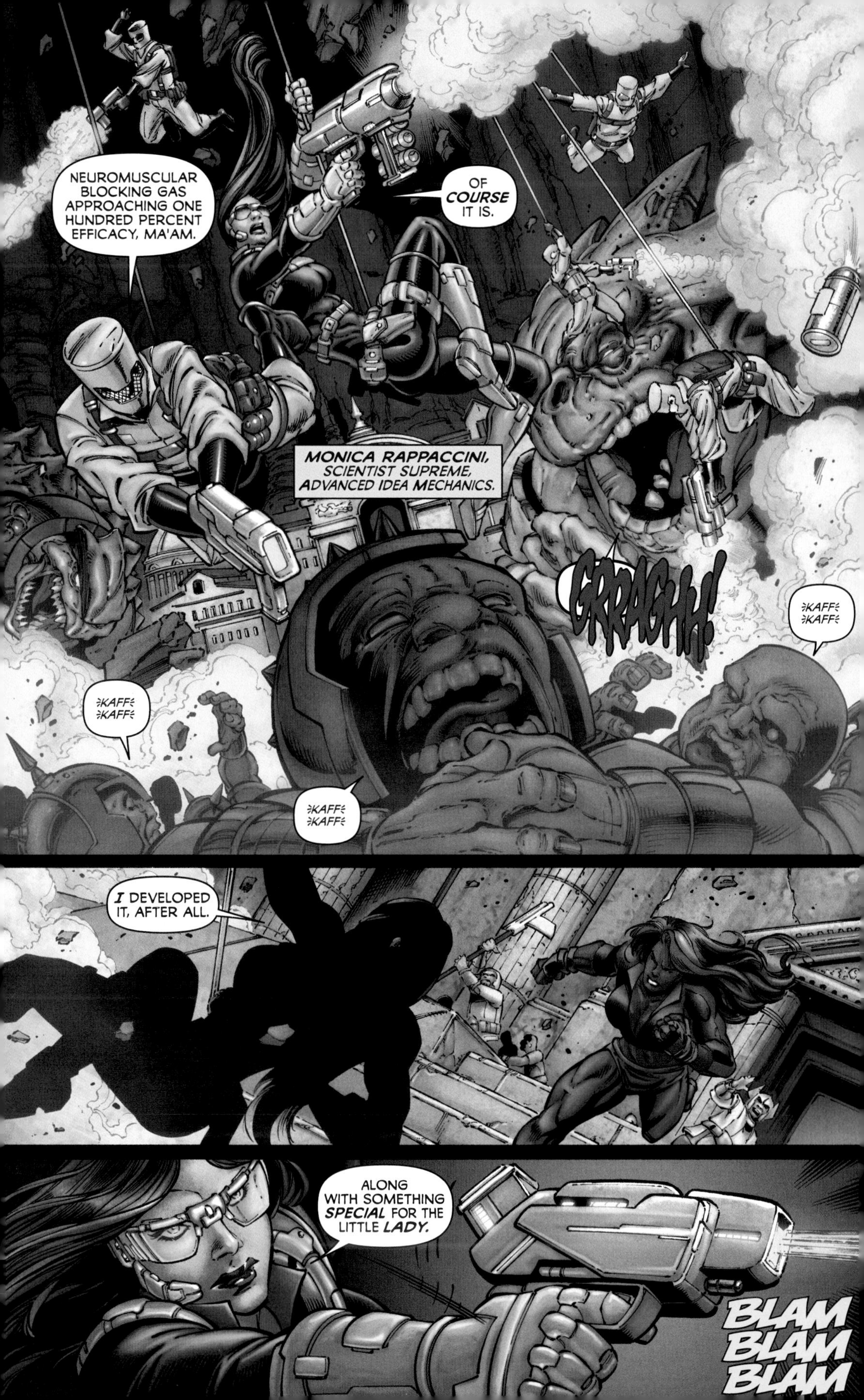
NEUROMUSCULAR BLOCKING GAS APPROACHING ONE HUNDRED PERCENT EFFICACY, MA'AM.
OF COURSE IT IS.
MONICA RAPPACCINI, SCIENTIST SUPREME, ADVANCED IDEA MECHANICS.
GRRAGHH!
KAFF KAFF
KAFF KAFF
KAFF KAFF
I DEVELOPED IT, AFTER ALL.
ALONG WITH SOMETHING SPECIAL FOR THE LITTLE LADY.
BLAM BLAM BLAM

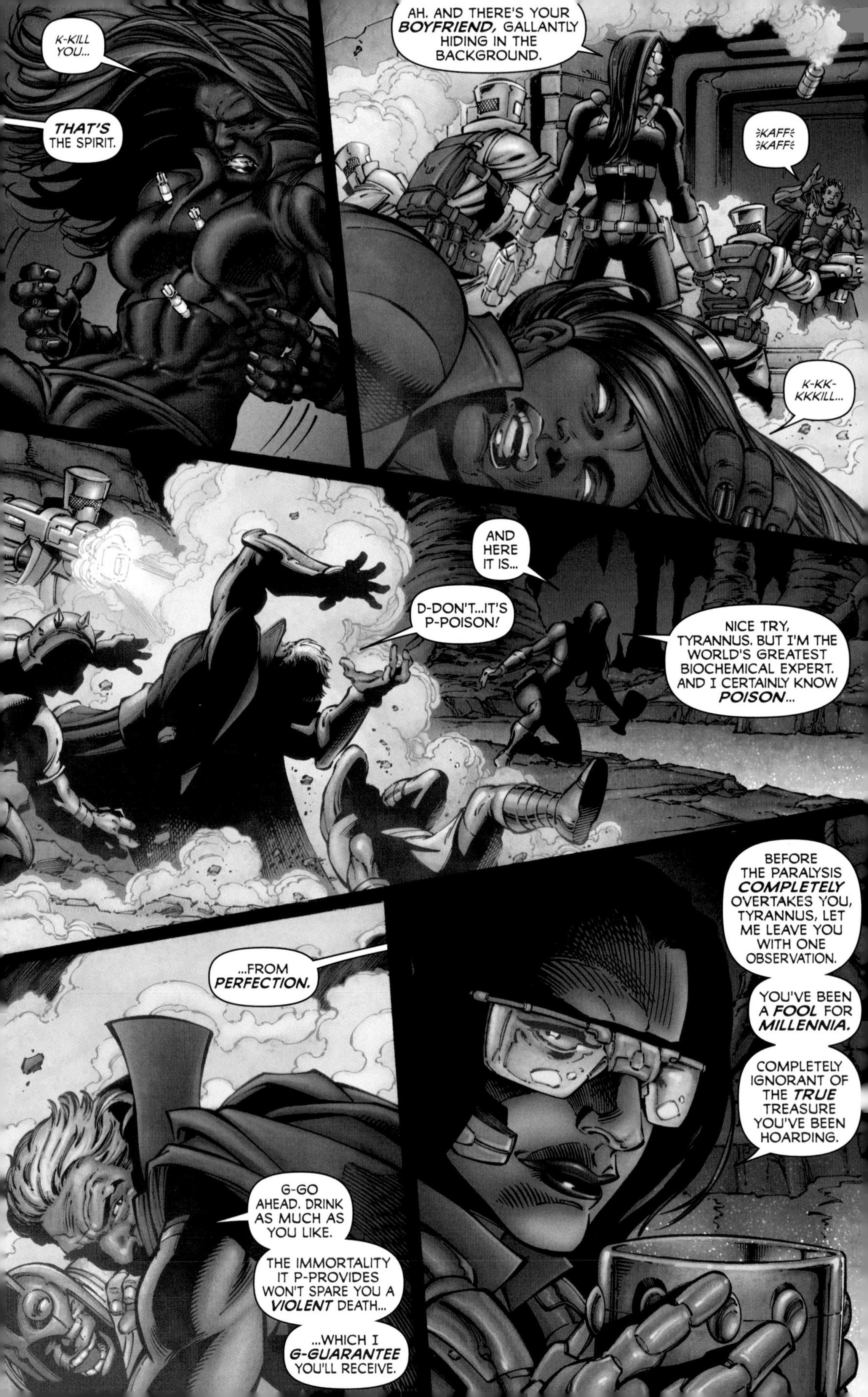
K-KILL YOU...
THAT'S THE SPIRIT.
AH. AND THERE'S YOUR BOYFRIEND, GALLANTLY HIDING IN THE BACKGROUND.
KAFF KAFF
K-KK-KKKILL...
D-DON'T...IT'S P-POISON!
AND HERE IT IS...
NICE TRY, TYRANNUS. BUT I'M THE WORLD'S GREATEST BIOCHEMICAL EXPERT. AND I CERTAINLY KNOW POISON...
...FROM PERFECTION.
BEFORE THE PARALYSIS COMPLETELY OVERTAKES YOU, TYRANNUS, LET ME LEAVE YOU WITH ONE OBSERVATION.
YOU'VE BEEN A FOOL FOR MILLENNIA.
COMPLETELY IGNORANT OF THE TRUE TREASURE YOU'VE BEEN HOARDING.
G-GO AHEAD. DRINK AS MUCH AS YOU LIKE.
THE IMMORTALITY IT P-PROVIDES WON'T SPARE YOU A VIOLENT DEATH...
...WHICH I G-GUARANTEE YOU'LL RECEIVE.

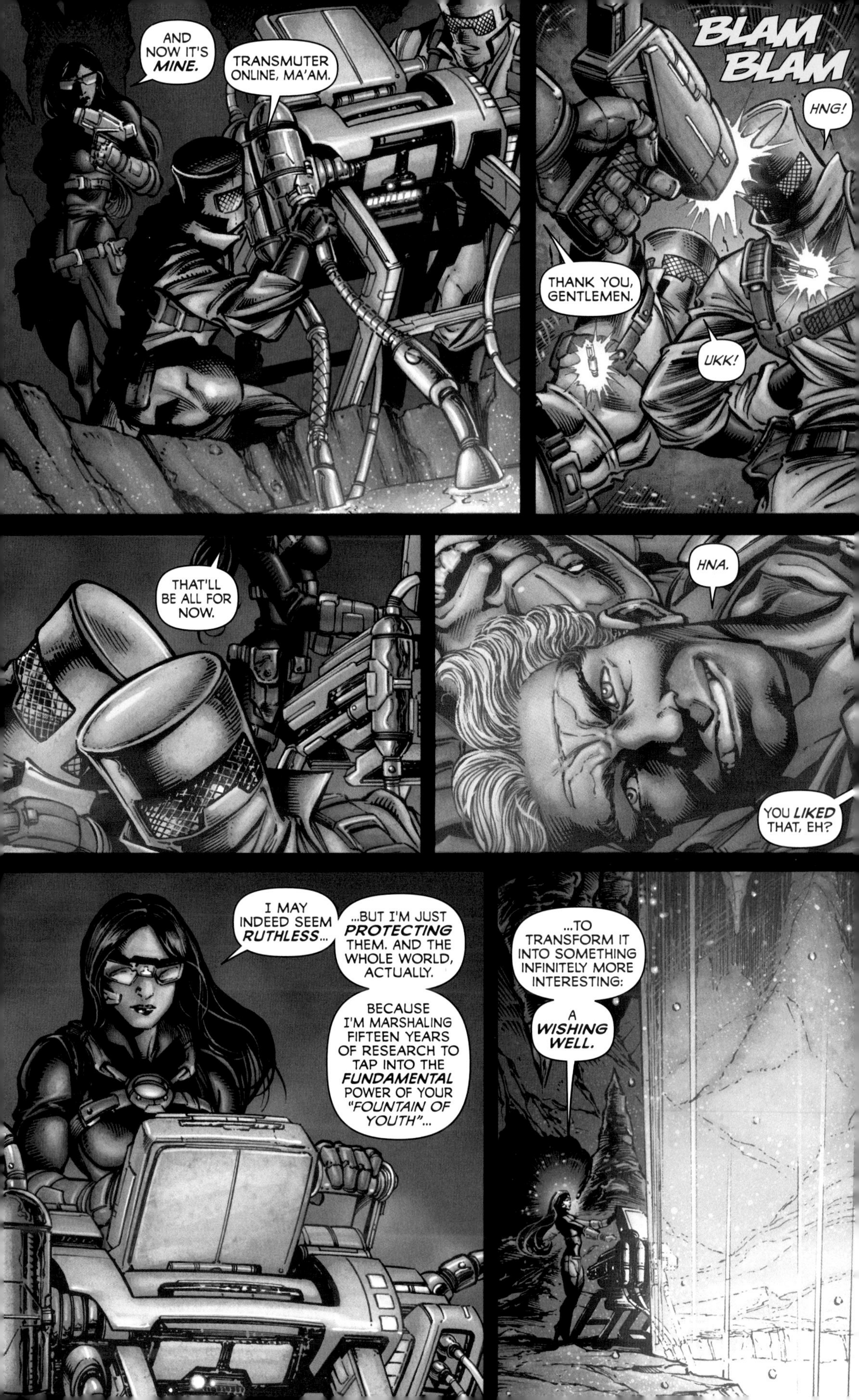
AND NOW IT'S *MINE.*
TRANSMUTER ONLINE, MA'AM.
BLAM BLAM
HNG!
THANK YOU, GENTLEMEN.
UKK!
THAT'LL BE ALL FOR NOW.
HNA.
YOU *LIKED* THAT, EH?
I MAY INDEED SEEM *RUTHLESS*...
...BUT I'M JUST *PROTECTING* THEM. AND THE WHOLE WORLD, ACTUALLY.
BECAUSE I'M MARSHALING FIFTEEN YEARS OF RESEARCH TO TAP INTO THE *FUNDAMENTAL* POWER OF YOUR *"FOUNTAIN OF YOUTH"*...
...TO TRANSFORM IT INTO SOMETHING INFINITELY MORE INTERESTING:
A *WISHING WELL.*

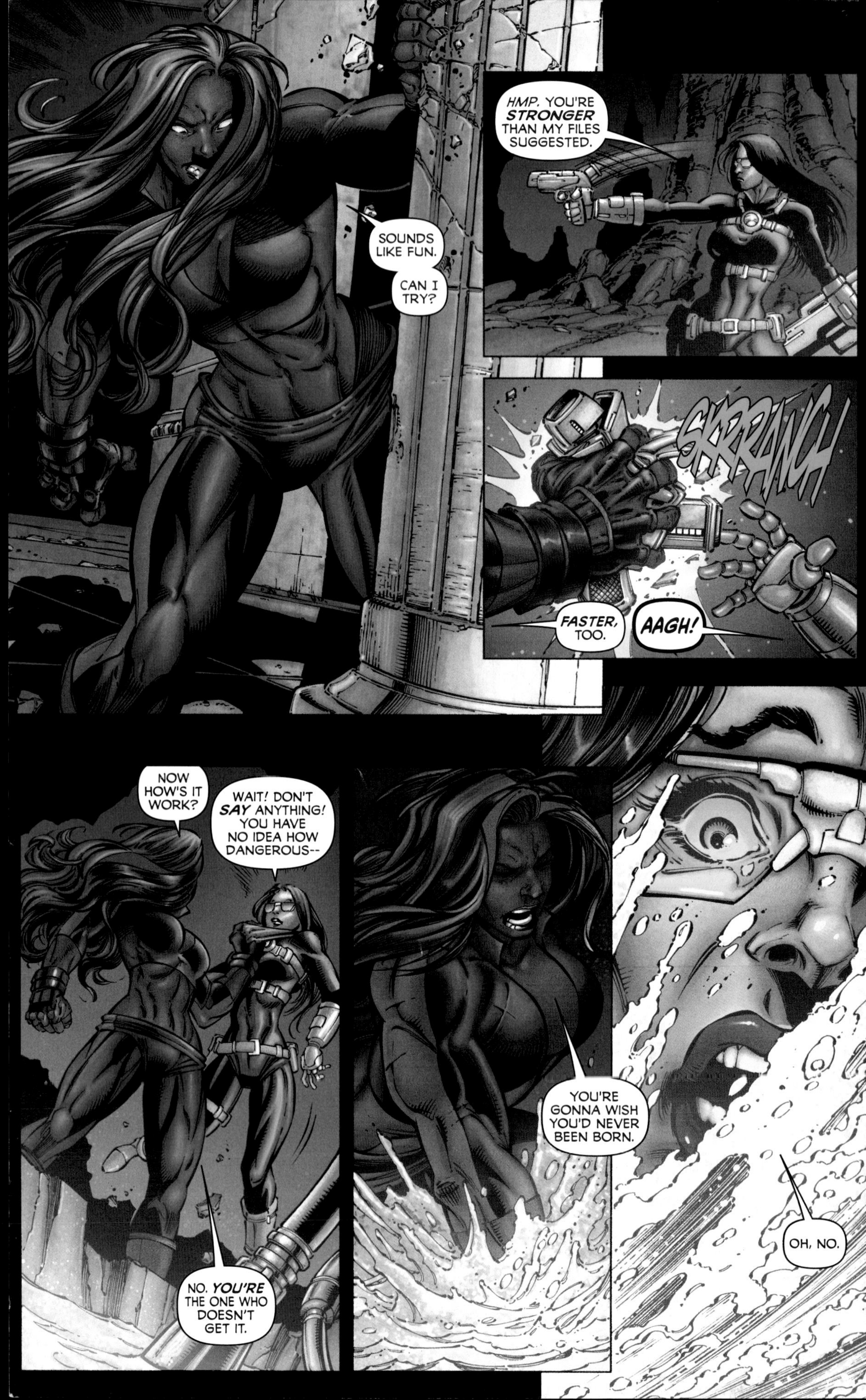
SOUNDS LIKE FUN.
CAN I TRY?
HMP. YOU'RE STRONGER THAN MY FILES SUGGESTED.
SKRRANCH
FASTER, TOO.
AAGH!
NOW HOW'S IT WORK?
WAIT! DON'T SAY ANYTHING! YOU HAVE NO IDEA HOW DANGEROUS--
NO. YOU'RE THE ONE WHO DOESN'T GET IT.
YOU'RE GONNA WISH YOU'D NEVER BEEN BORN.
OH, NO.

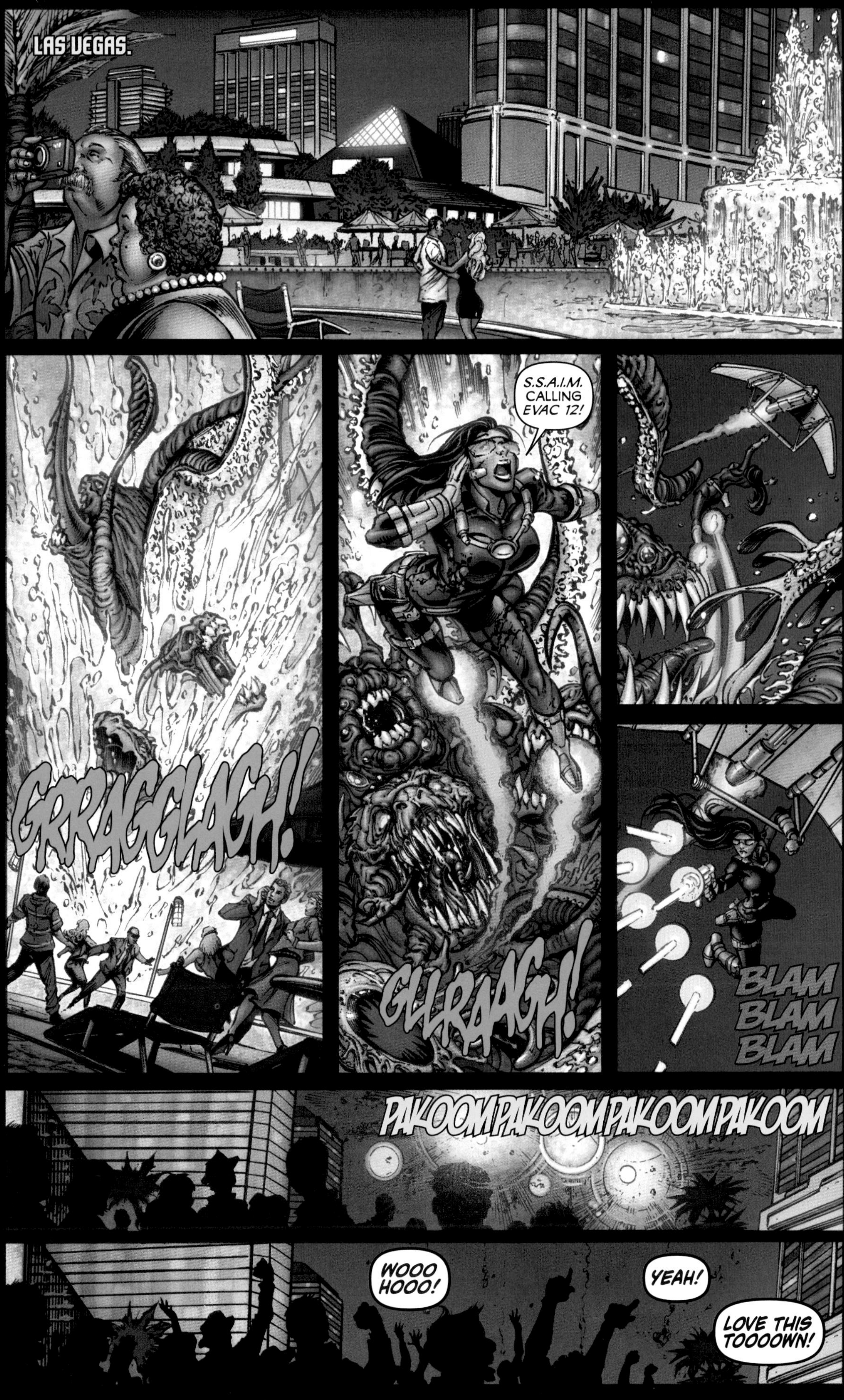
LAS VEGAS.
GRRAGGLAGH!
S.S.A.I.M. CALLING EVAC 12!
GLLRAAGH!
BLAM BLAM BLAM
PAKOOM PAKOOM PAKOOM PAKOOM
WOOO HOOO!
YEAH!
LOVE THIS TOOOOWN!

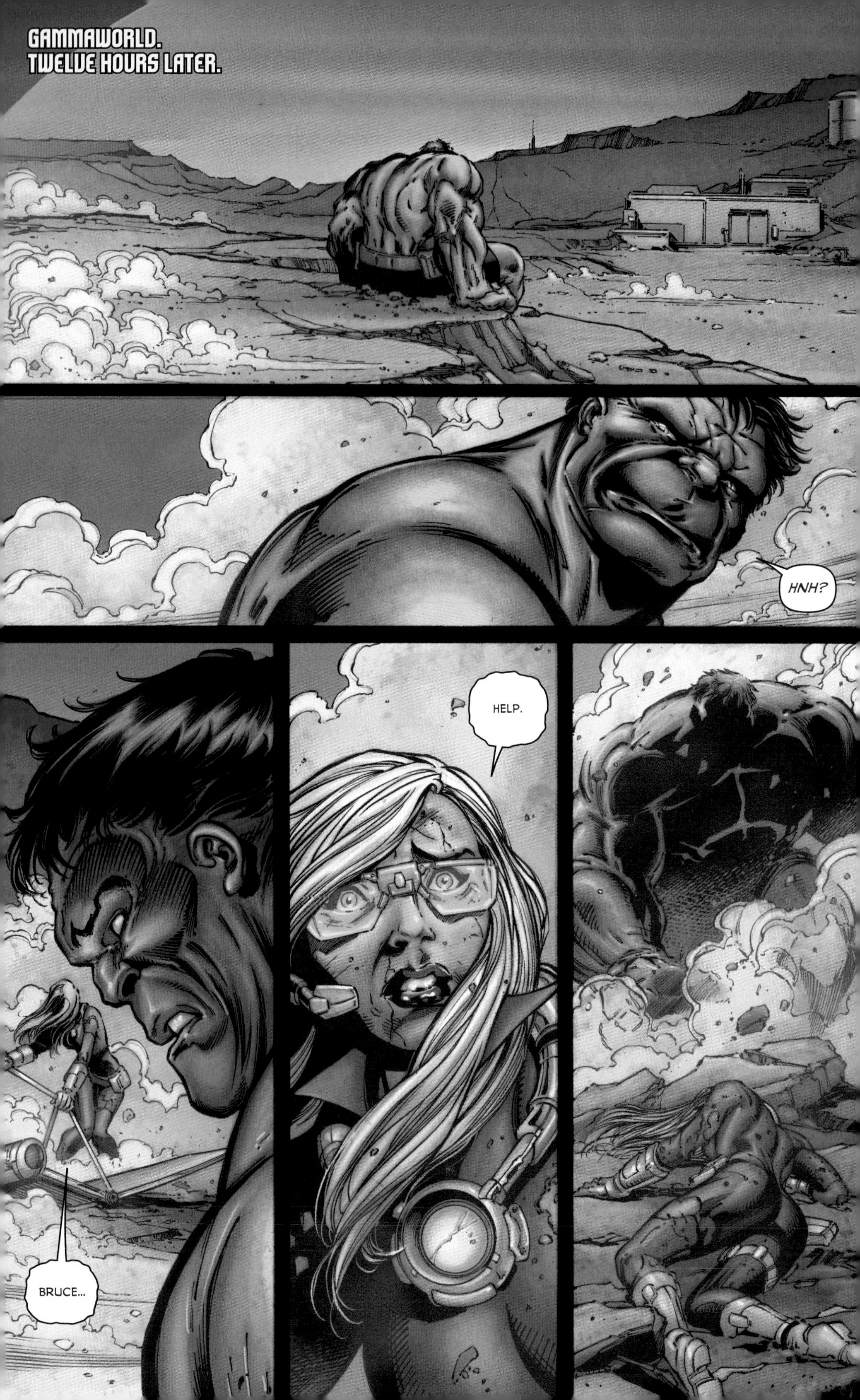
GAMMAWORLD.
TWELVE HOURS LATER.
HNH?
BRUCE...
HELP.

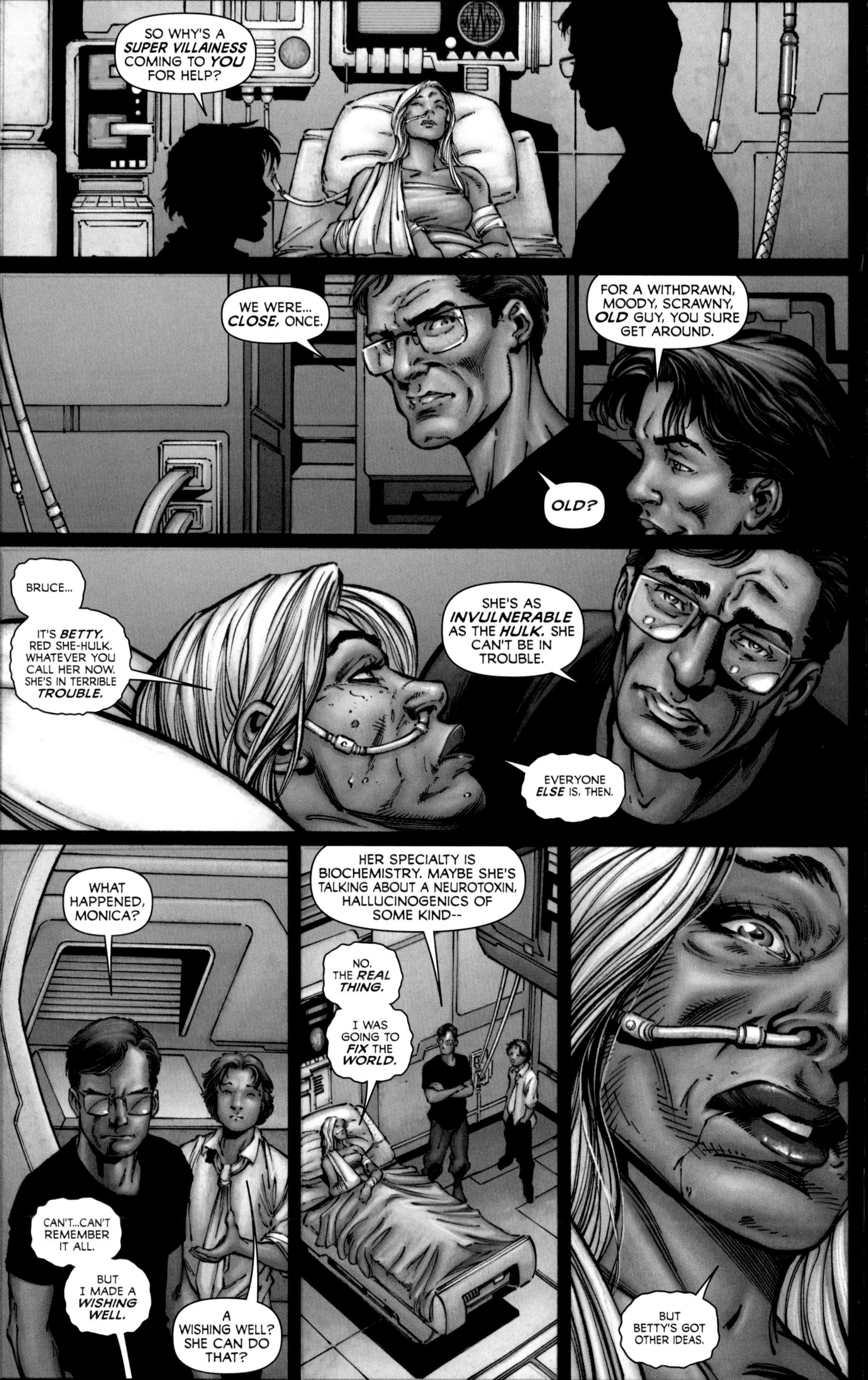
SO WHY'S A SUPER VILLAINESS COMING TO YOU FOR HELP?
WE WERE... CLOSE, ONCE.
FOR A WITHDRAWN, MOODY, SCRAWNY, OLD GUY, YOU SURE GET AROUND.
OLD?
BRUCE...
IT'S BETTY. RED SHE-HULK. WHATEVER YOU CALL HER NOW. SHE'S IN TERRIBLE TROUBLE.
SHE'S AS INVULNERABLE AS THE HULK. SHE CAN'T BE IN TROUBLE.
EVERYONE ELSE IS, THEN.
WHAT HAPPENED, MONICA?
CAN'T...CAN'T REMEMBER IT ALL.
BUT I MADE A WISHING WELL.
A WISHING WELL? SHE CAN DO THAT?
HER SPECIALTY IS BIOCHEMISTRY. MAYBE SHE'S TALKING ABOUT A NEUROTOXIN, HALLUCINOGENICS OF SOME KIND--
NO. THE REAL THING.
I WAS GOING TO FIX THE WORLD.
BUT BETTY'S GOT OTHER IDEAS.

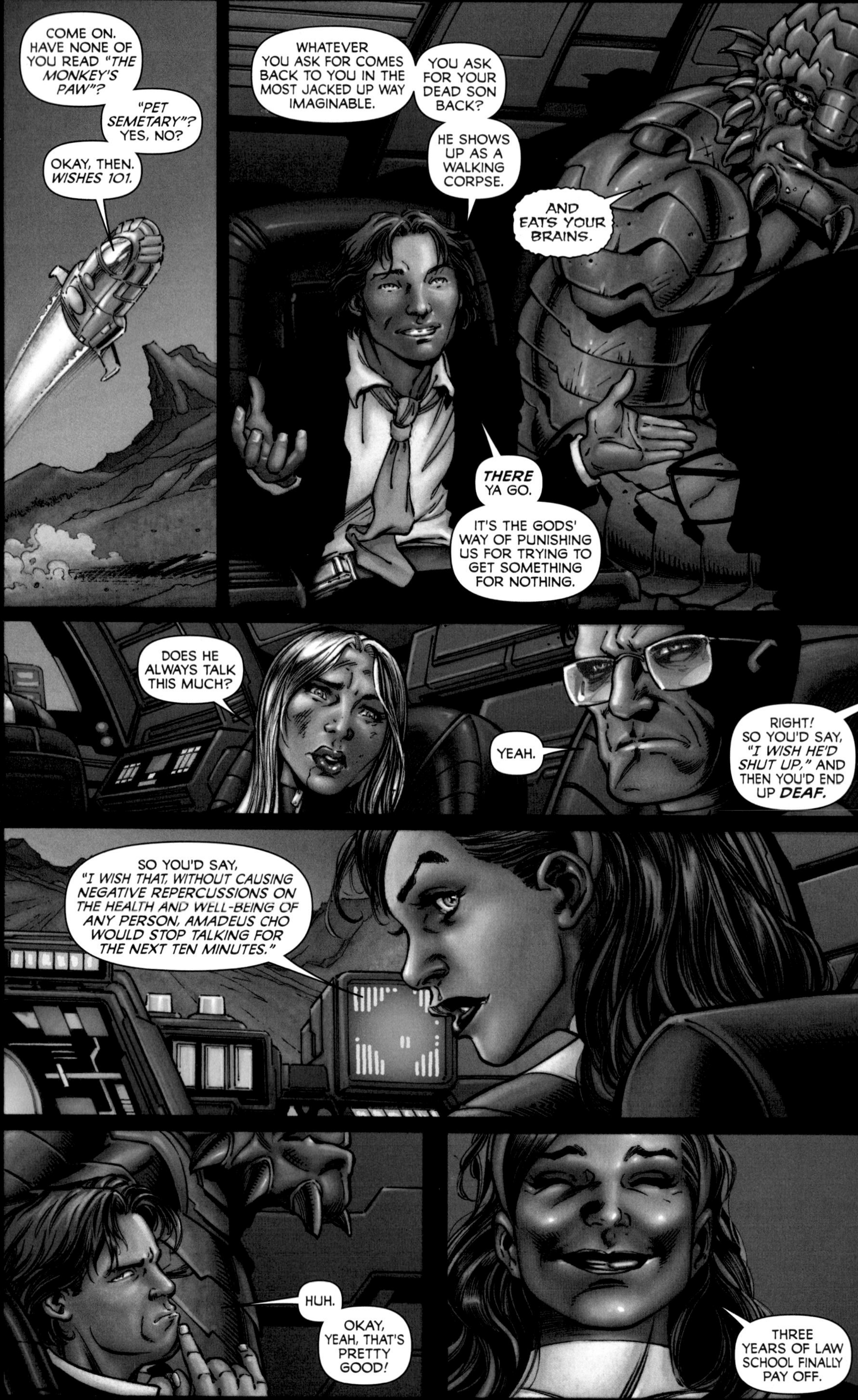
COME ON. HAVE NONE OF YOU READ *"THE MONKEY'S PAW"*?
"PET SEMETARY"? YES, NO?
OKAY, THEN. *WISHES 101.*
WHATEVER YOU ASK FOR COMES BACK TO YOU IN THE MOST JACKED UP WAY IMAGINABLE.
YOU ASK FOR YOUR DEAD SON BACK?
HE SHOWS UP AS A WALKING CORPSE.
AND EATS YOUR BRAINS.
THERE YA GO.
IT'S THE GODS' WAY OF PUNISHING US FOR TRYING TO GET SOMETHING FOR NOTHING.
DOES HE ALWAYS TALK THIS MUCH?
YEAH.
RIGHT! SO YOU'D SAY, *"I WISH HE'D SHUT UP,"* AND THEN YOU'D END UP ***DEAF.***
SO YOU'D SAY, *"I WISH THAT, WITHOUT CAUSING NEGATIVE REPERCUSSIONS ON THE HEALTH AND WELL-BEING OF ANY PERSON, AMADEUS CHO WOULD STOP TALKING FOR THE NEXT TEN MINUTES."*
HUH.
OKAY, YEAH, THAT'S PRETTY GOOD!
THREE YEARS OF LAW SCHOOL FINALLY PAY OFF.

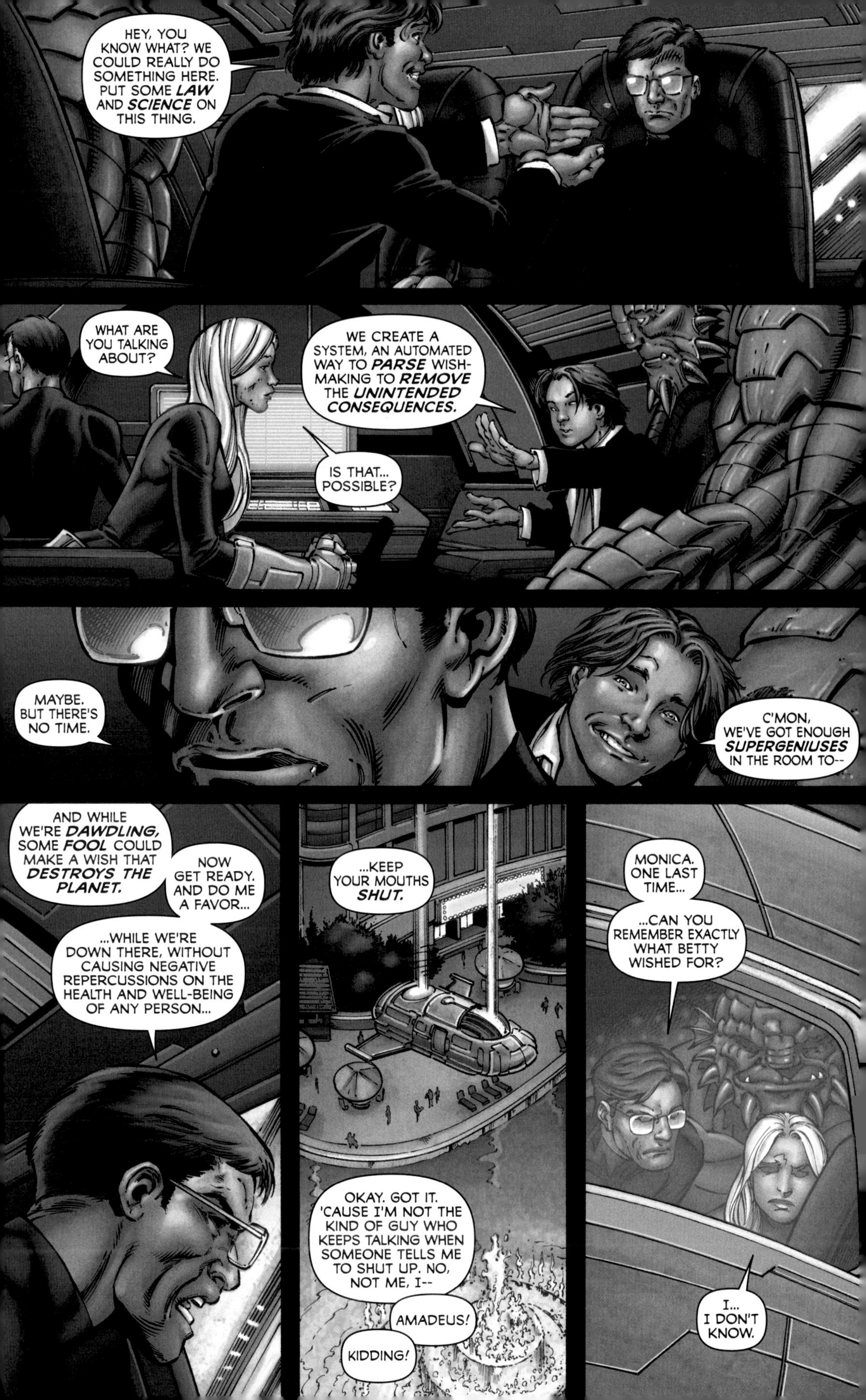
HEY, YOU KNOW WHAT? WE COULD REALLY DO SOMETHING HERE. PUT SOME LAW AND SCIENCE ON THIS THING.
WHAT ARE YOU TALKING ABOUT?
WE CREATE A SYSTEM, AN AUTOMATED WAY TO PARSE WISH-MAKING TO REMOVE THE UNINTENDED CONSEQUENCES.
IS THAT... POSSIBLE?
MAYBE. BUT THERE'S NO TIME.
C'MON, WE'VE GOT ENOUGH SUPERGENIUSES IN THE ROOM TO--
AND WHILE WE'RE DAWDLING, SOME FOOL COULD MAKE A WISH THAT DESTROYS THE PLANET.
NOW GET READY. AND DO ME A FAVOR...
...WHILE WE'RE DOWN THERE, WITHOUT CAUSING NEGATIVE REPERCUSSIONS ON THE HEALTH AND WELL-BEING OF ANY PERSON...
...KEEP YOUR MOUTHS SHUT.
OKAY. GOT IT. 'CAUSE I'M NOT THE KIND OF GUY WHO KEEPS TALKING WHEN SOMEONE TELLS ME TO SHUT UP. NO, NOT ME, I--
AMADEUS!
KIDDING!
MONICA. ONE LAST TIME...
...CAN YOU REMEMBER EXACTLY WHAT BETTY WISHED FOR?
I... I DON'T KNOW.

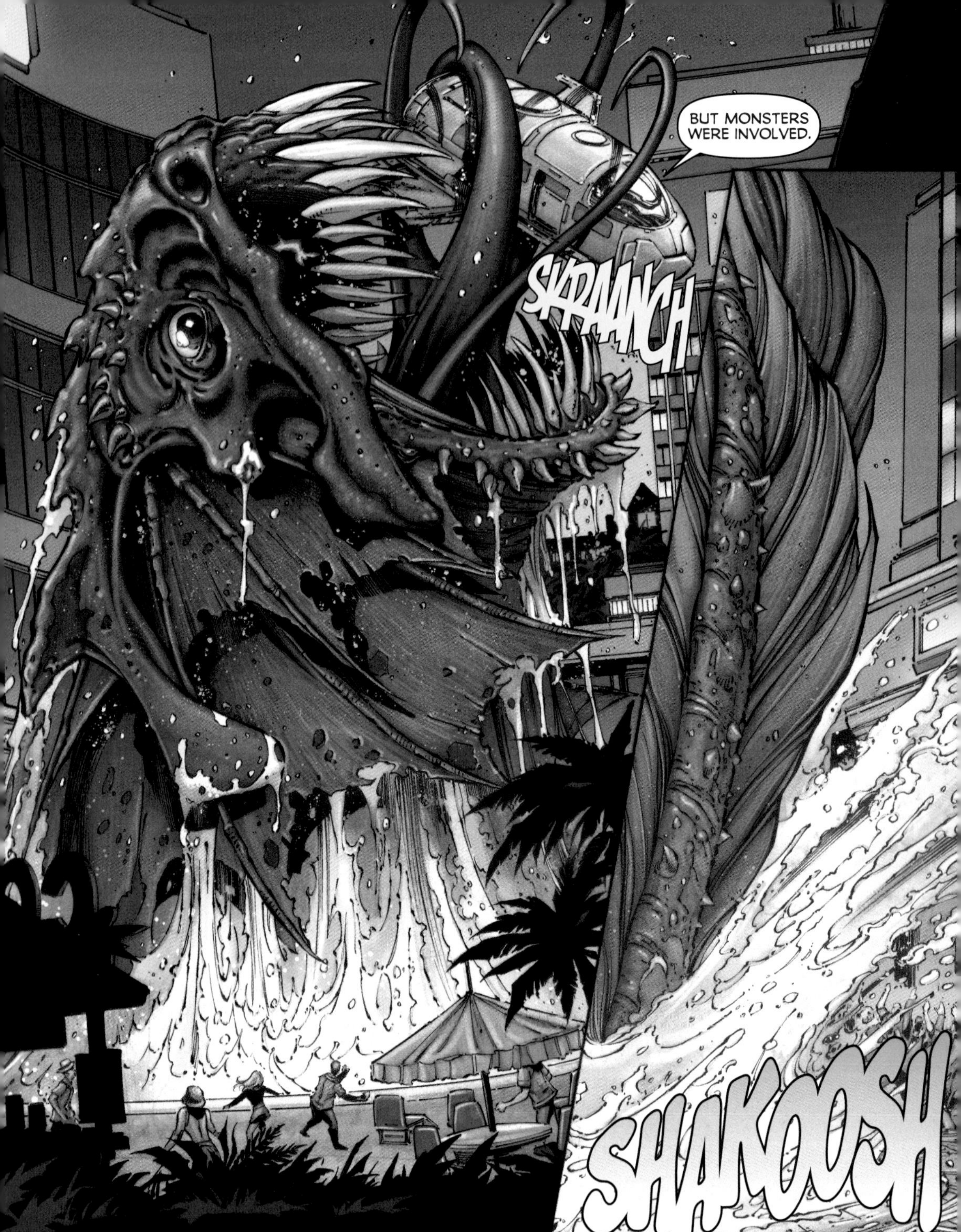
BUT MONSTERS WERE INVOLVED.
SKRAANCH
SHAKOOSH

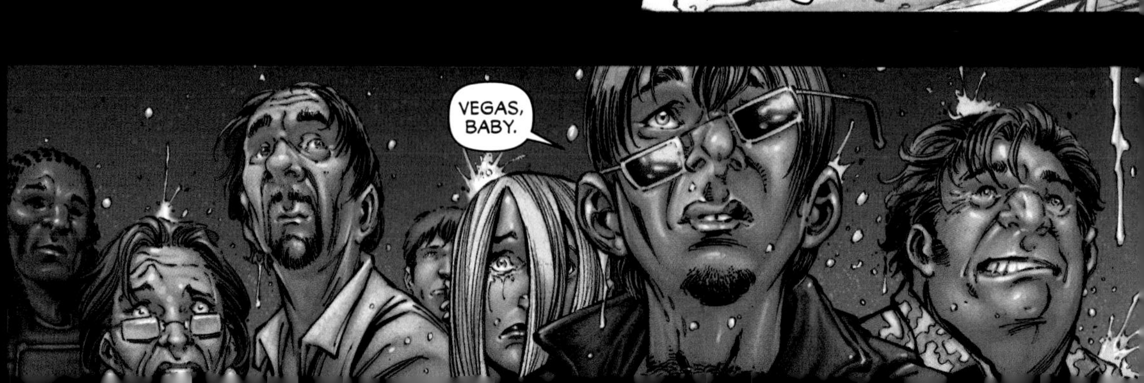
VEGAS, BABY.

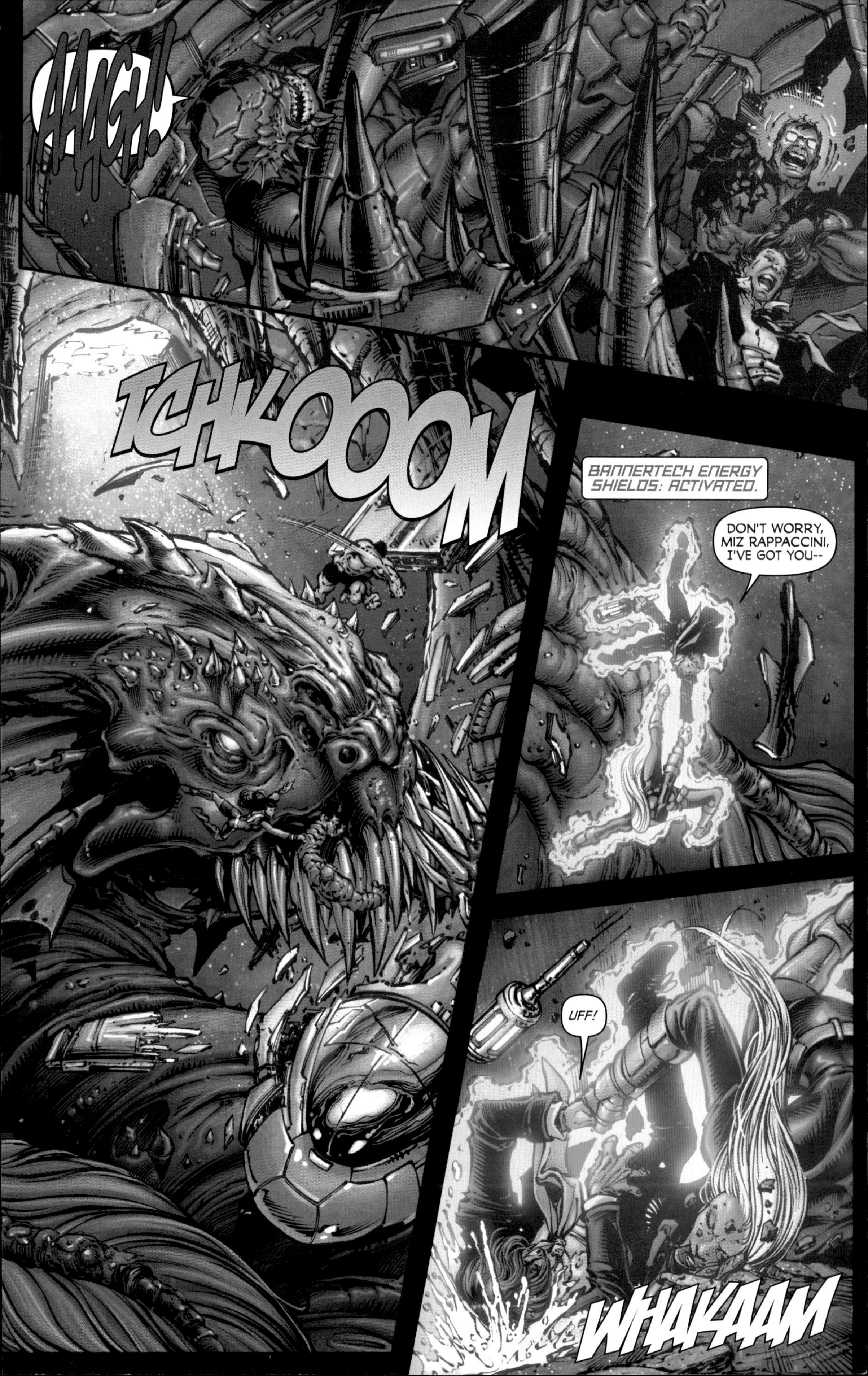
AAAGH!
TCHKOOOM
BANNERTECH ENERGY SHIELDS: ACTIVATED.
DON'T WORRY, MIZ RAPPACCINI, I'VE GOT YOU--
UFF!
WHAKAAM

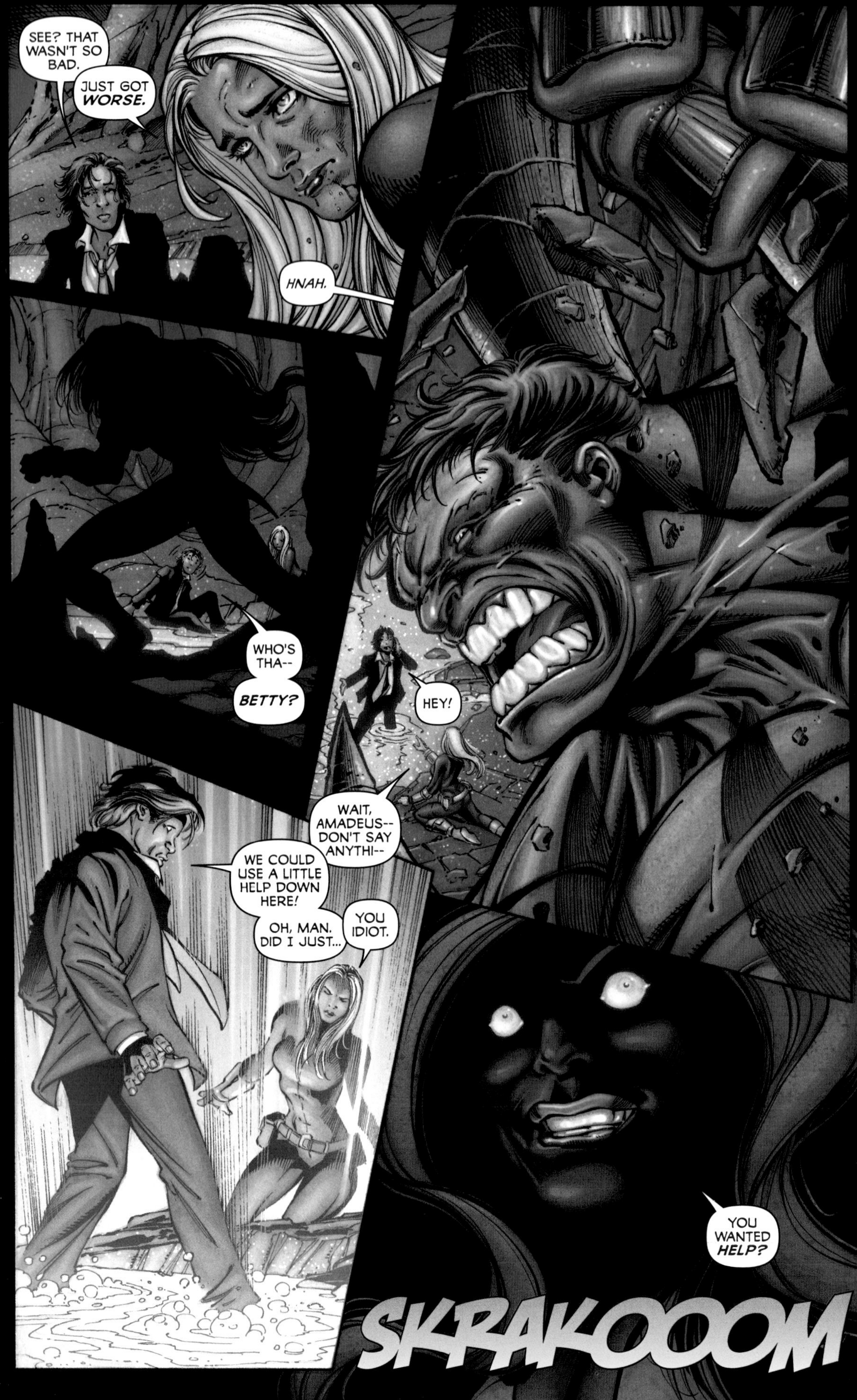
SEE? THAT WASN'T SO BAD.
JUST GOT *WORSE.*
HNAH.
WHO'S THA--
BETTY?
HEY!
WAIT, AMADEUS-- DON'T SAY ANYTHI--
WE COULD USE A LITTLE HELP DOWN HERE!
OH, MAN. DID I JUST...
YOU IDIOT.
YOU WANTED *HELP?*
SKRAKOOOM

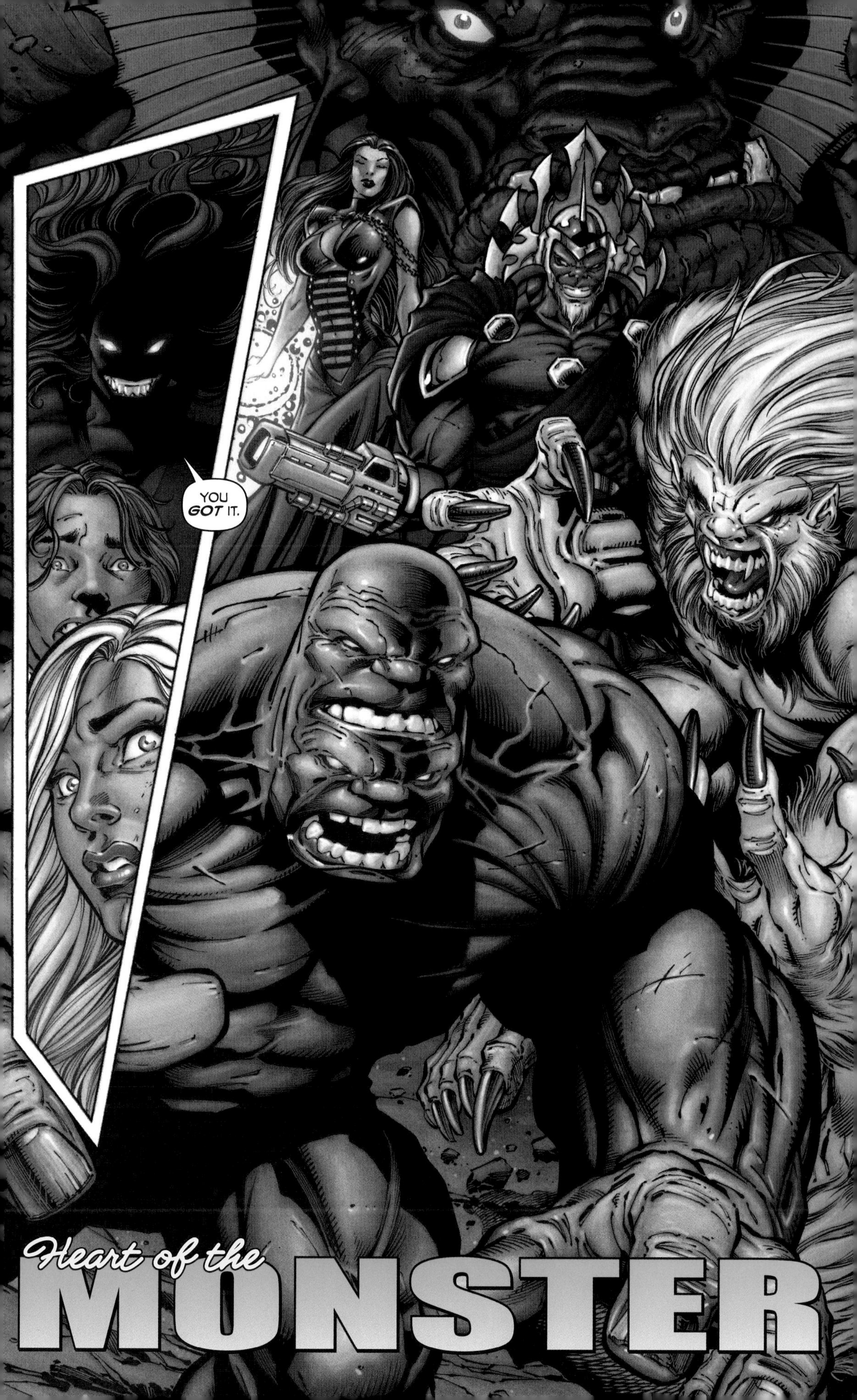
YOU GOT IT.
Heart of the
MONSTER

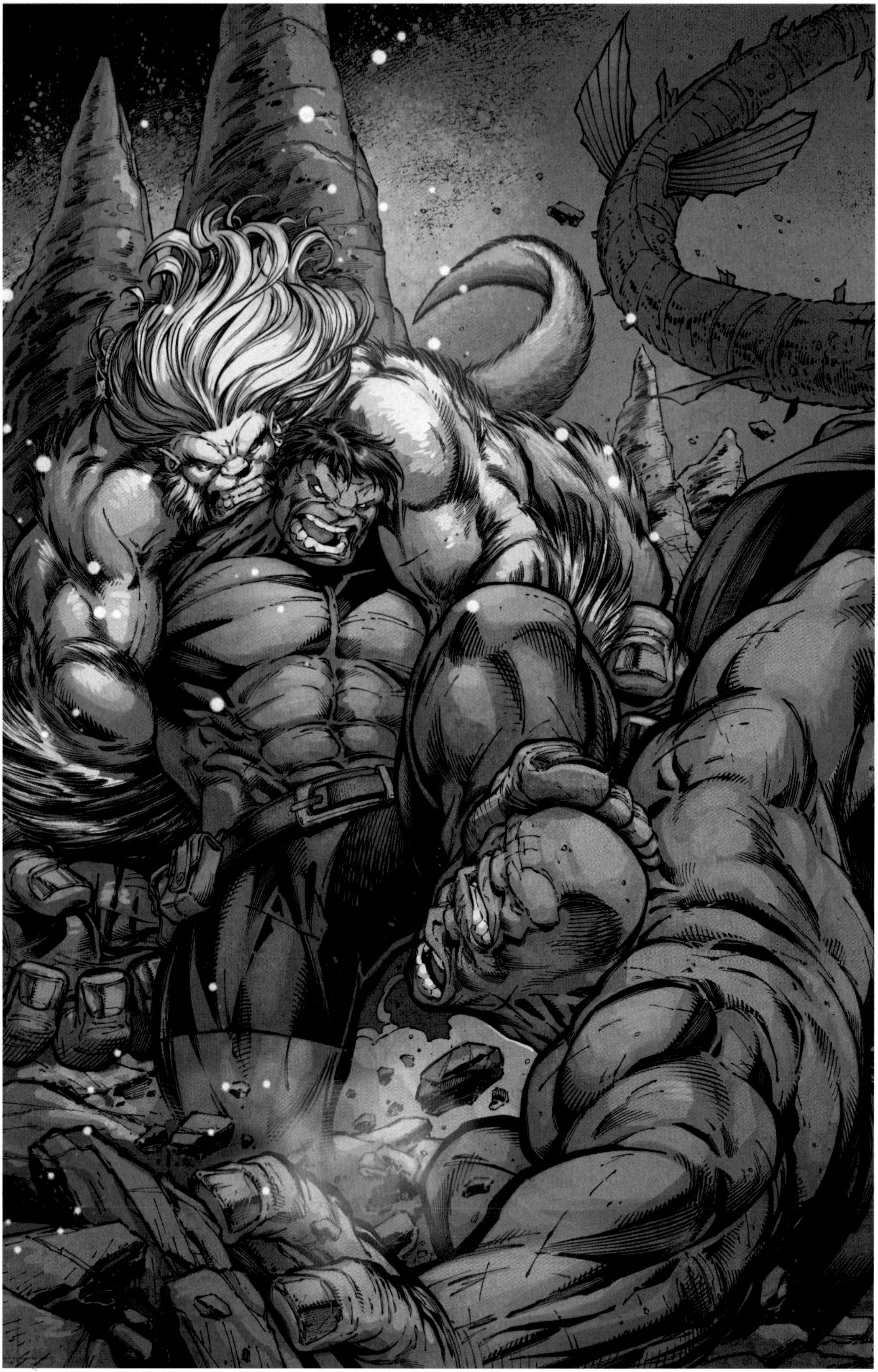

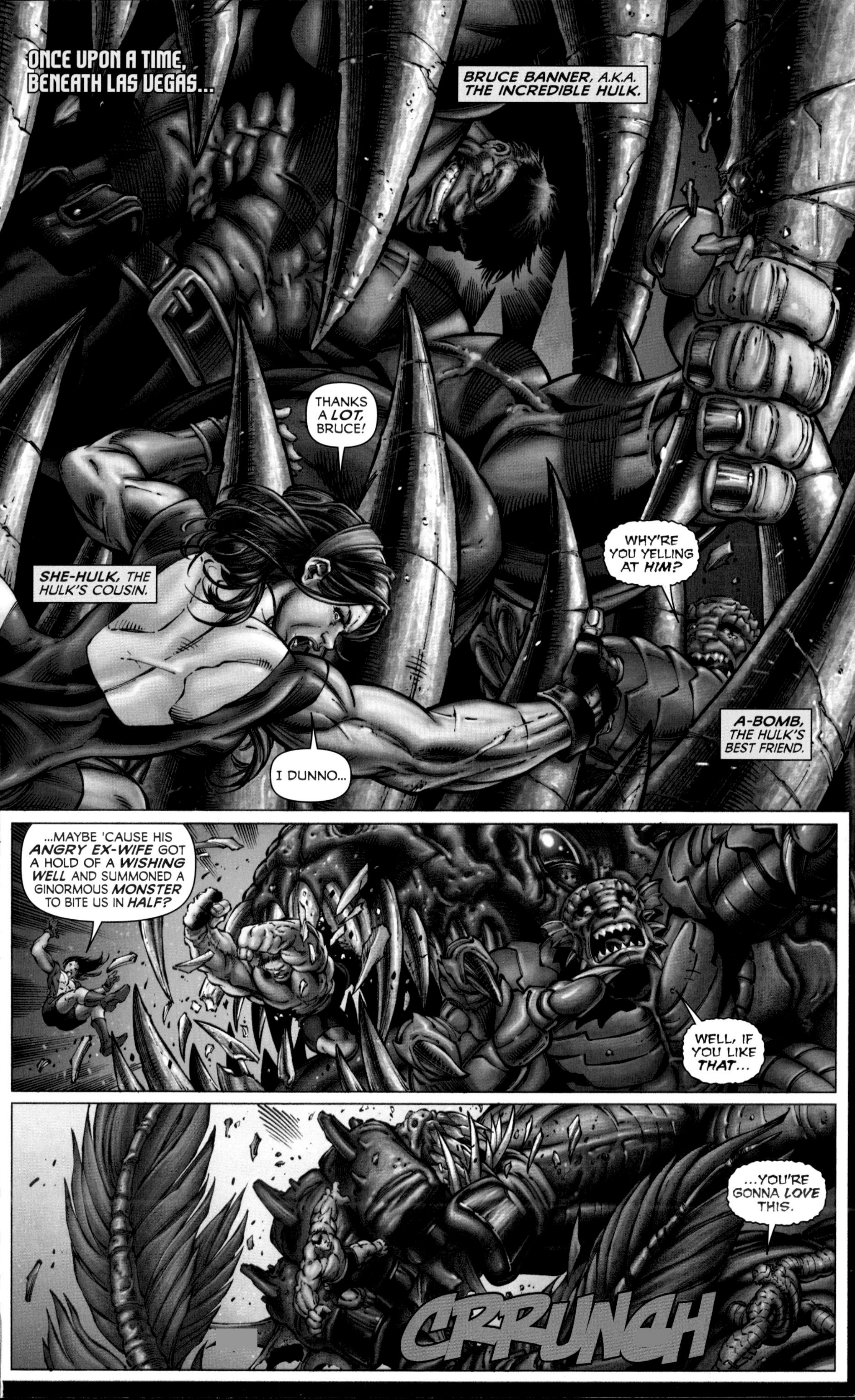
ONCE UPON A TIME, BENEATH LAS VEGAS...
BRUCE BANNER, A.K.A. THE INCREDIBLE HULK.
THANKS A LOT, BRUCE!
SHE-HULK, THE HULK'S COUSIN.
WHY'RE YOU YELLING AT HIM?
I DUNNO...
A-BOMB, THE HULK'S BEST FRIEND.
...MAYBE 'CAUSE HIS ANGRY EX-WIFE GOT A HOLD OF A WISHING WELL AND SUMMONED A GINORMOUS MONSTER TO BITE US IN HALF?
WELL, IF YOU LIKE THAT...
...YOU'RE GONNA LOVE THIS.
CRRUNCH

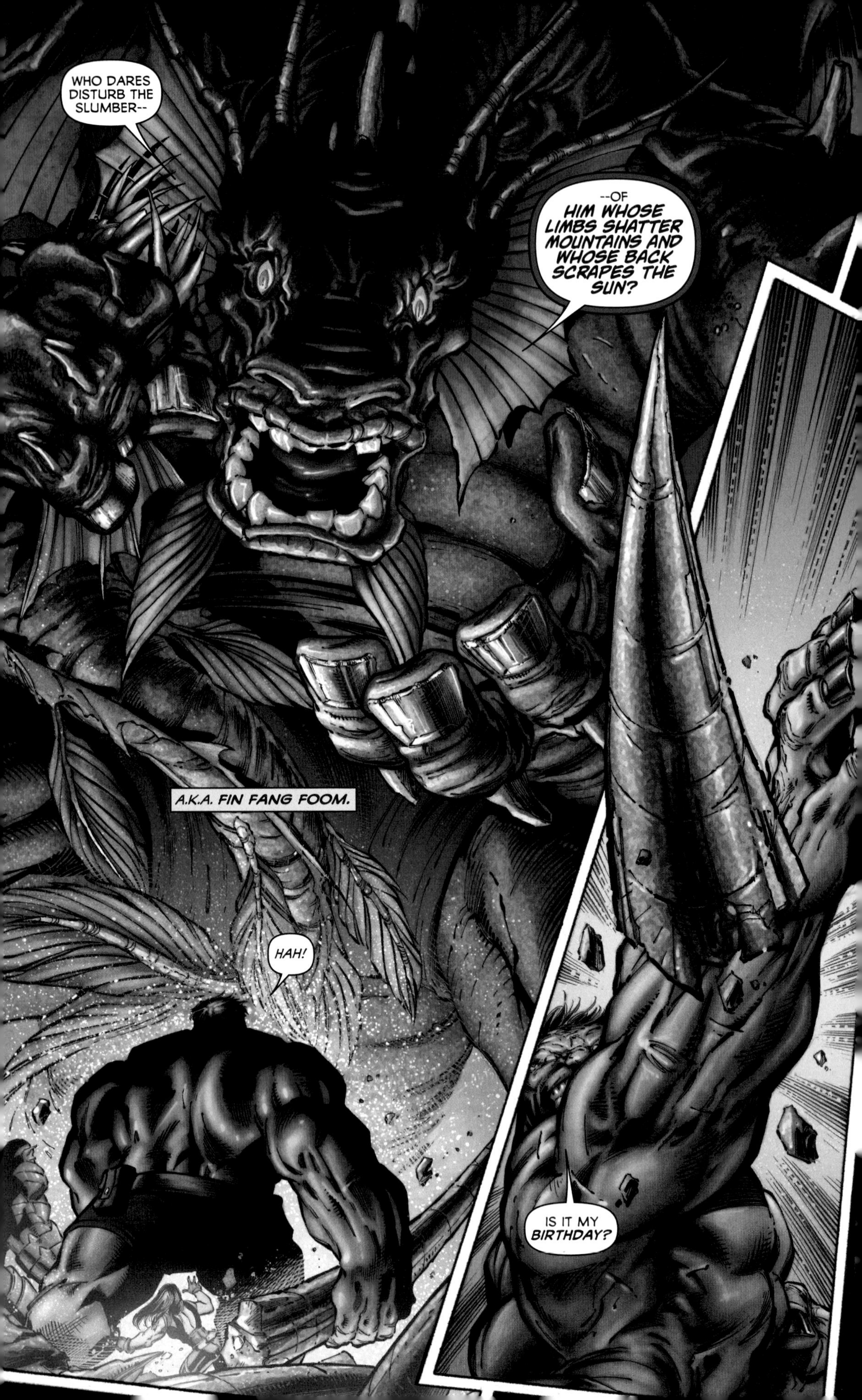
WHO DARES DISTURB THE SLUMBER--
--OF HIM WHOSE LIMBS SHATTER MOUNTAINS AND WHOSE BACK SCRAPES THE SUN?
A.K.A. FIN FANG FOOM.
HAH!
IS IT MY BIRTHDAY?

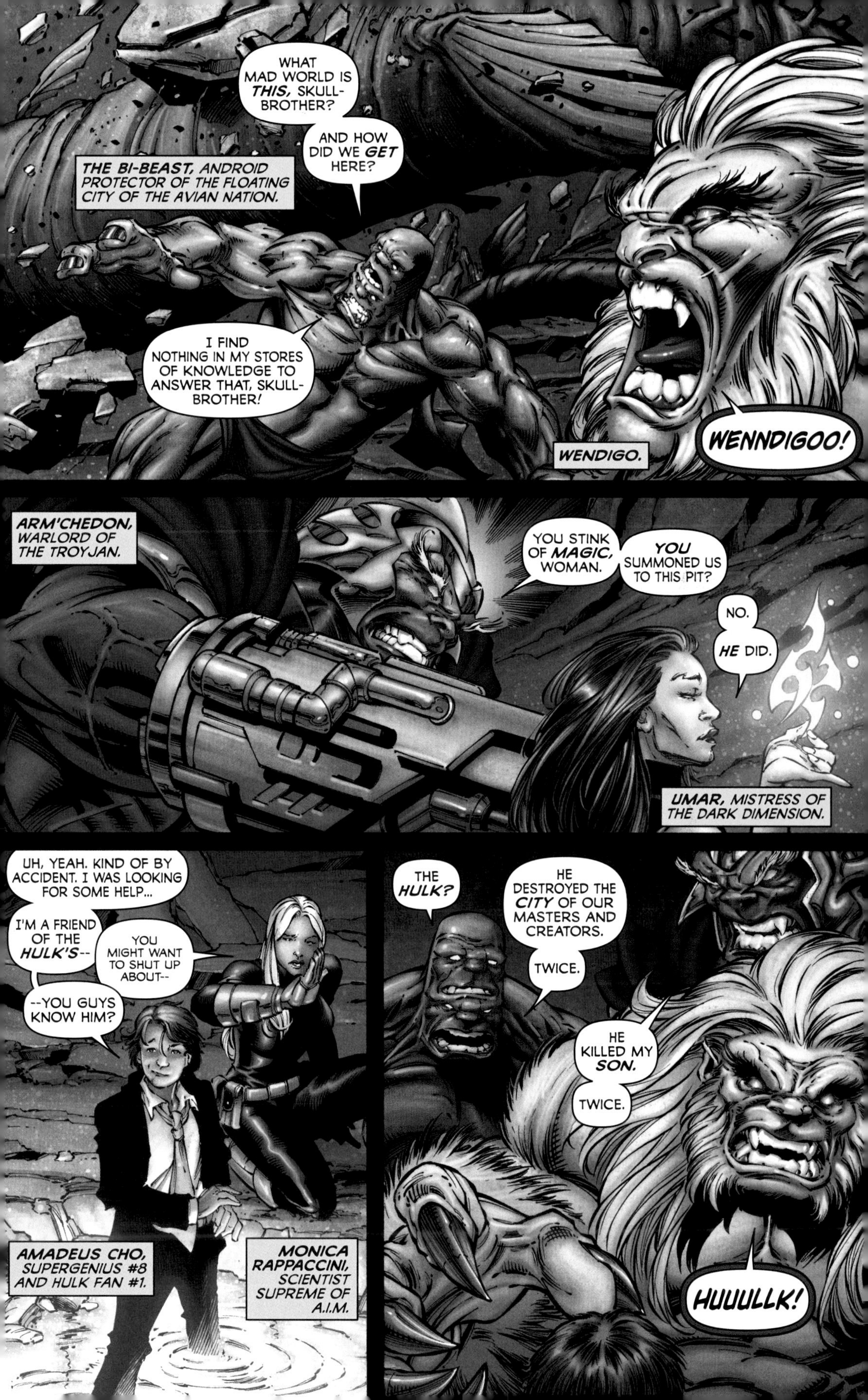
WHAT MAD WORLD IS *THIS,* SKULL-BROTHER?
AND HOW DID WE *GET* HERE?
THE BI-BEAST, ANDROID PROTECTOR OF THE FLOATING CITY OF THE AVIAN NATION.
I FIND NOTHING IN MY STORES OF KNOWLEDGE TO ANSWER THAT, SKULL-BROTHER!
WENDIGO.
WENNDIGOO!
ARM'CHEDON, WARLORD OF THE TROYJAN.
YOU STINK OF *MAGIC,* WOMAN.
YOU SUMMONED US TO THIS PIT?
NO.
HE DID.
UMAR, MISTRESS OF THE DARK DIMENSION.
UH, YEAH. KIND OF BY ACCIDENT. I WAS LOOKING FOR SOME HELP...
I'M A FRIEND OF THE *HULK'S*--
YOU MIGHT WANT TO SHUT UP ABOUT--
--YOU GUYS KNOW HIM?
AMADEUS CHO, SUPERGENIUS #8 AND HULK FAN #1.
MONICA RAPPACCINI, SCIENTIST SUPREME OF A.I.M.
THE *HULK?*
HE DESTROYED THE *CITY* OF OUR MASTERS AND CREATORS.
TWICE.
HE KILLED MY *SON.*
TWICE.
HUUULLK!

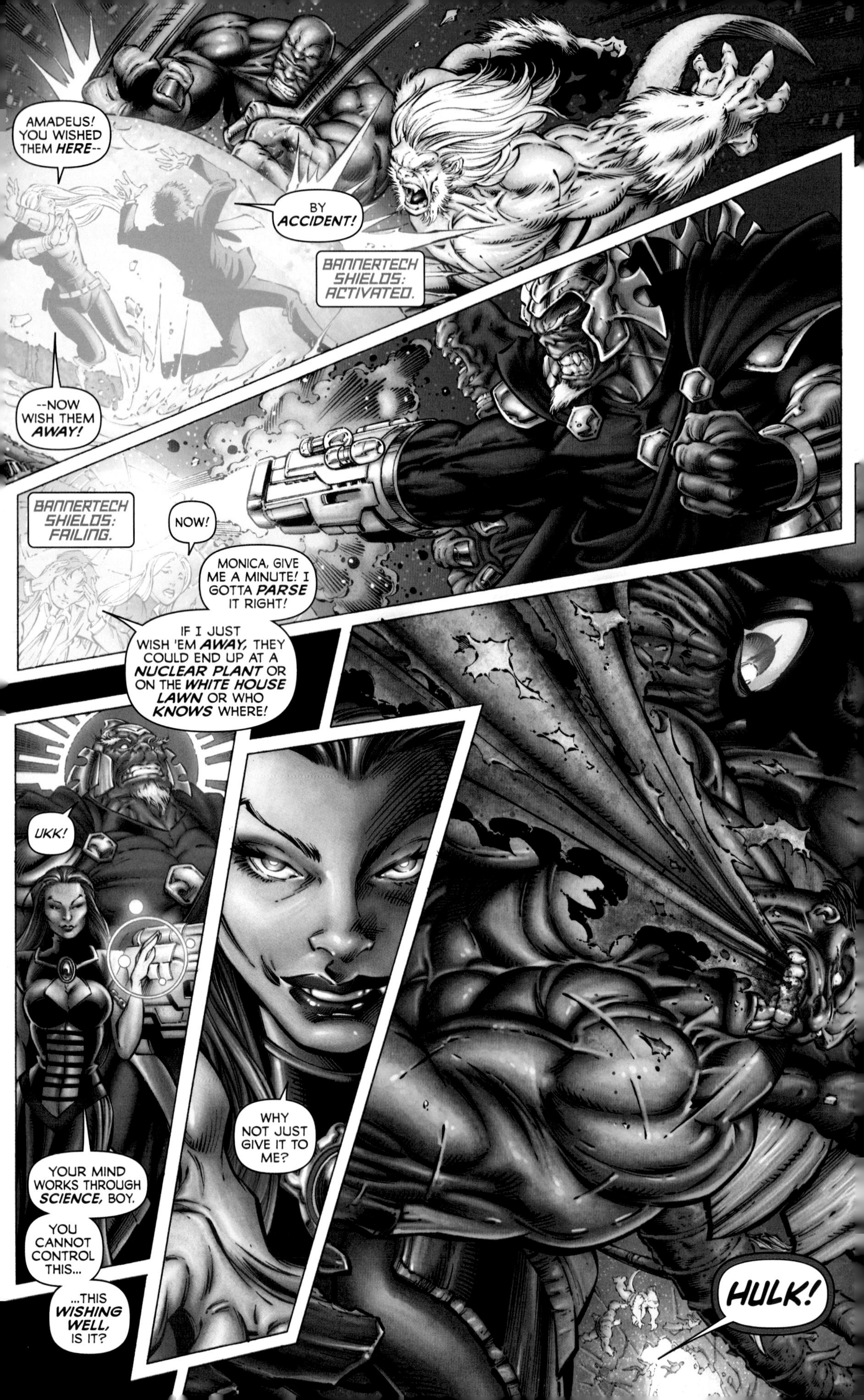
AMADEUS! YOU WISHED THEM HERE--
BY ACCIDENT!
--NOW WISH THEM AWAY!
BANNERTECH SHIELDS: ACTIVATED.
BANNERTECH SHIELDS: FAILING.
NOW!
MONICA, GIVE ME A MINUTE! I GOTTA PARSE IT RIGHT!
IF I JUST WISH 'EM AWAY, THEY COULD END UP AT A NUCLEAR PLANT OR ON THE WHITE HOUSE LAWN OR WHO KNOWS WHERE!
UKK!
YOUR MIND WORKS THROUGH SCIENCE, BOY.
YOU CANNOT CONTROL THIS...
...THIS WISHING WELL, IS IT?
WHY NOT JUST GIVE IT TO ME?
HULK!

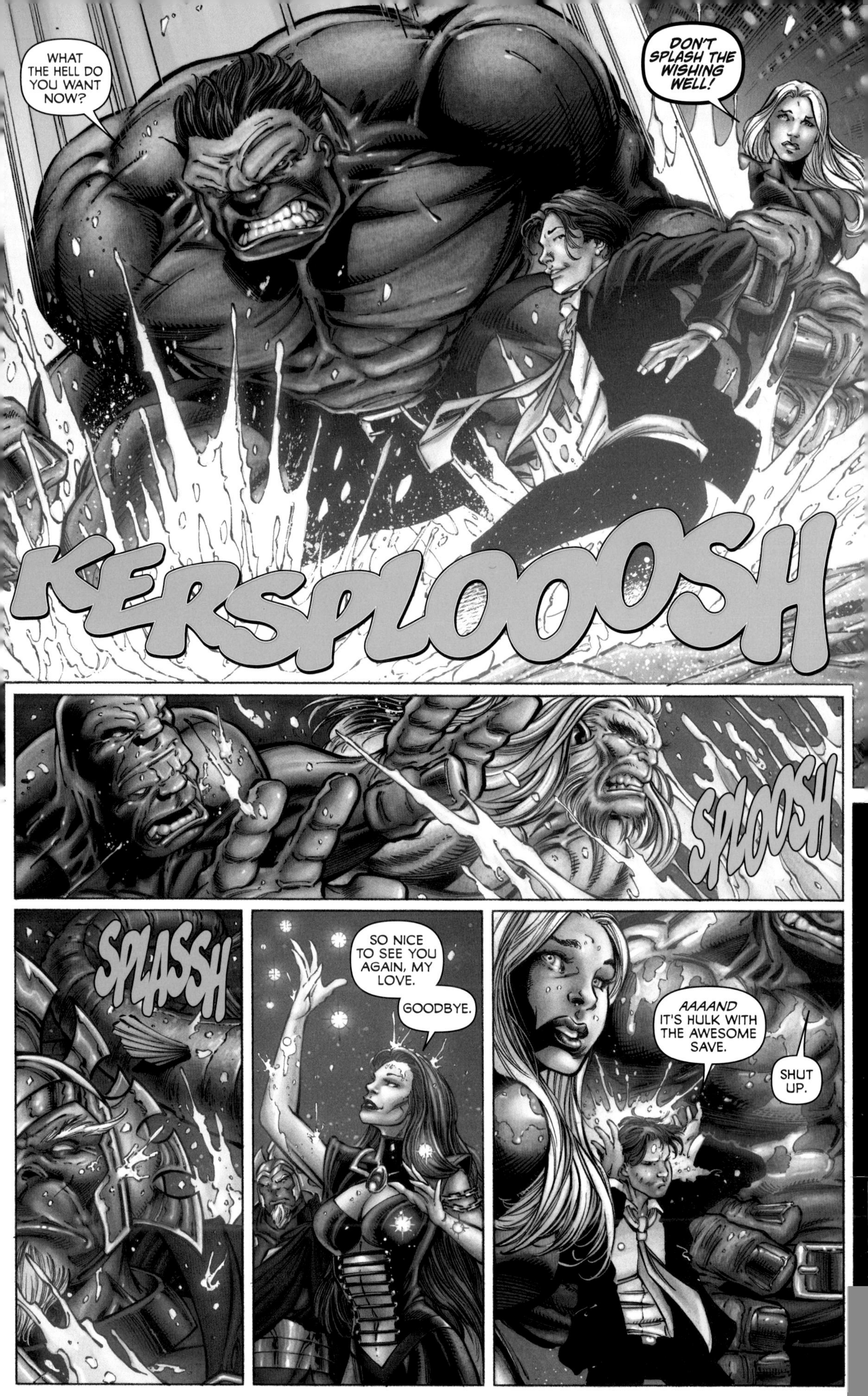
WHAT THE HELL DO YOU WANT NOW?
DON'T SPLASH THE WISHING WELL!
KERSPLOOOSH
SPLOOSH
SPLASSH
SO NICE TO SEE YOU AGAIN, MY LOVE.
GOODBYE.
AAAAND IT'S HULK WITH THE AWESOME SAVE.
SHUT UP.

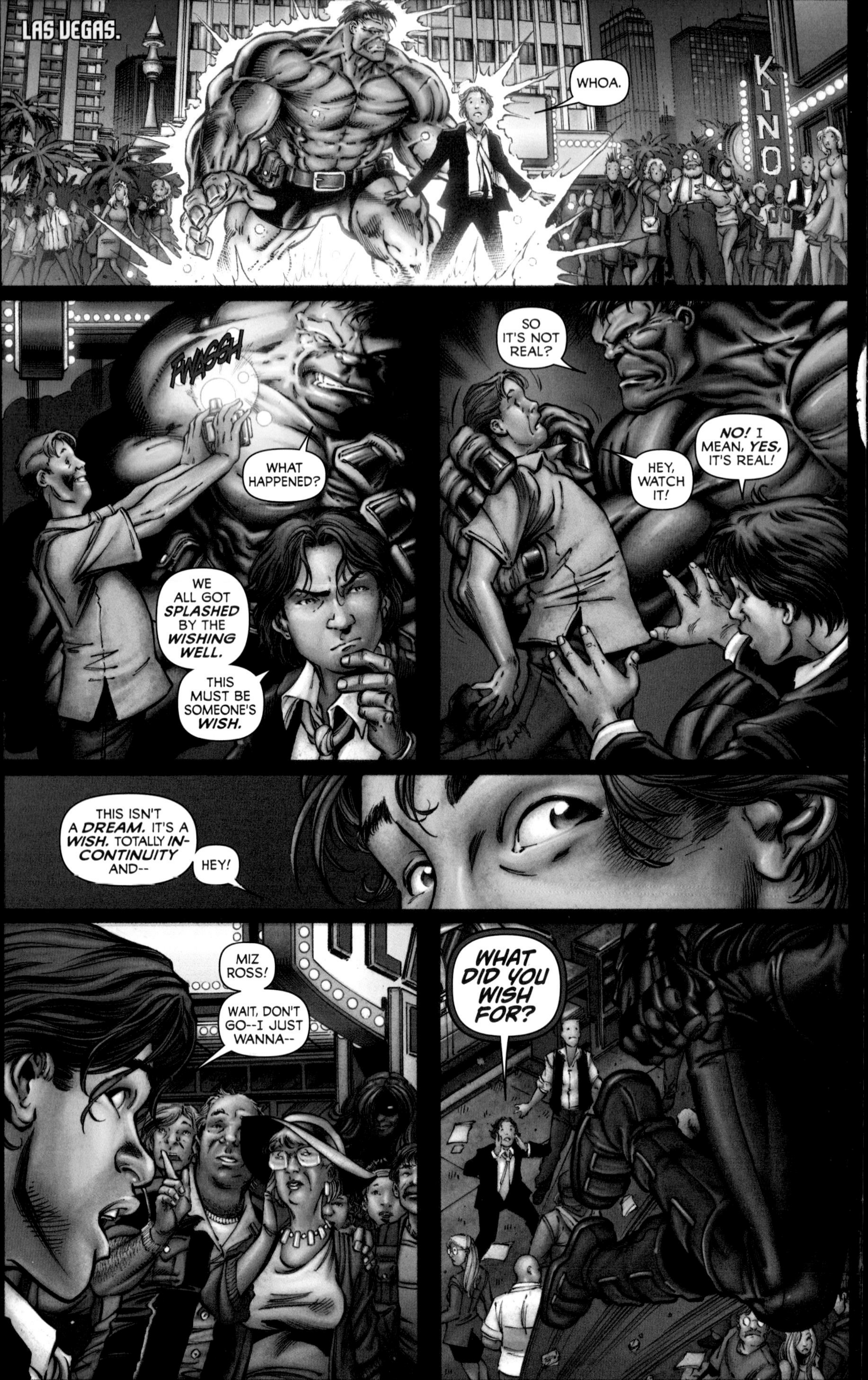
LAS VEGAS.
WHOA.
FWASSH
WHAT HAPPENED?
WE ALL GOT SPLASHED BY THE WISHING WELL.
THIS MUST BE SOMEONE'S WISH.
SO IT'S NOT REAL?
HEY, WATCH IT!
NO! I MEAN, YES, IT'S REAL!
THIS ISN'T A DREAM. IT'S A WISH. TOTALLY IN-CONTINUITY AND--
HEY!
MIZ ROSS!
WAIT, DON'T GO--I JUST WANNA--
WHAT DID YOU WISH FOR?

COME ON, HULK! WE GOTTA CATCH HER!

WHY? SHE SEEMS HAPPY ENOUGH.

COME ON! IF WE WANT TO GET TO THE *BOTTOM* OF THIS, WE *NEED* HER!

ACCORDING TO MONICA, BETTY WAS THE FIRST PERSON TO MAKE A WISH FROM THE WELL.

SO?

SO I'M THEORIZING THAT WHATEVER ANYONE *ELSE* WISHES BECOMES A SUBSET OF *HER* WISH.

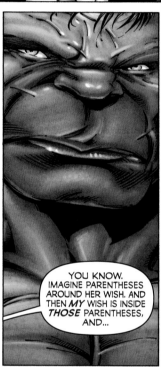

YOU KNOW. IMAGINE PARENTHESES AROUND HER WISH. AND THEN *MY* WISH IS INSIDE *THOSE* PARENTHESES, AND...

...UH...

...AH, HELL.

CAN I JUST TALK TO BANNER?

AAAGH!

MAYBE LATER.

KRAKOOM

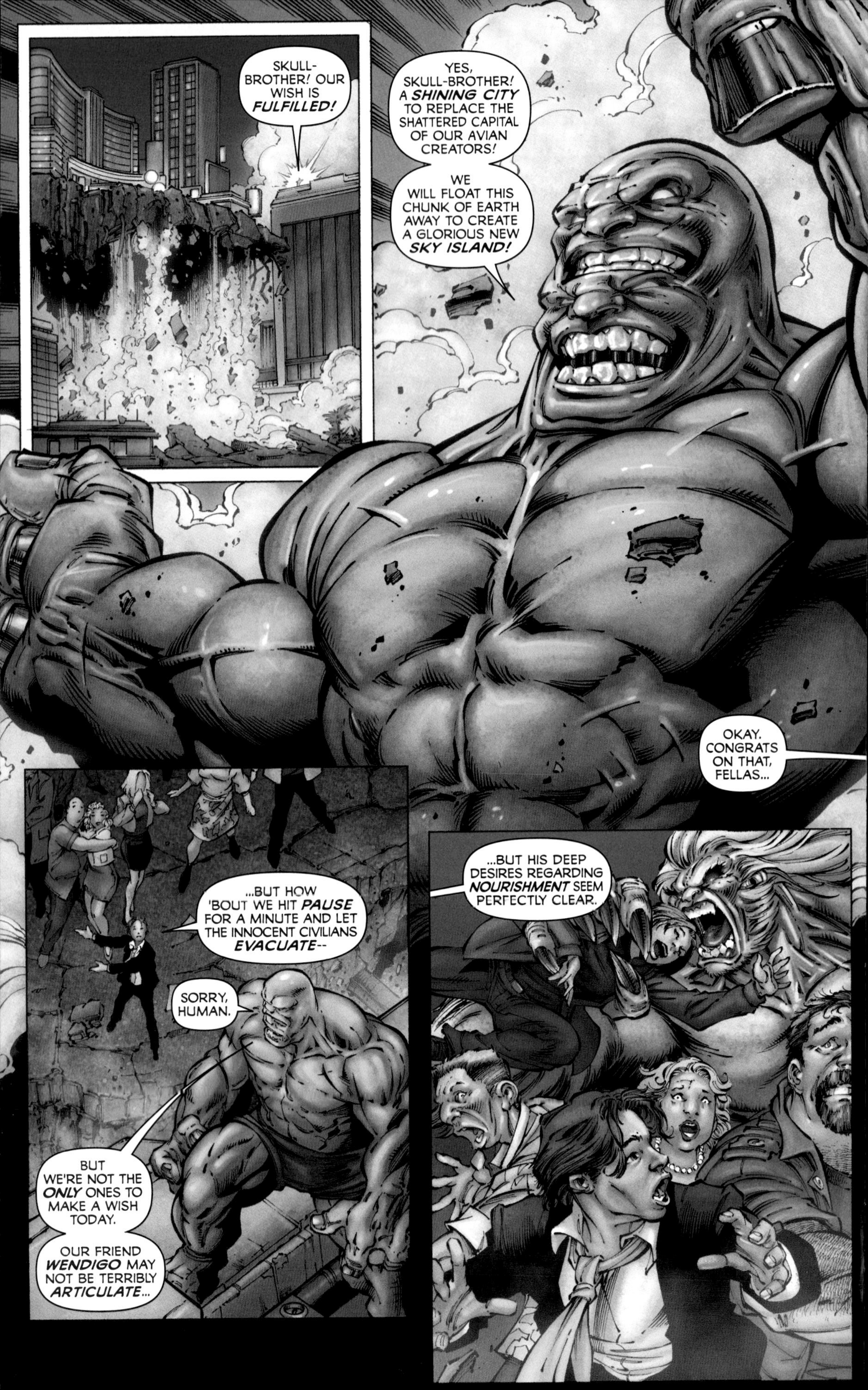
SKULL-BROTHER! OUR WISH IS *FULFILLED!*
YES, SKULL-BROTHER! A *SHINING CITY* TO REPLACE THE SHATTERED CAPITAL OF OUR AVIAN CREATORS!
WE WILL FLOAT THIS CHUNK OF EARTH AWAY TO CREATE A GLORIOUS NEW *SKY ISLAND!*
OKAY. CONGRATS ON THAT, FELLAS...
...BUT HOW 'BOUT WE HIT *PAUSE* FOR A MINUTE AND LET THE INNOCENT CIVILIANS *EVACUATE*--
SORRY, HUMAN.
BUT WE'RE NOT THE *ONLY* ONES TO MAKE A WISH TODAY.
OUR FRIEND *WENDIGO* MAY NOT BE TERRIBLY *ARTICULATE*...
...BUT HIS DEEP DESIRES REGARDING *NOURISHMENT* SEEM PERFECTLY CLEAR.

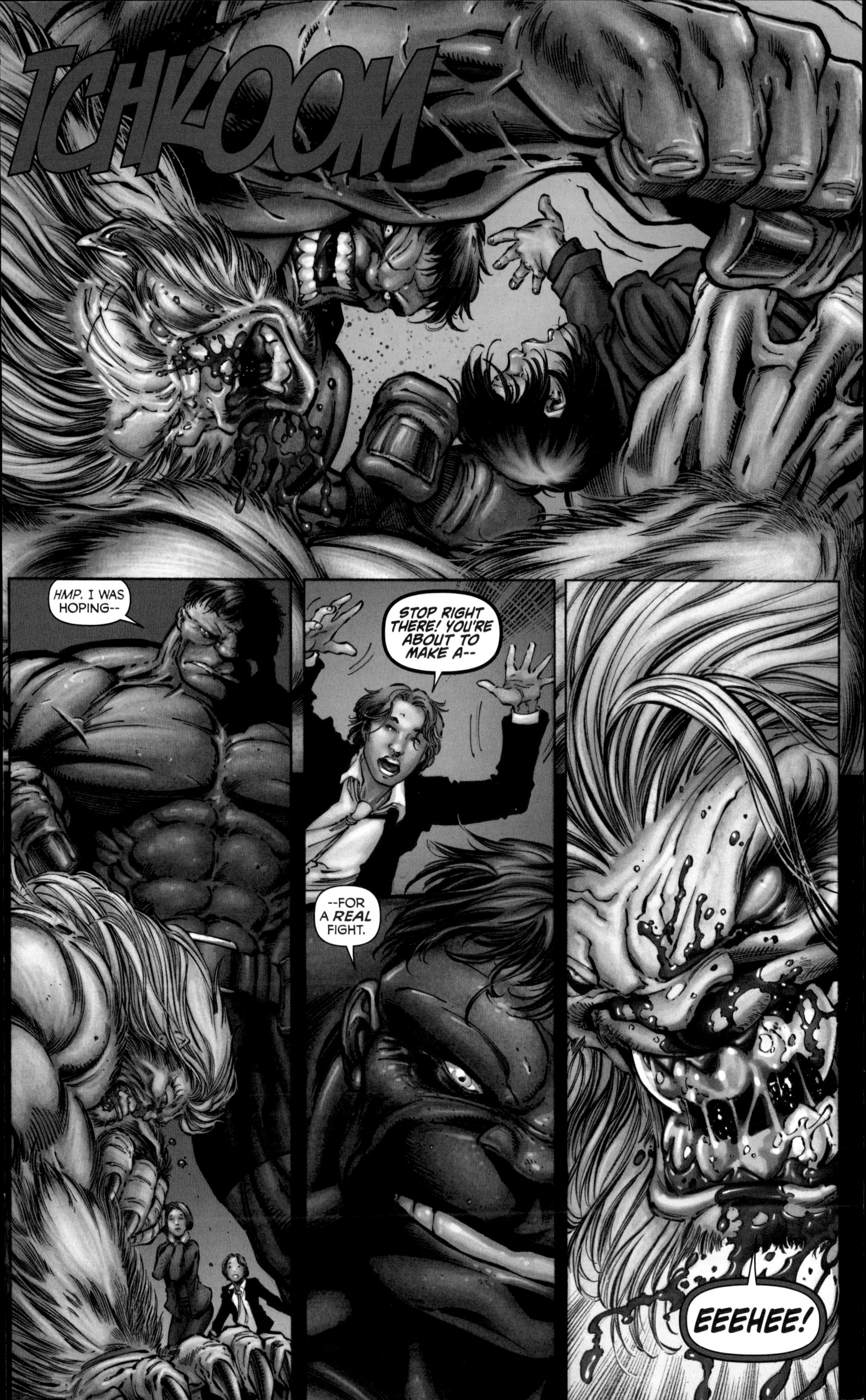
TCHKOOM
HMP. I WAS HOPING--
STOP RIGHT THERE! YOU'RE ABOUT TO MAKE A--
--FOR A REAL FIGHT.
EEEHEE!

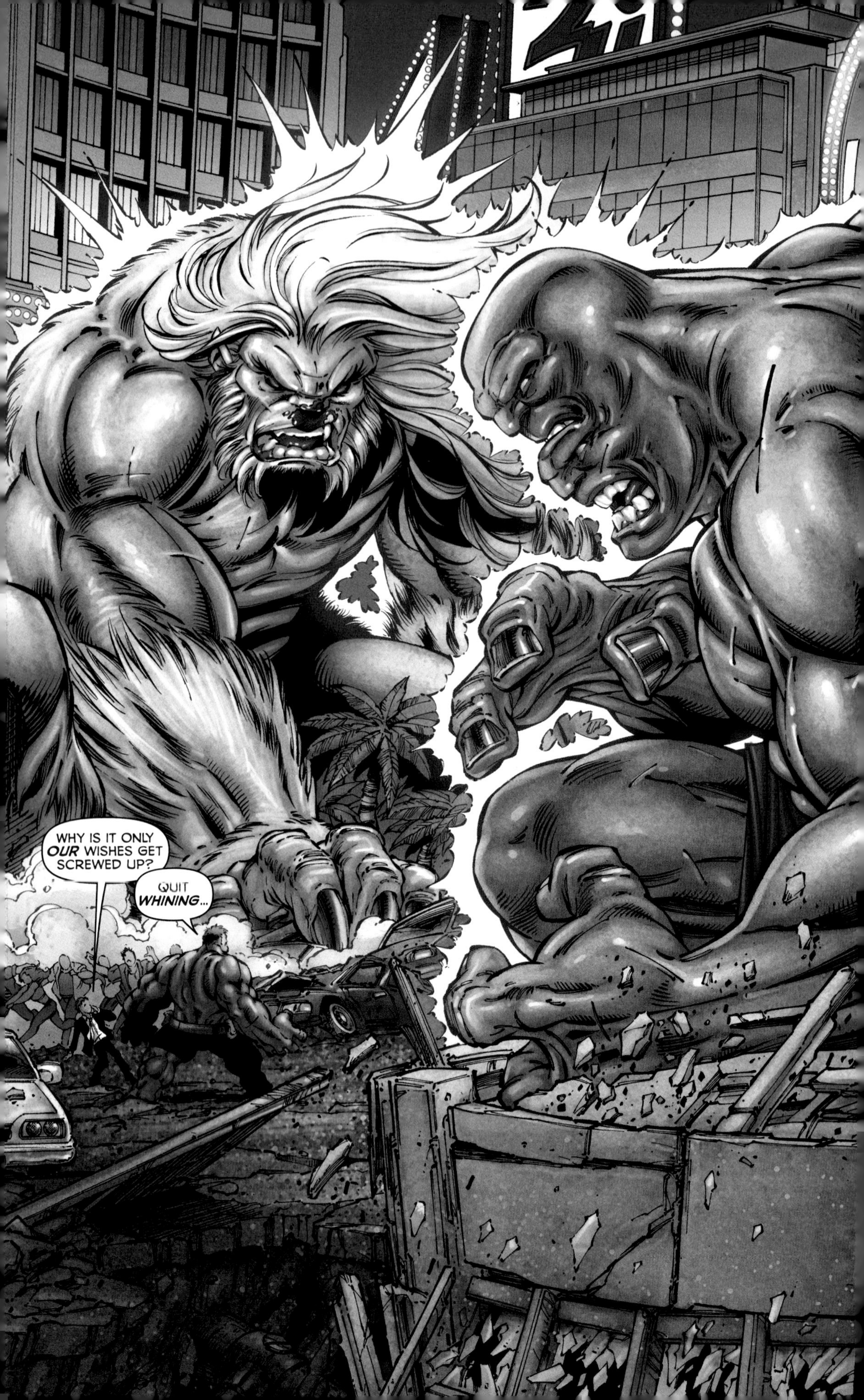
WHY IS IT ONLY *OUR* WISHES GET SCREWED UP?
QUIT *WHINING*...

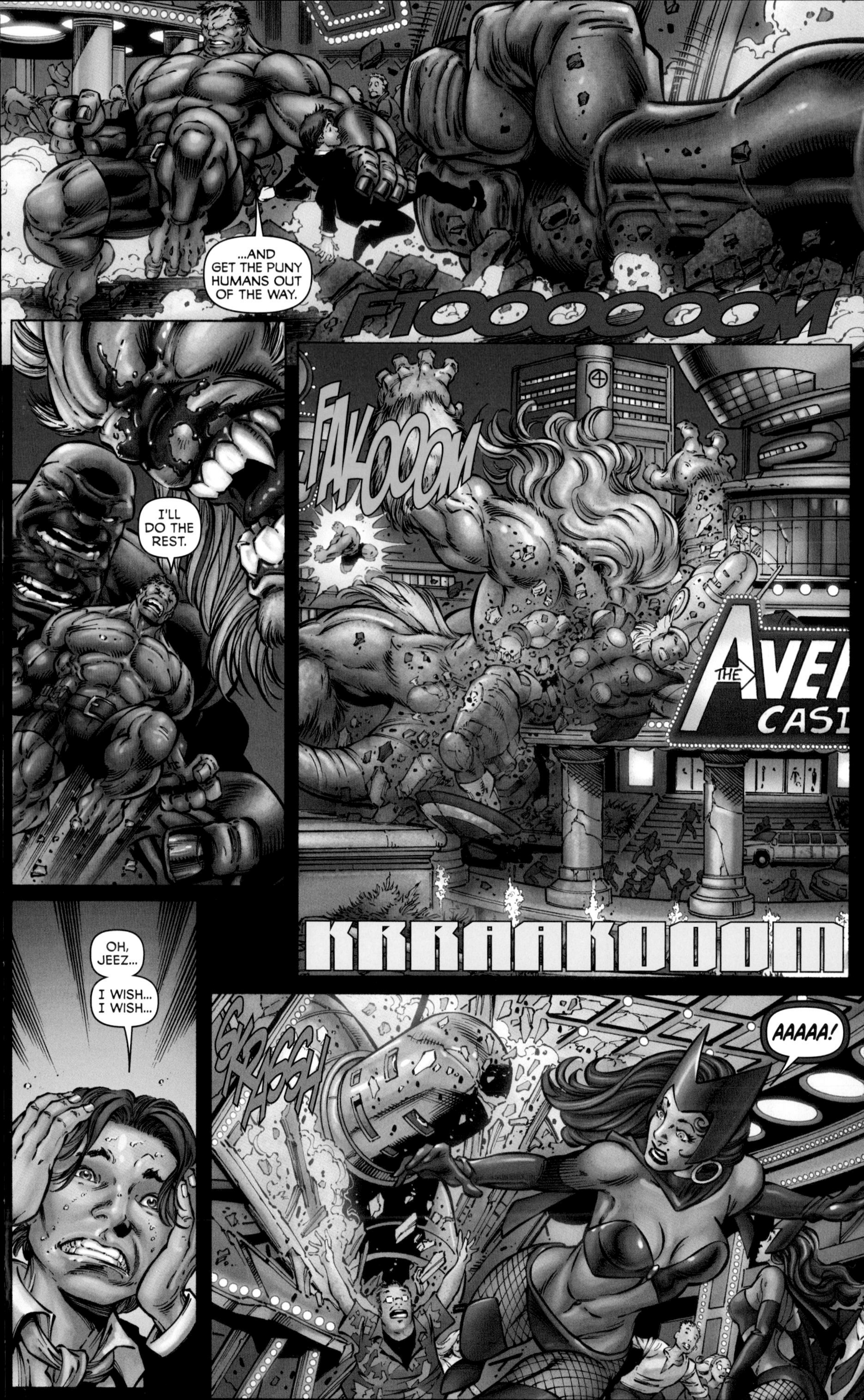
...AND GET THE PUNY HUMANS OUT OF THE WAY.
FTOOOOOOOM
I'LL DO THE REST.
FAKOOOM
THE AVE
CASI
KRRAAKOOOOM
OH, JEEZ...
I WISH... I WISH...
AAAAA!

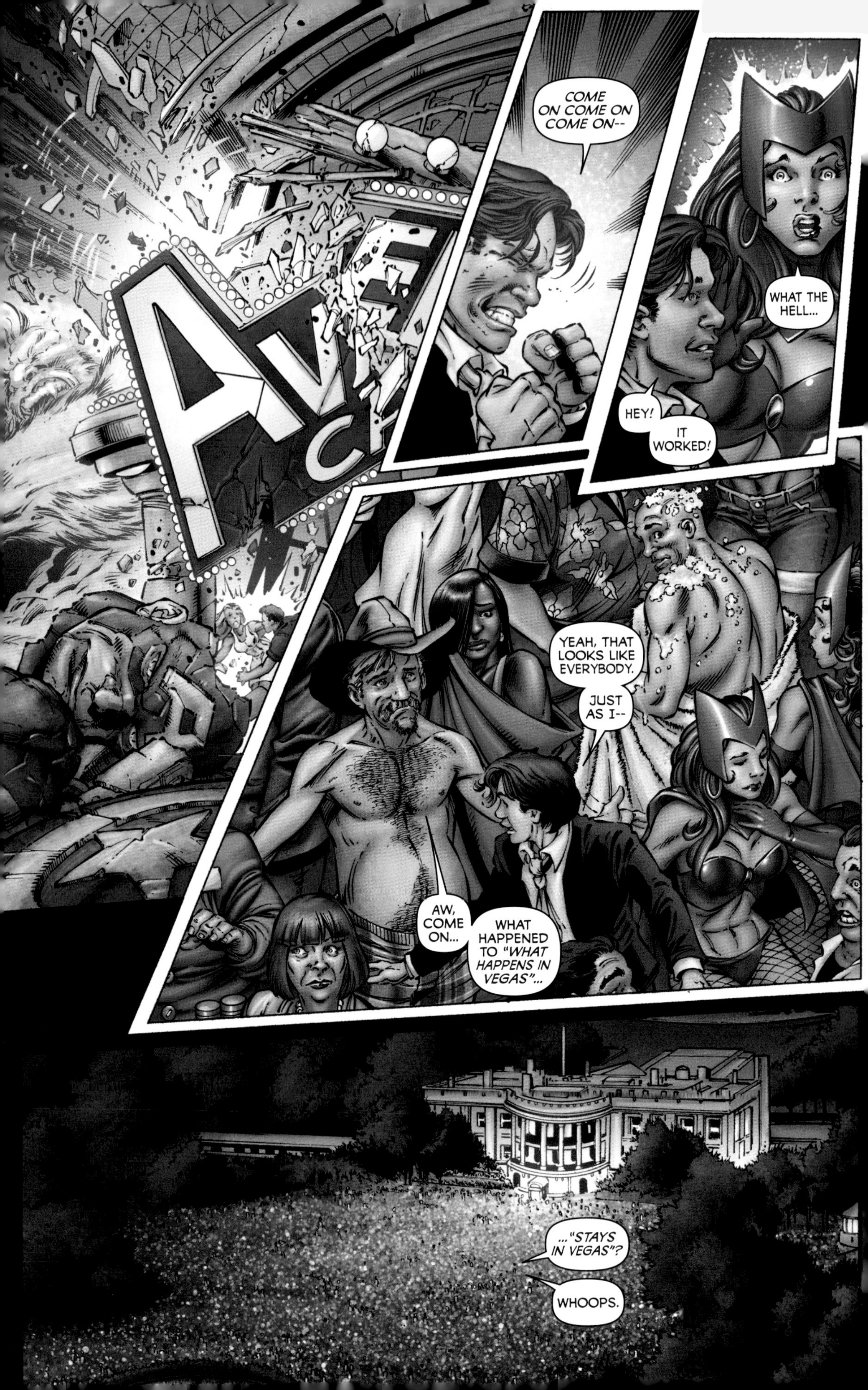
COME ON COME ON COME ON--
WHAT THE HELL...
HEY!
IT WORKED!
YEAH, THAT LOOKS LIKE EVERYBODY.
JUST AS I--
AW, COME ON...
WHAT HAPPENED TO "WHAT HAPPENS IN VEGAS"...
..."STAYS IN VEGAS"?
WHOOPS.

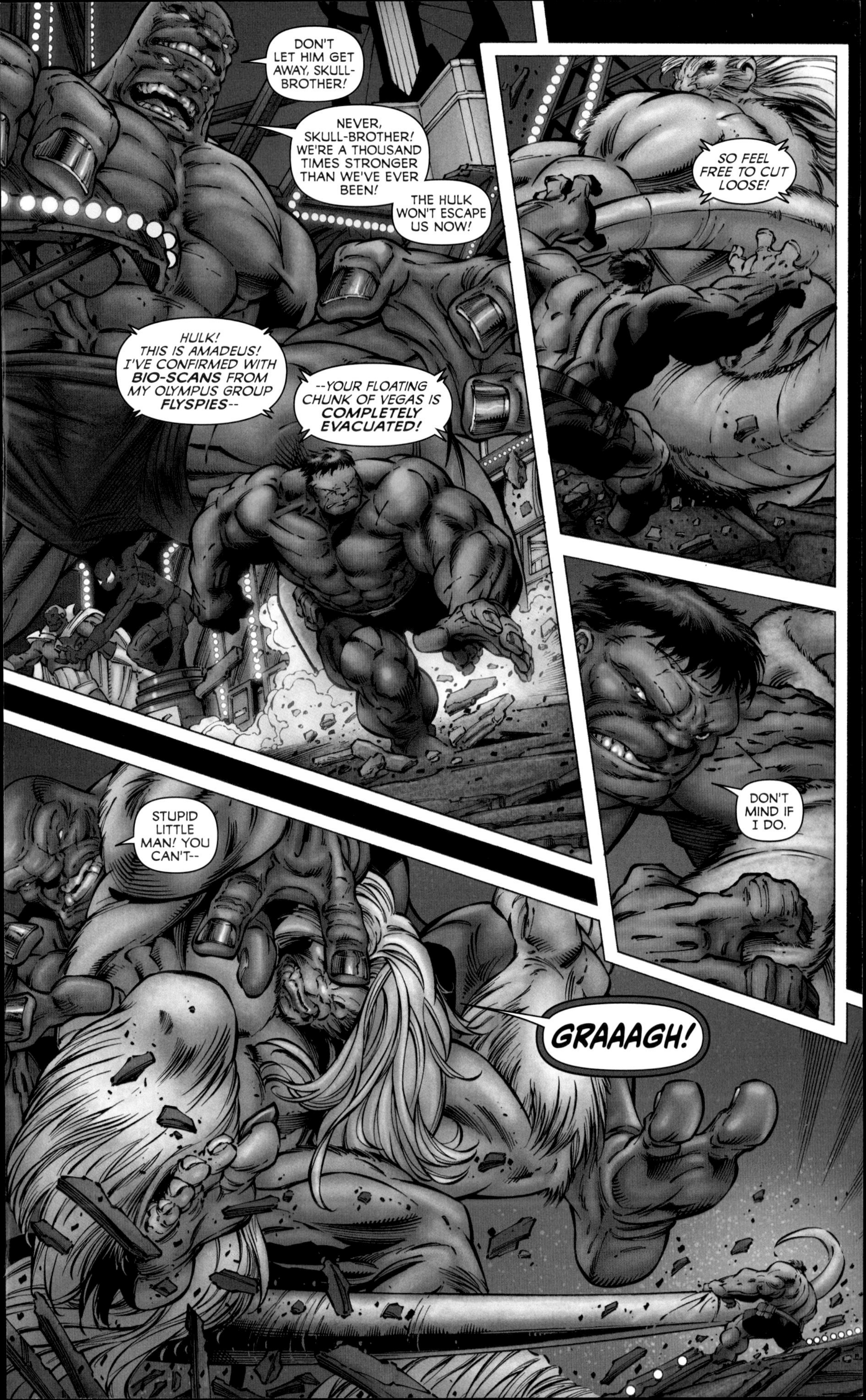
DON'T LET HIM GET AWAY, SKULL-BROTHER!
NEVER, SKULL-BROTHER! WE'RE A THOUSAND TIMES STRONGER THAN WE'VE EVER BEEN!
THE HULK WON'T ESCAPE US NOW!
HULK! THIS IS AMADEUS! I'VE CONFIRMED WITH BIO-SCANS FROM MY OLYMPUS GROUP FLYSPIES--
--YOUR FLOATING CHUNK OF VEGAS IS COMPLETELY EVACUATED!
SO FEEL FREE TO CUT LOOSE!
DON'T MIND IF I DO.
STUPID LITTLE MAN! YOU CAN'T--
GRAAAGH!

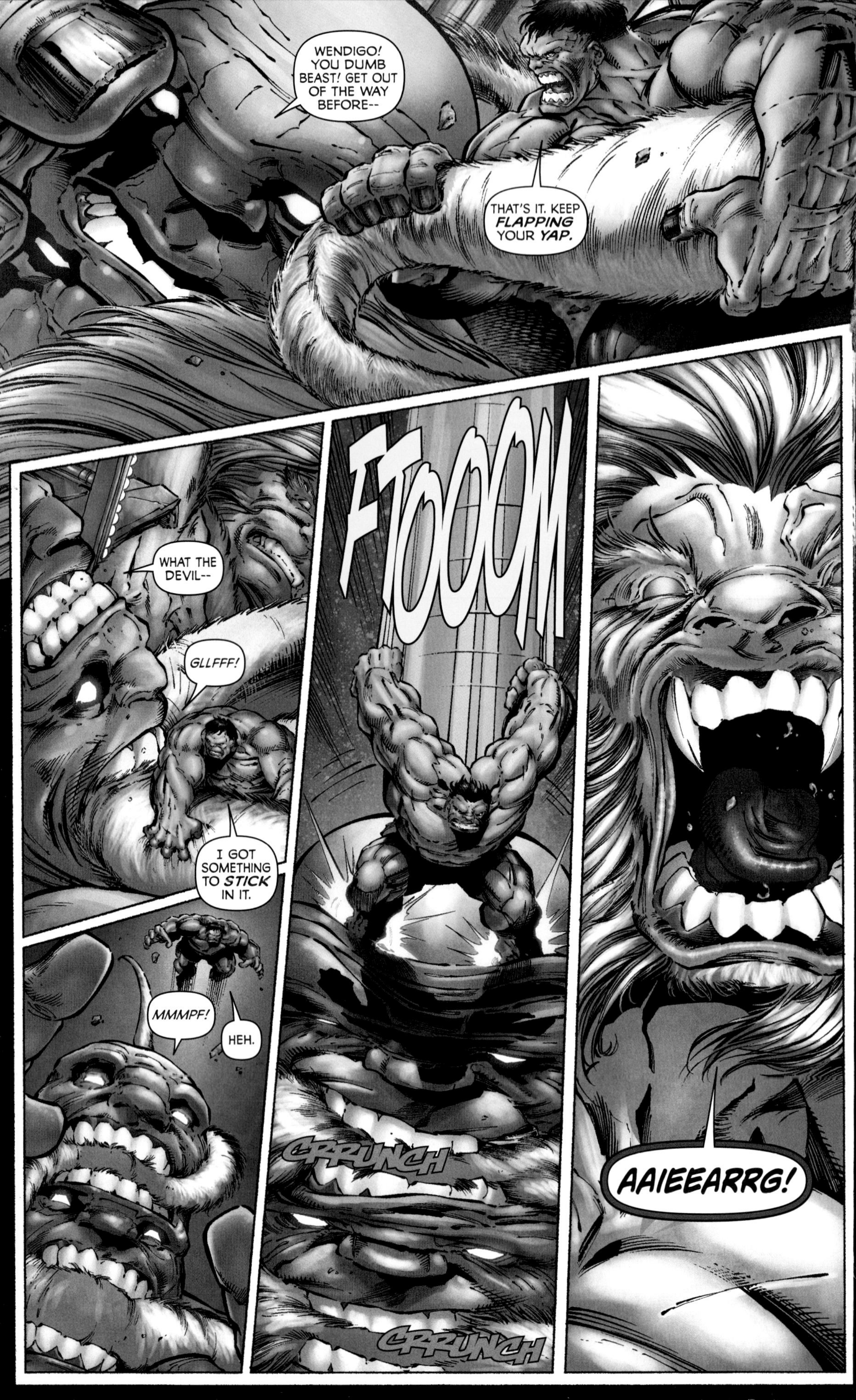
WENDIGO! YOU DUMB BEAST! GET OUT OF THE WAY BEFORE--
THAT'S IT. KEEP FLAPPING YOUR YAP.
WHAT THE DEVIL--
GLLFFF!
I GOT SOMETHING TO STICK IN IT.
MMMPF!
HEH.
FTOOOM
CRRUNCH
CRRUNCH
AAIEEARRG!

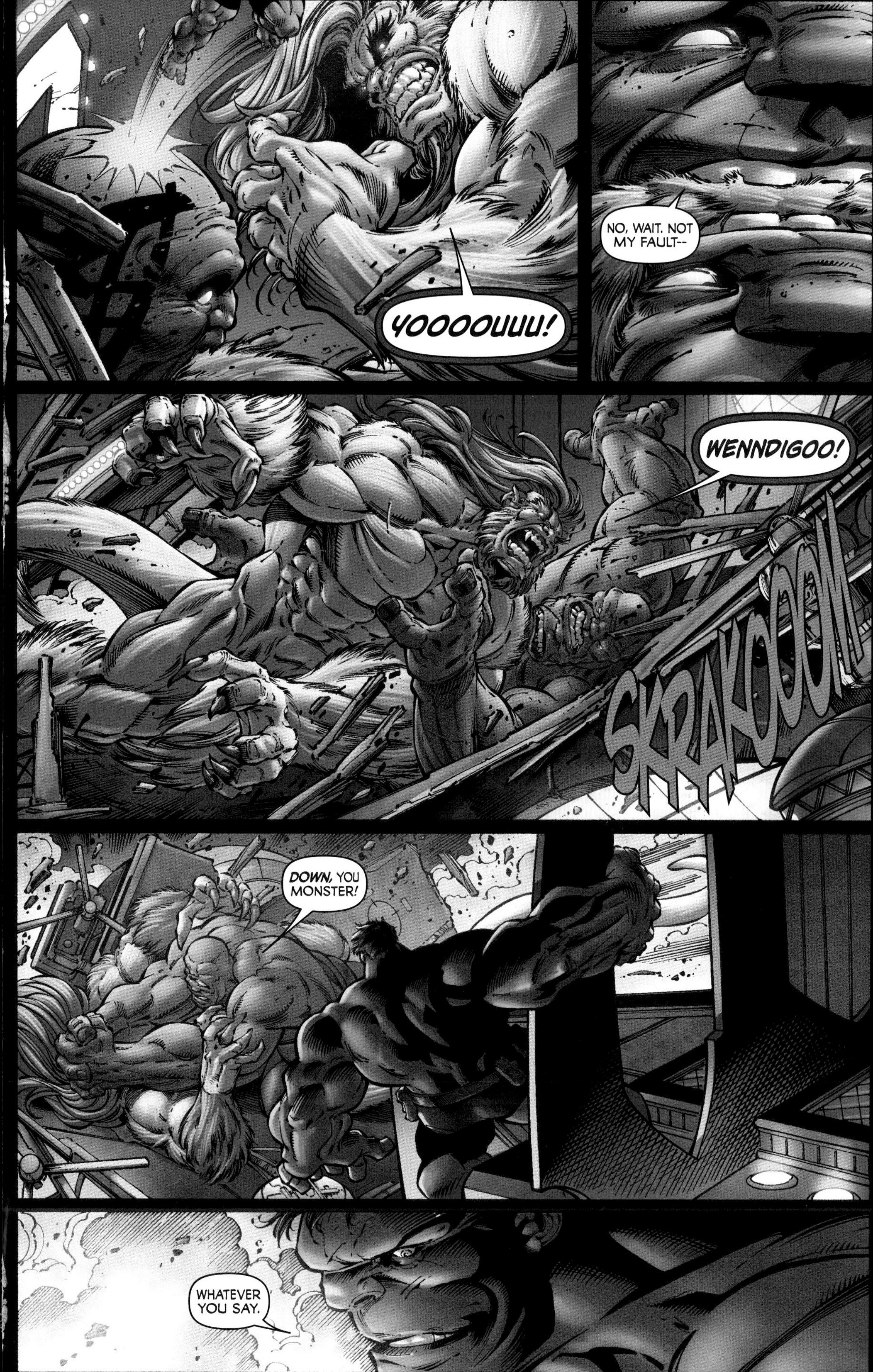
YOOOOUUU!
NO, WAIT. NOT MY FAULT--
WENNDIGOO!
SKRAKOOOM
DOWN, YOU MONSTER!
WHATEVER YOU SAY.

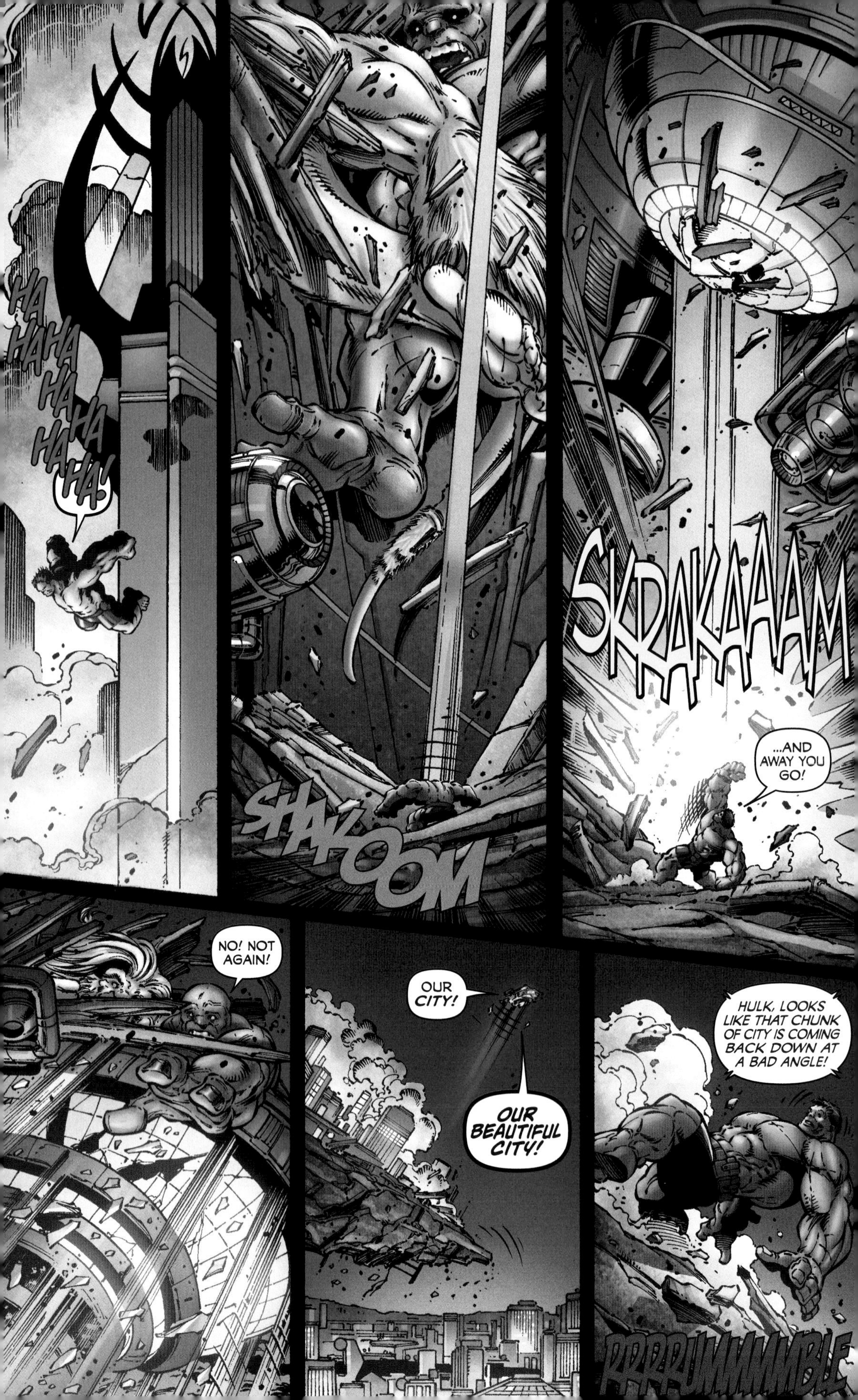
HA HA HA HA HA HA HA!
SHAKOOM
SKRAKAAAM
...AND AWAY YOU GO!
NO! NOT AGAIN!
OUR CITY!
OUR BEAUTIFUL CITY!
HULK, LOOKS LIKE THAT CHUNK OF CITY IS COMING BACK DOWN AT A BAD ANGLE!
RRRRUMMMMBLE

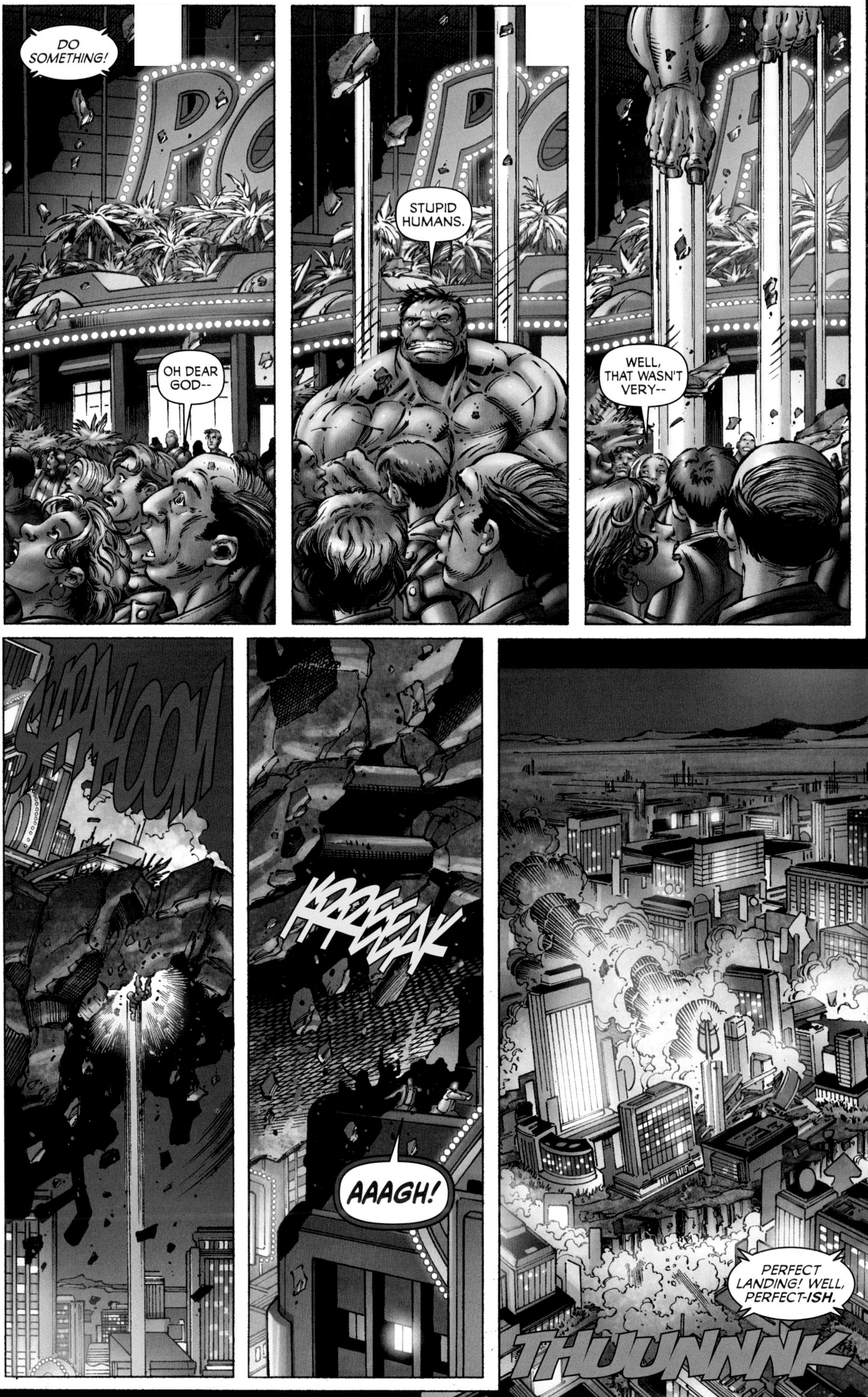
DO SOMETHING!
OH DEAR GOD--
STUPID HUMANS.
WELL, THAT WASN'T VERY--
SHPAHOOM
KRREEEAK
AAAGH!
PERFECT LANDING! WELL, PERFECT-ISH.
THUUNNNK

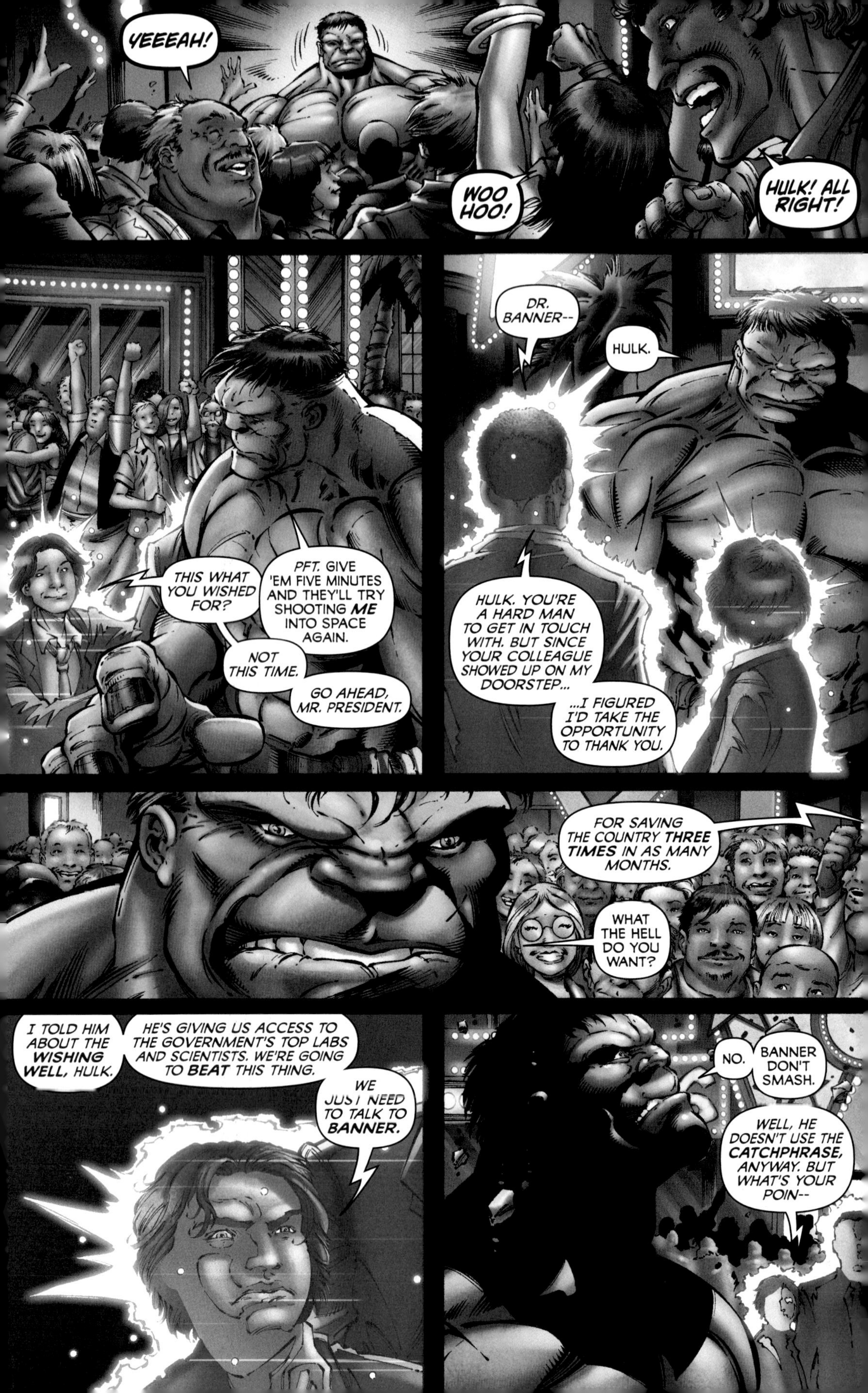
YEEEAH!
WOO HOO!
HULK! ALL RIGHT!
THIS WHAT YOU WISHED FOR?
PFT. GIVE 'EM FIVE MINUTES AND THEY'LL TRY SHOOTING ME INTO SPACE AGAIN.
NOT THIS TIME.
GO AHEAD, MR. PRESIDENT.
DR. BANNER--
HULK.
HULK. YOU'RE A HARD MAN TO GET IN TOUCH WITH. BUT SINCE YOUR COLLEAGUE SHOWED UP ON MY DOORSTEP...
...I FIGURED I'D TAKE THE OPPORTUNITY TO THANK YOU.
FOR SAVING THE COUNTRY THREE TIMES IN AS MANY MONTHS.
WHAT THE HELL DO YOU WANT?
I TOLD HIM ABOUT THE WISHING WELL, HULK.
HE'S GIVING US ACCESS TO THE GOVERNMENT'S TOP LABS AND SCIENTISTS. WE'RE GOING TO BEAT THIS THING.
WE JUST NEED TO TALK TO BANNER.
NO.
BANNER DON'T SMASH.
WELL, HE DOESN'T USE THE CATCHPHRASE, ANYWAY. BUT WHAT'S YOUR POIN--

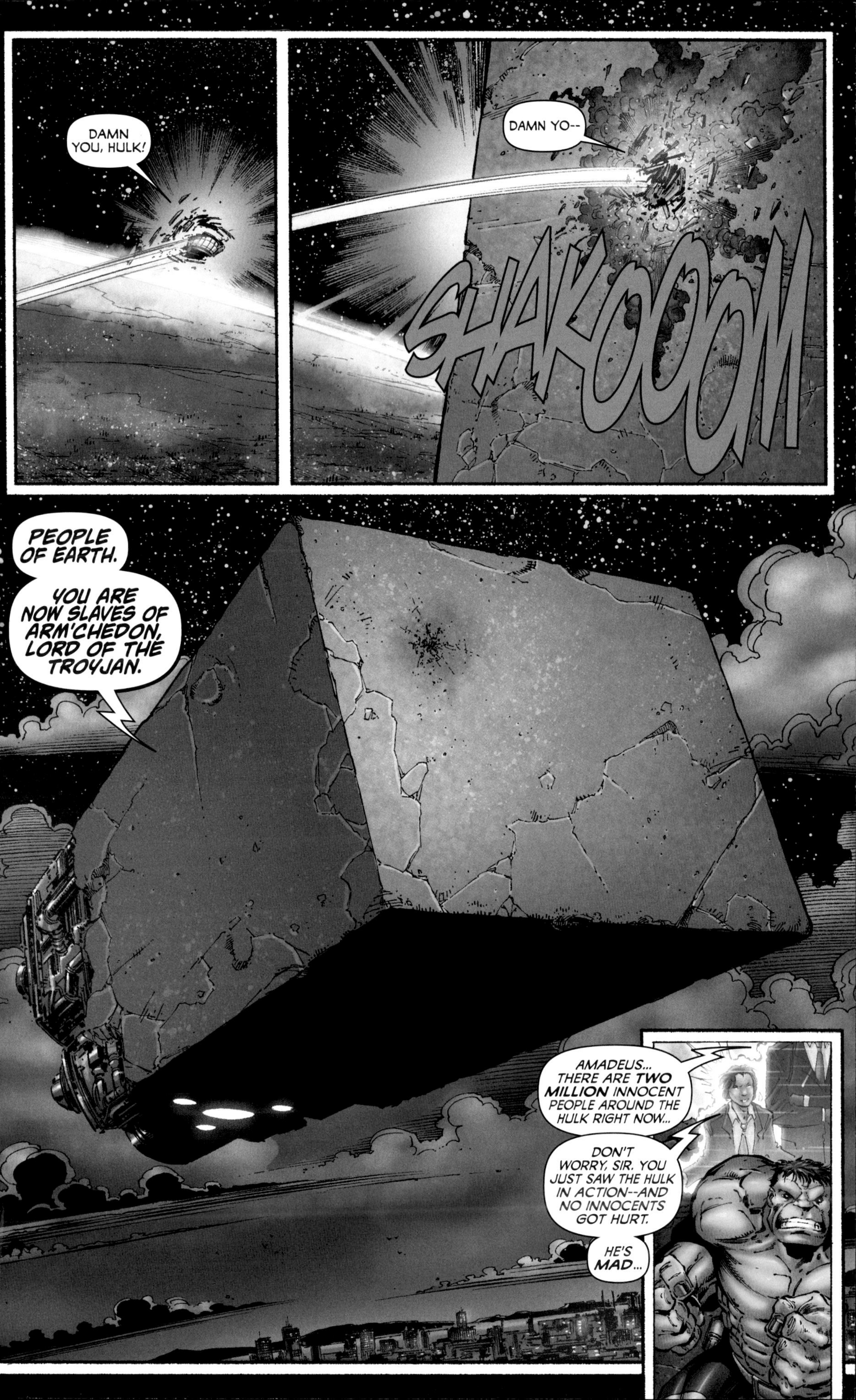

DAMN YOU, HULK!
DAMN YO--
SHAKOOOM
PEOPLE OF EARTH.
YOU ARE NOW SLAVES OF ARM'CHEDON, LORD OF THE TROYJAN.
AMADEUS... THERE ARE TWO MILLION INNOCENT PEOPLE AROUND THE HULK RIGHT NOW...
DON'T WORRY, SIR. YOU JUST SAW THE HULK IN ACTION--AND NO INNOCENTS GOT HURT.
HE'S MAD...

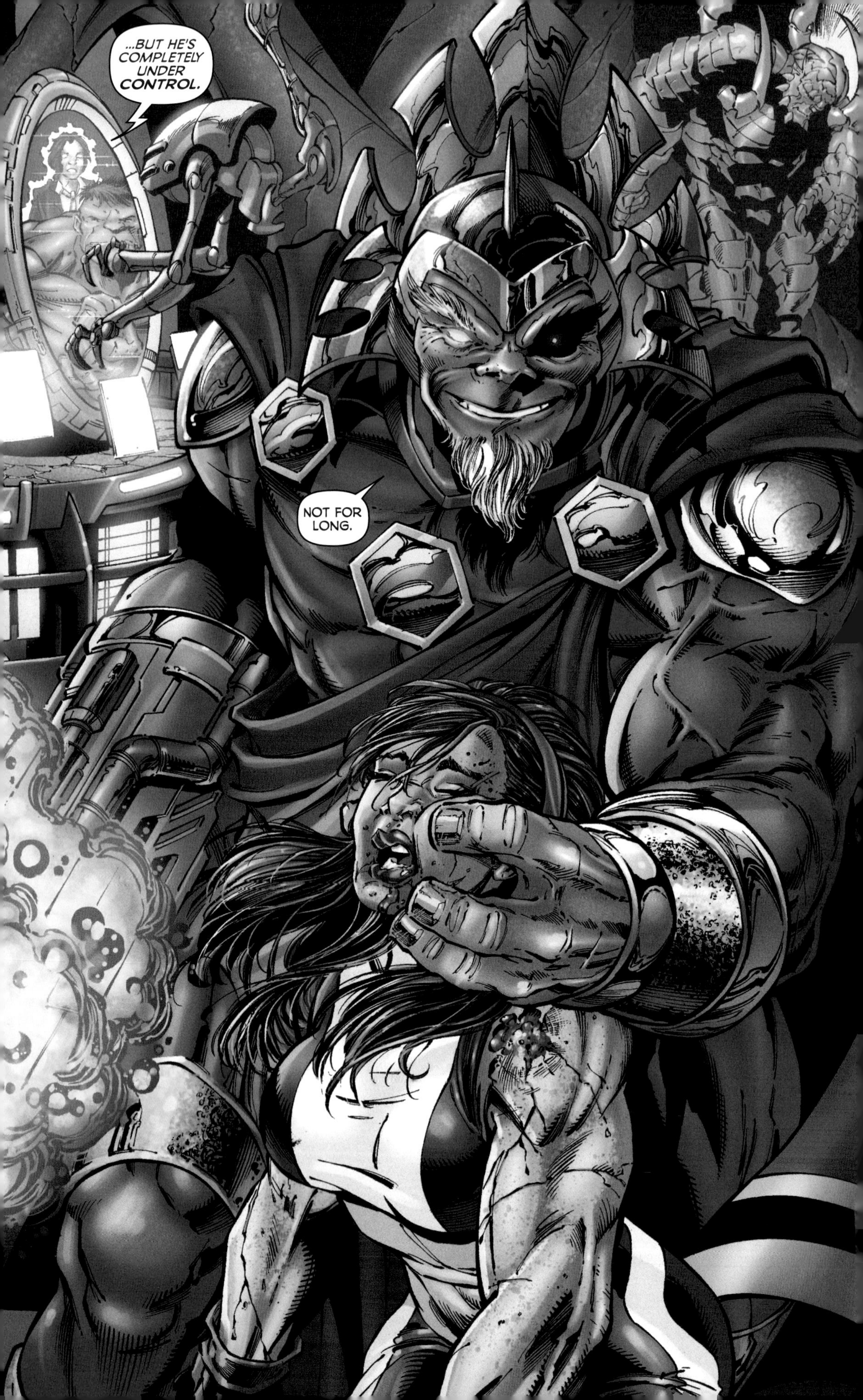
...BUT HE'S COMPLETELY UNDER CONTROL.
NOT FOR LONG.

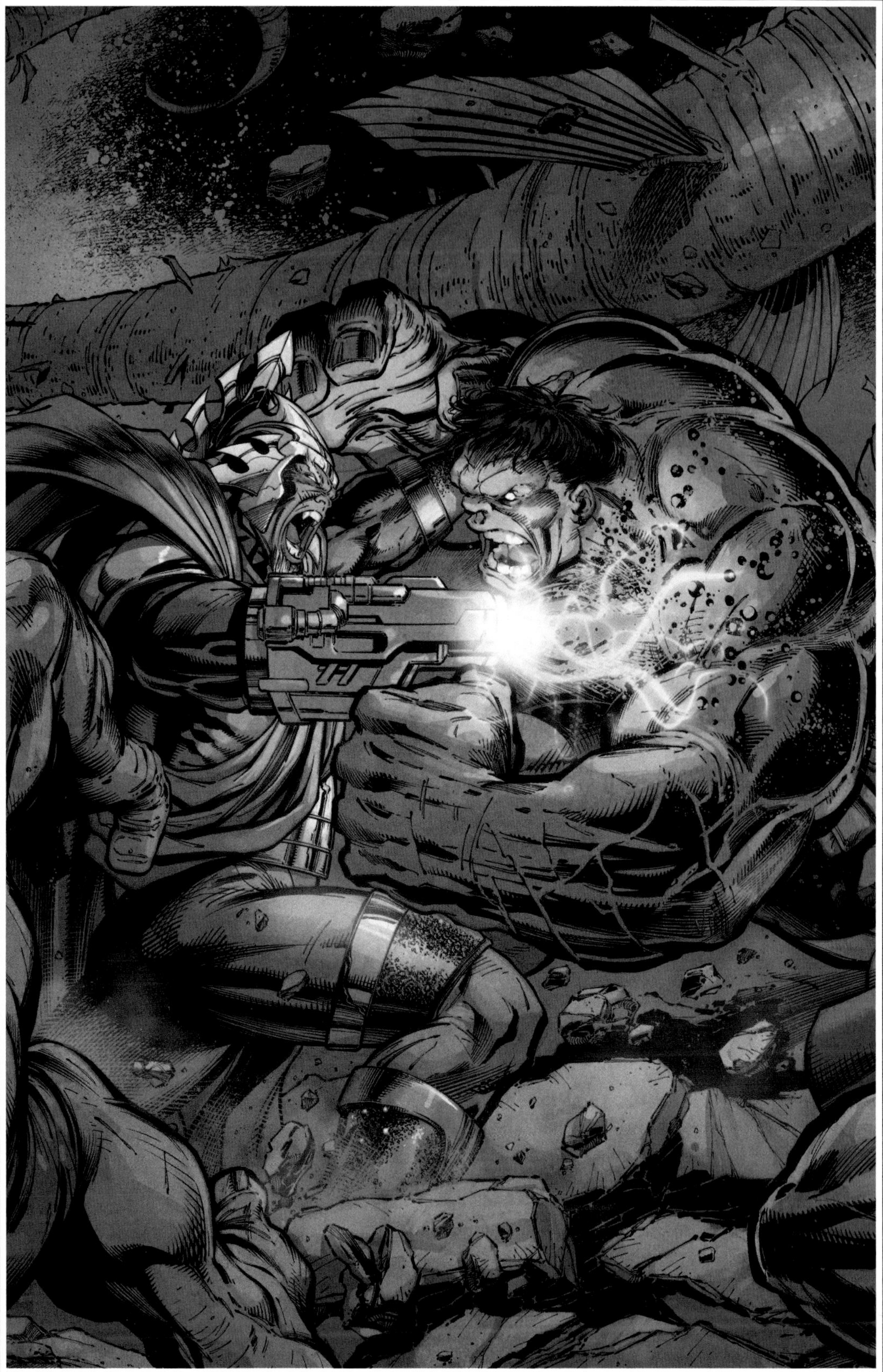

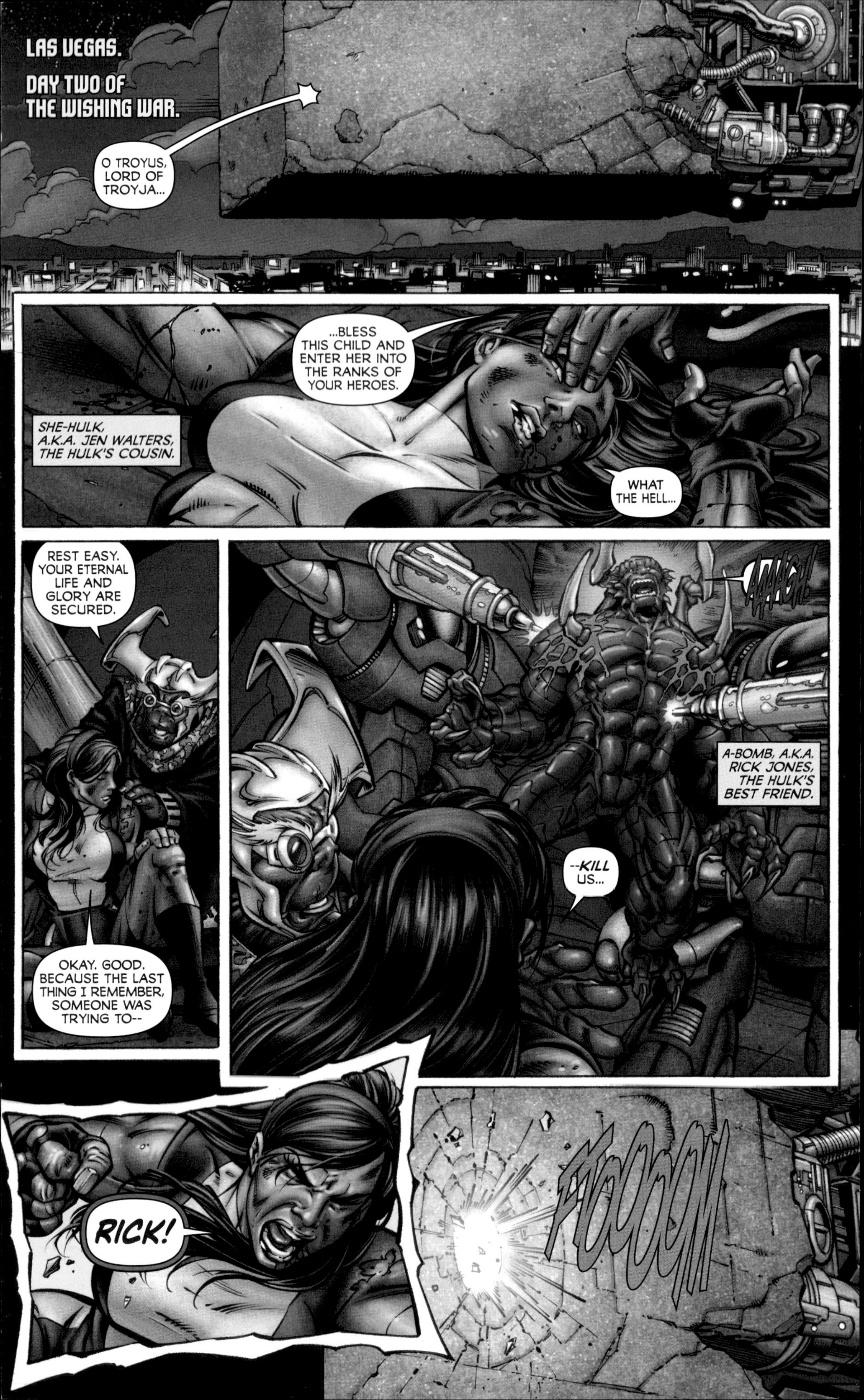
LAS VEGAS.
DAY TWO OF THE WISHING WAR.
O TROYUS, LORD OF TROYJA...
...BLESS THIS CHILD AND ENTER HER INTO THE RANKS OF YOUR HEROES.
SHE-HULK, A.K.A. JEN WALTERS, THE HULK'S COUSIN.
WHAT THE HELL...
REST EASY. YOUR ETERNAL LIFE AND GLORY ARE SECURED.
OKAY. GOOD. BECAUSE THE LAST THING I REMEMBER, SOMEONE WAS TRYING TO--
--KILL US...
AAAAGH!
A-BOMB, A.K.A. RICK JONES, THE HULK'S BEST FRIEND.
RICK!
FTOOOOM

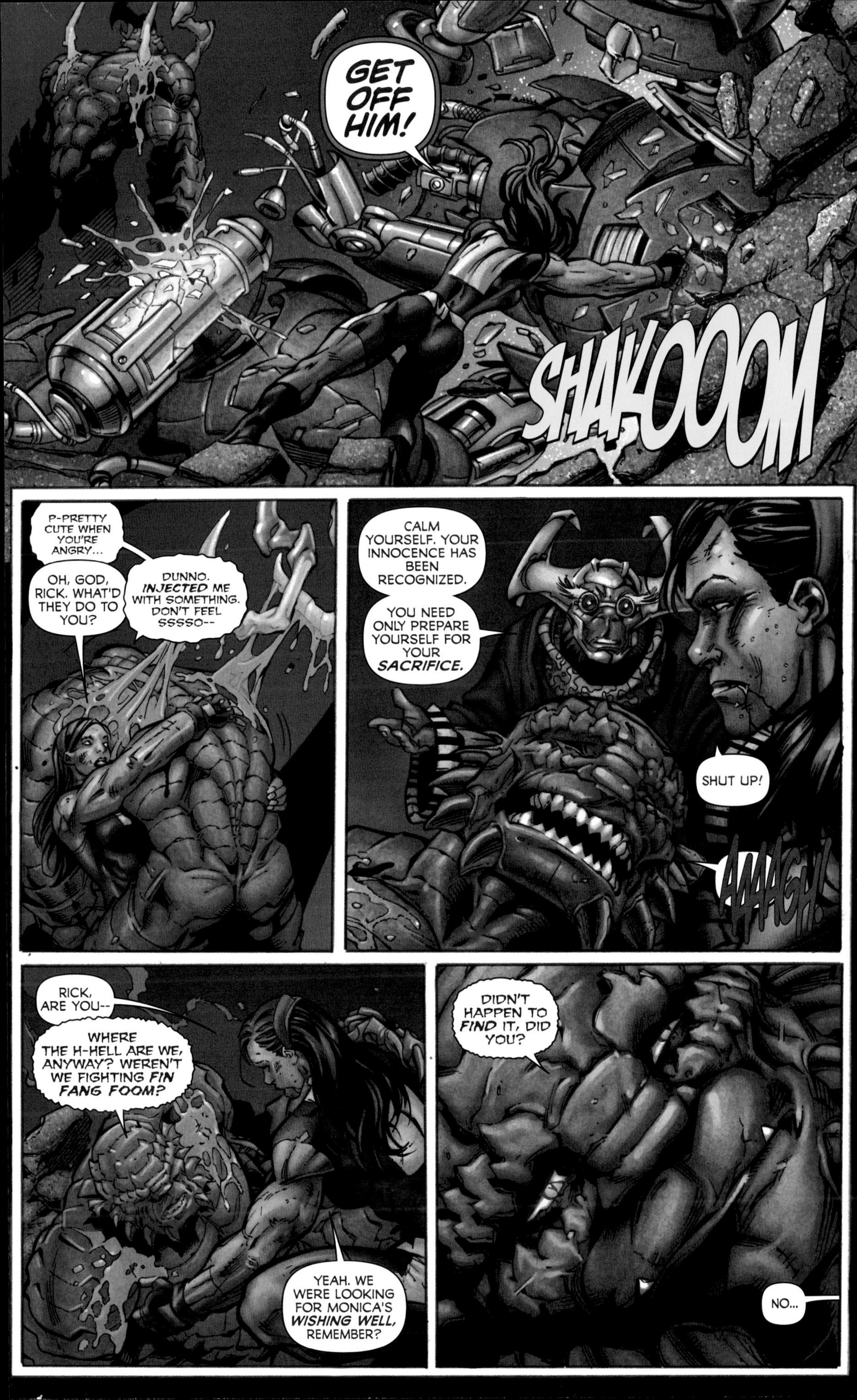
GET OFF HIM!
SHAKOOOM
P-PRETTY CUTE WHEN YOU'RE ANGRY...
OH, GOD, RICK. WHAT'D THEY DO TO YOU?
DUNNO. INJECTED ME WITH SOMETHING. DON'T FEEL SSSSO--
CALM YOURSELF. YOUR INNOCENCE HAS BEEN RECOGNIZED.
YOU NEED ONLY PREPARE YOURSELF FOR YOUR SACRIFICE.
SHUT UP!
AAAAGH!
RICK, ARE YOU--
WHERE THE H-HELL ARE WE, ANYWAY? WEREN'T WE FIGHTING FIN FANG FOOM?
YEAH. WE WERE LOOKING FOR MONICA'S WISHING WELL, REMEMBER?
DIDN'T HAPPEN TO FIND IT, DID YOU?
NO...

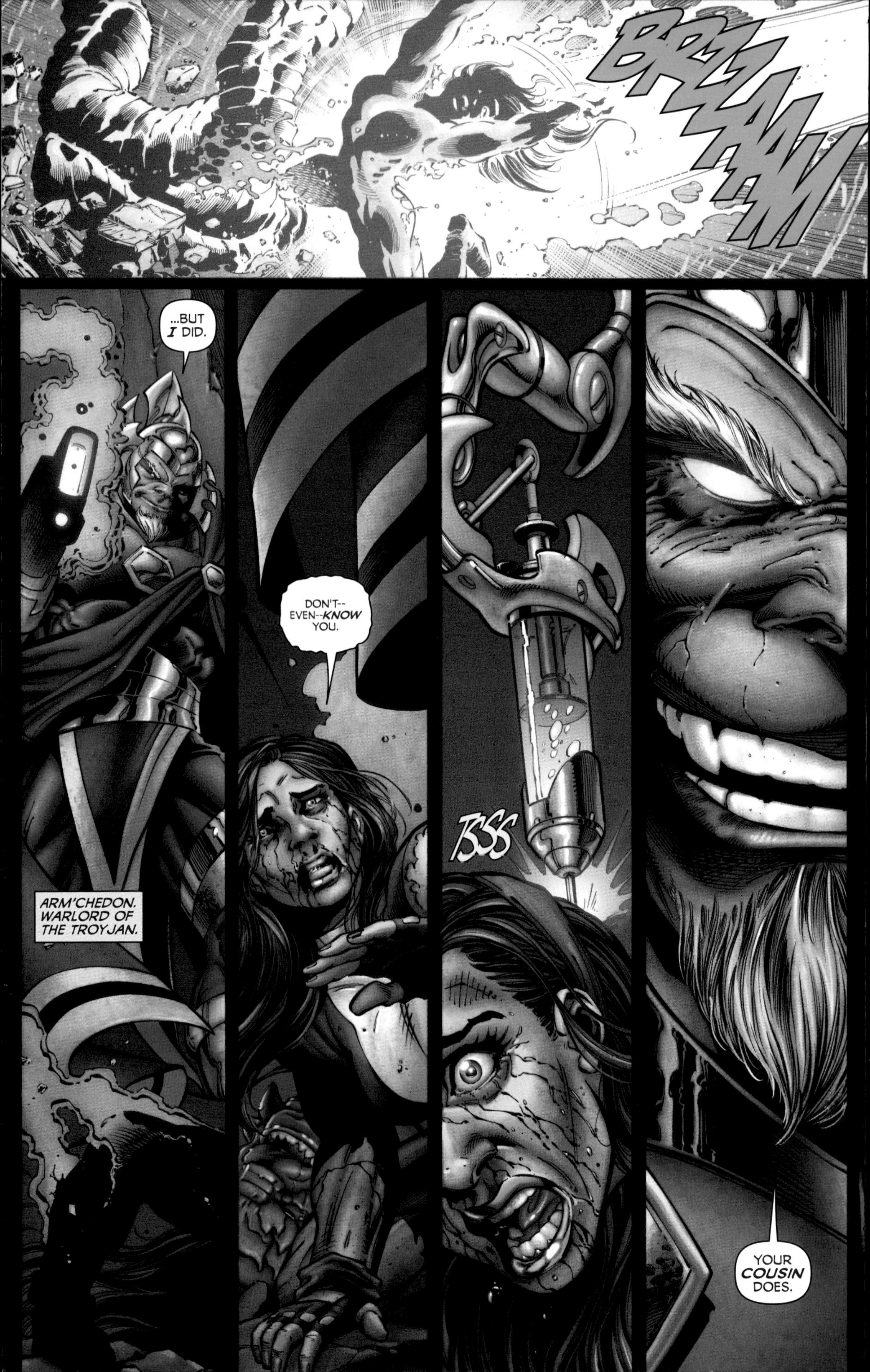
BRZZAAM
...BUT *I* DID.
ARM'CHEDON. WARLORD OF THE TROYJAN.
DON'T-- EVEN--*KNOW* YOU.
TSSS
YOUR *COUSIN* DOES.

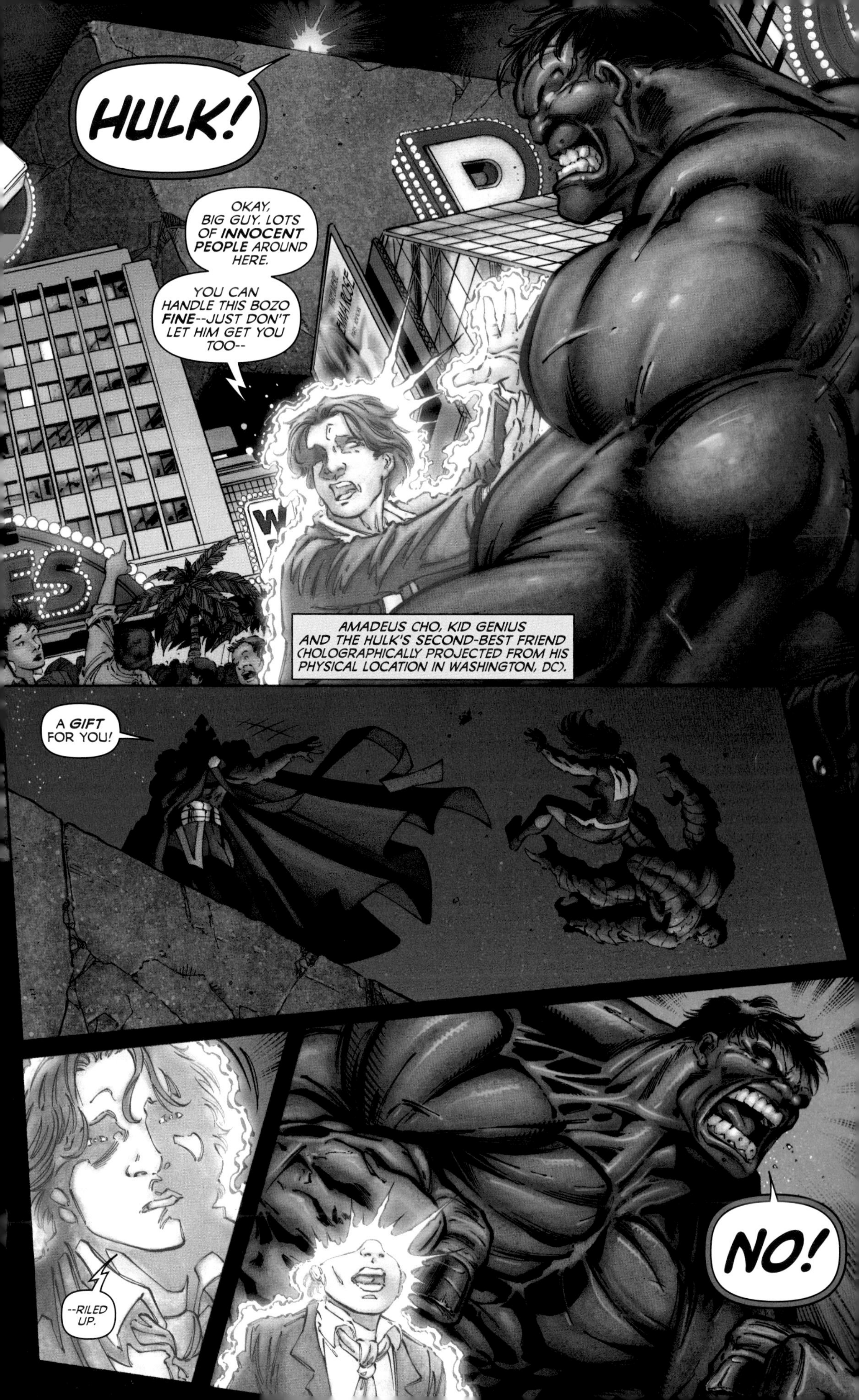
HULK!
OKAY, BIG GUY. LOTS OF **INNOCENT PEOPLE** AROUND HERE.
YOU CAN HANDLE THIS BOZO **FINE**--JUST DON'T LET HIM GET YOU TOO--
AMADEUS CHO, KID GENIUS AND THE HULK'S SECOND-BEST FRIEND (HOLOGRAPHICALLY PROJECTED FROM HIS PHYSICAL LOCATION IN WASHINGTON, DC).
A *GIFT* FOR YOU!
--RILED UP.
NO!

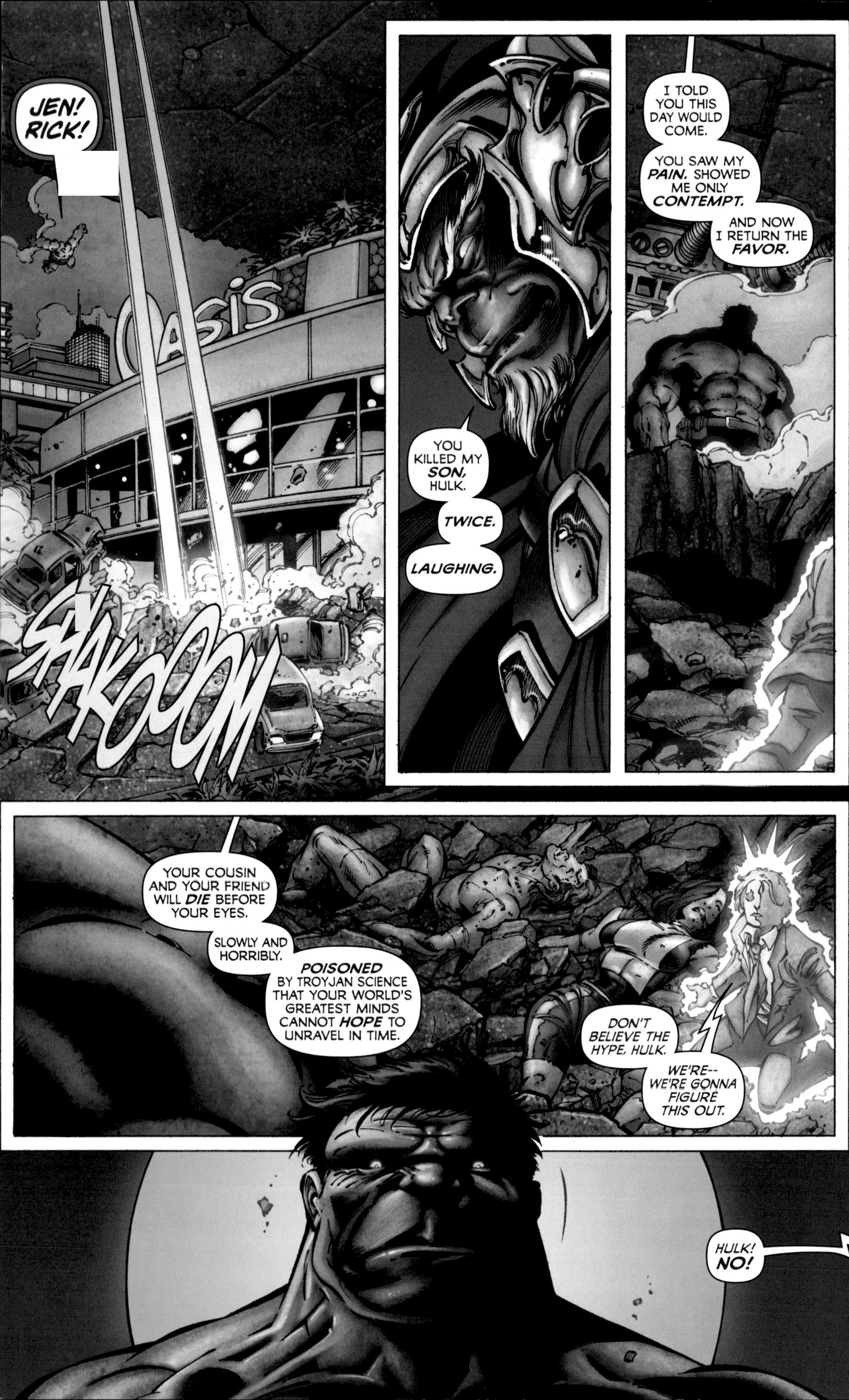
JEN! RICK!
SHAKOOOM
YOU KILLED MY *SON,* HULK.
TWICE.
LAUGHING.
I TOLD YOU THIS DAY WOULD COME.
YOU SAW MY *PAIN.* SHOWED ME ONLY *CONTEMPT.*
AND NOW I RETURN THE *FAVOR.*
YOUR COUSIN AND YOUR FRIEND WILL *DIE* BEFORE YOUR EYES.
SLOWLY AND HORRIBLY.
POISONED BY TROYJAN SCIENCE THAT YOUR WORLD'S GREATEST MINDS CANNOT *HOPE* TO UNRAVEL IN TIME.
DON'T BELIEVE THE HYPE, HULK.
WE'RE-- WE'RE GONNA FIGURE THIS OUT.
HULK! *NO!*

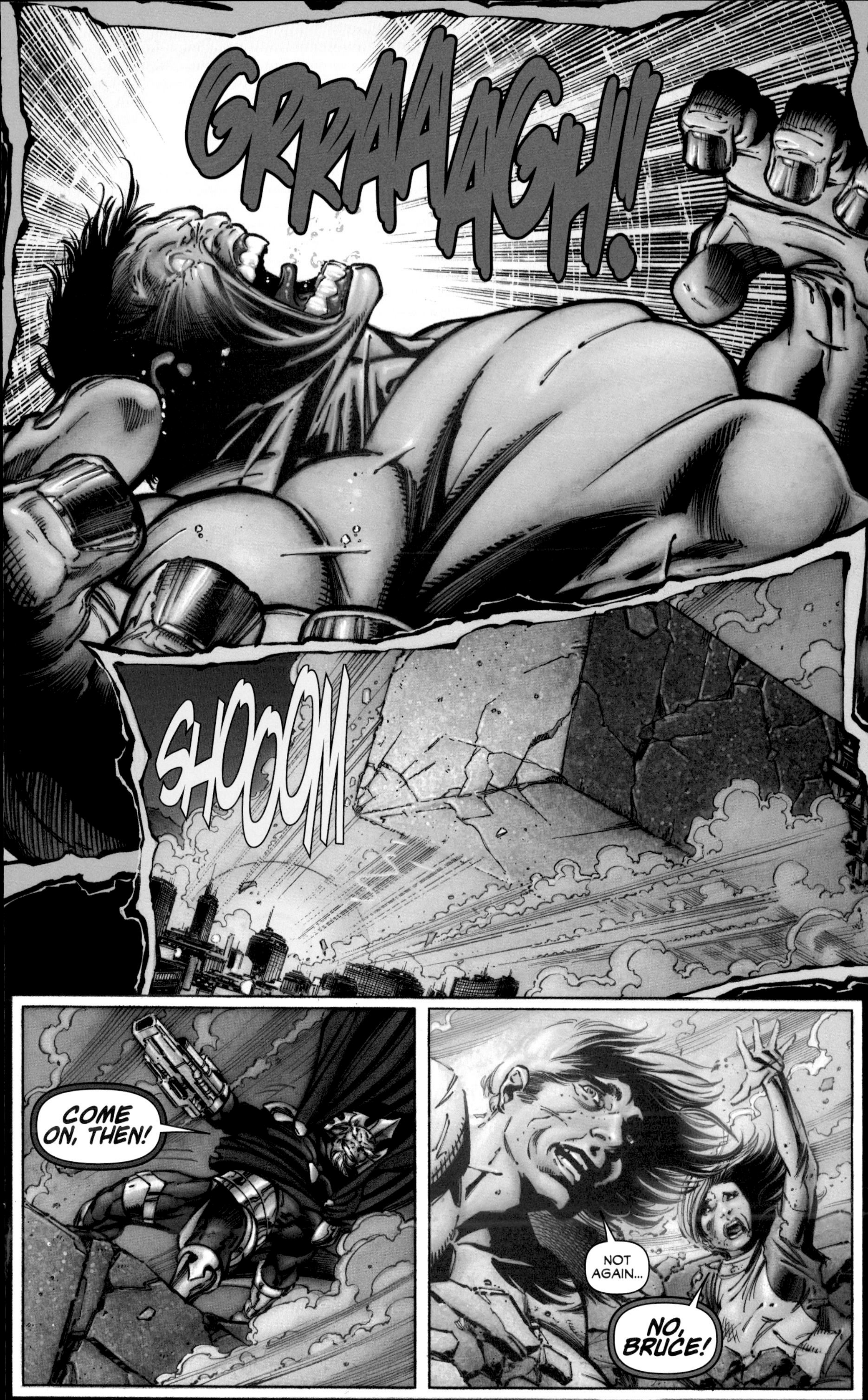
GRRAAAAGH!!
SHOOOM
COME ON, THEN!
NOT AGAIN...
NO, BRUCE!

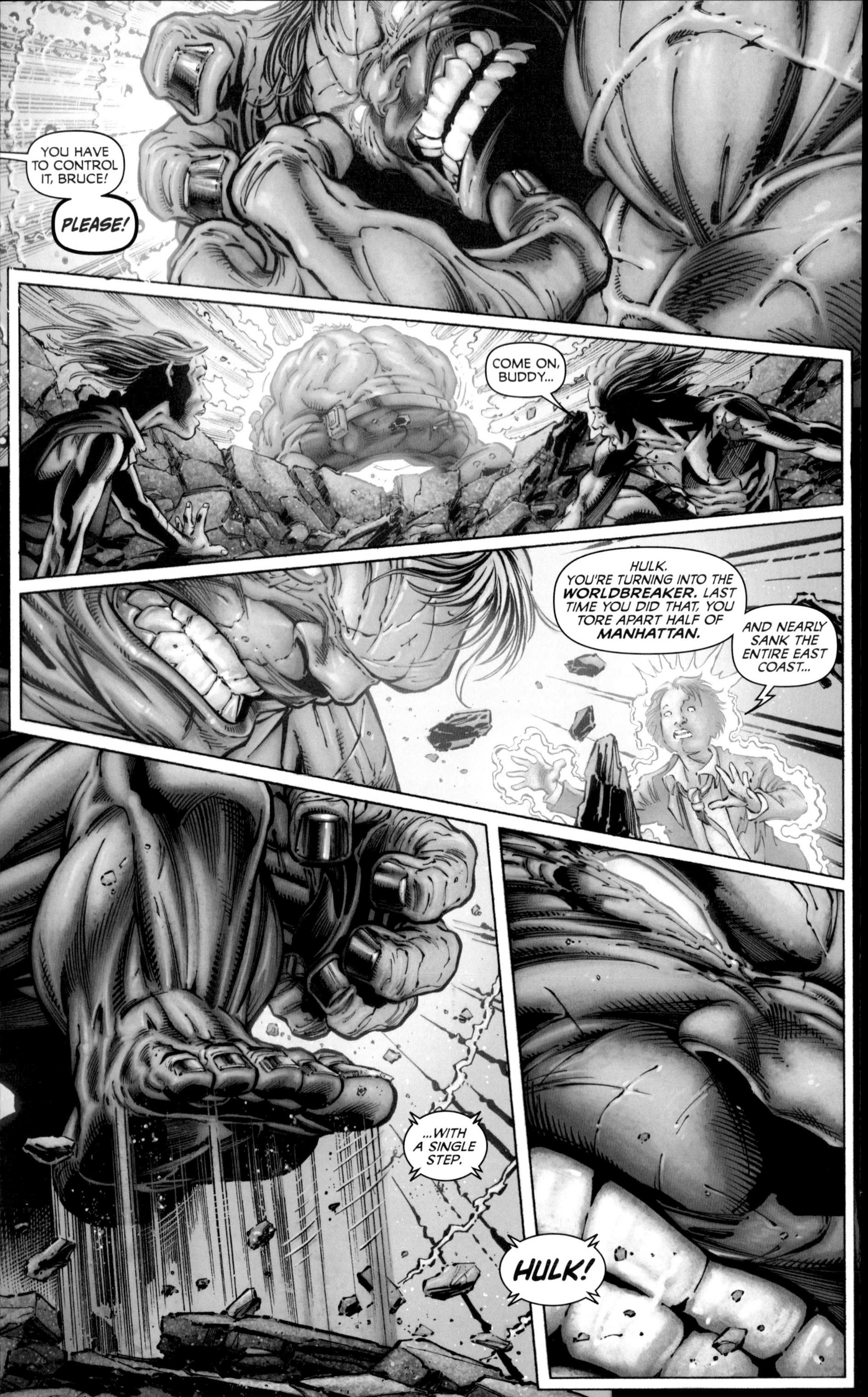
YOU HAVE TO CONTROL IT, BRUCE!
PLEASE!
COME ON, BUDDY...
HULK. YOU'RE TURNING INTO THE WORLDBREAKER. LAST TIME YOU DID THAT, YOU TORE APART HALF OF MANHATTAN.
AND NEARLY SANK THE ENTIRE EAST COAST...
...WITH A SINGLE STEP.
HULK!

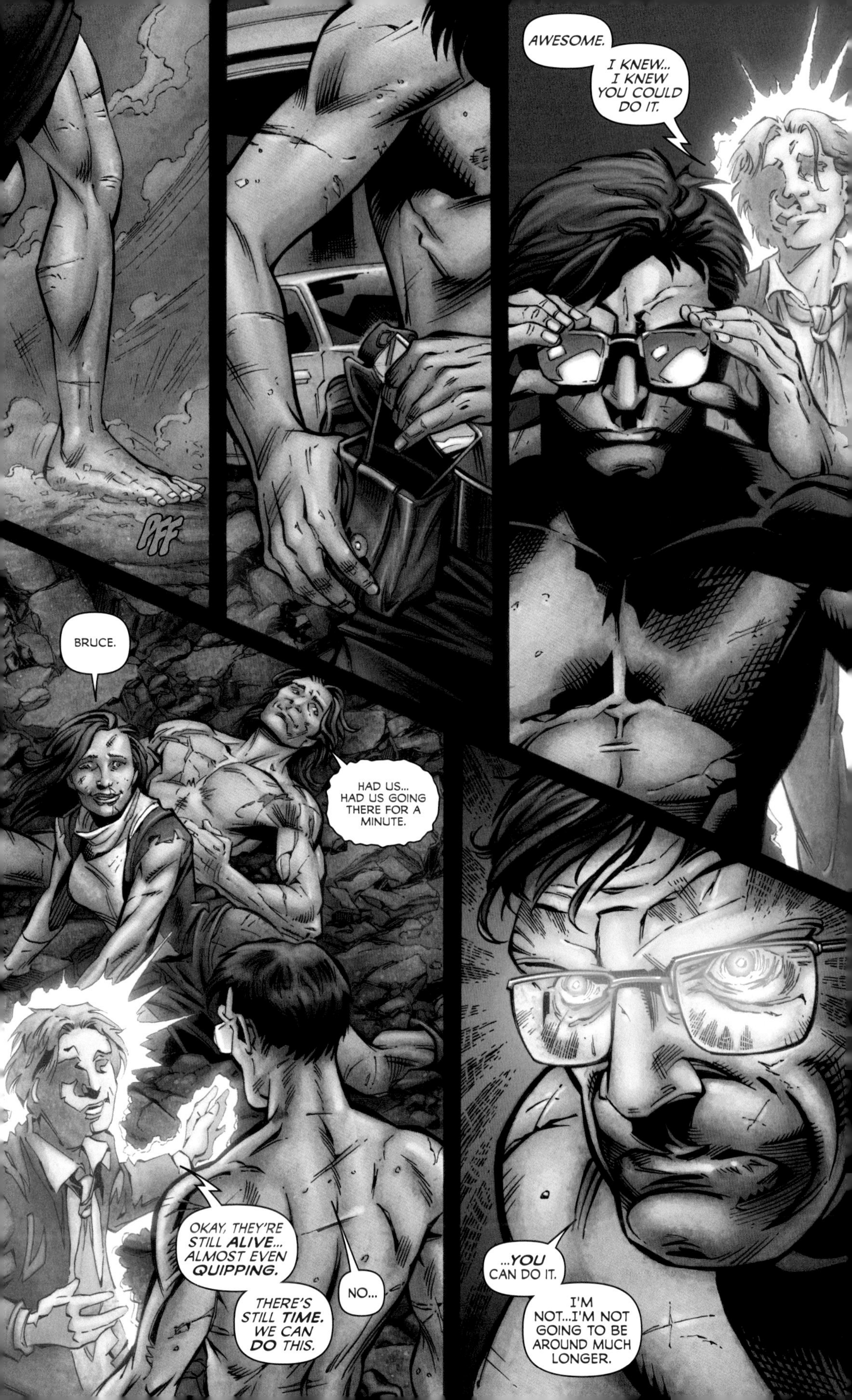
PFF
AWESOME.
I KNEW... I KNEW YOU COULD DO IT.
BRUCE.
HAD US... HAD US GOING THERE FOR A MINUTE.
OKAY, THEY'RE STILL ALIVE... ALMOST EVEN QUIPPING.
THERE'S STILL TIME. WE CAN DO THIS.
NO...
...YOU CAN DO IT.
I'M NOT...I'M NOT GOING TO BE AROUND MUCH LONGER.

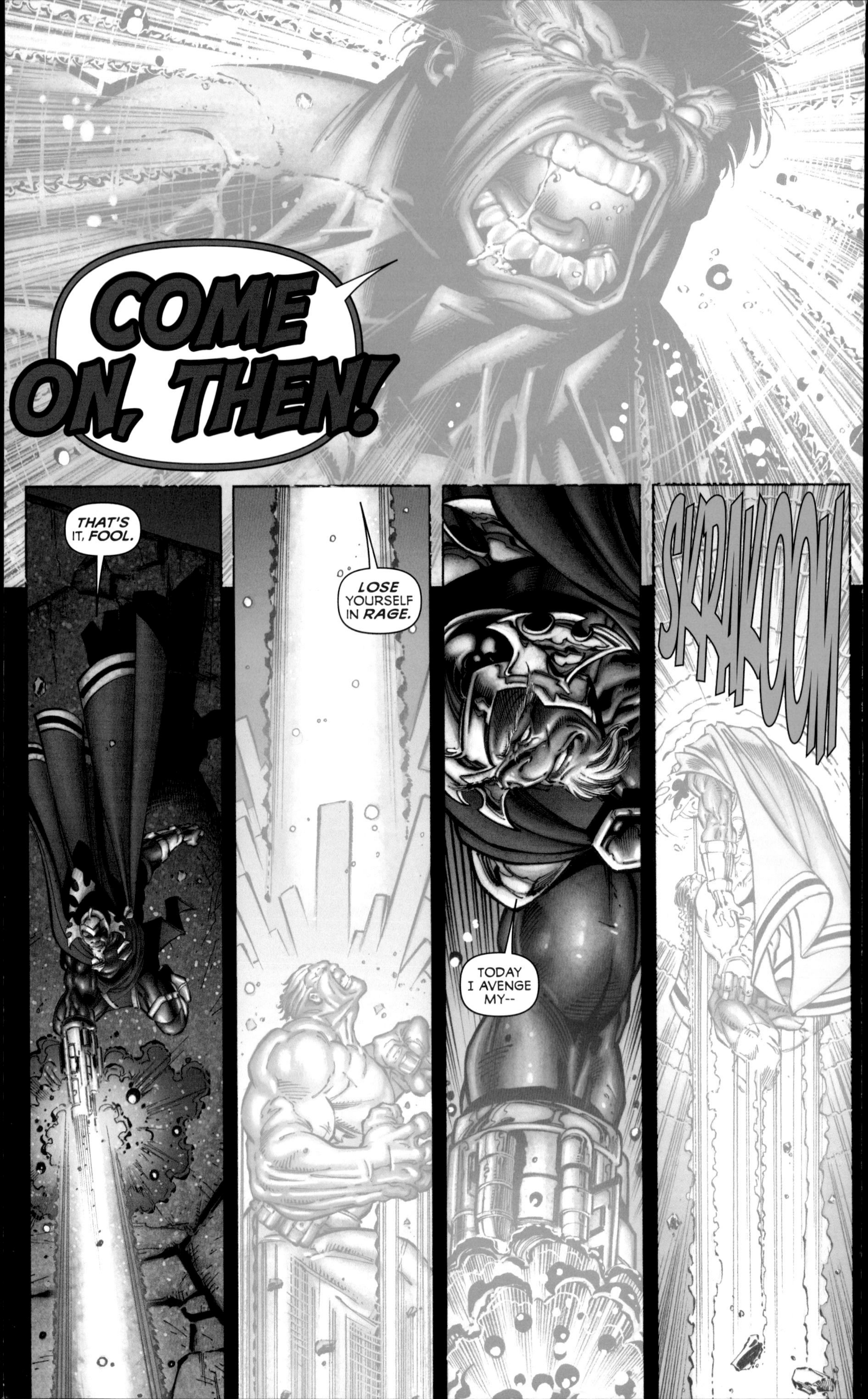
COME ON, THEN!
THAT'S IT, FOOL.
LOSE YOURSELF IN RAGE.
TODAY I AVENGE MY--
SKRAKOOM

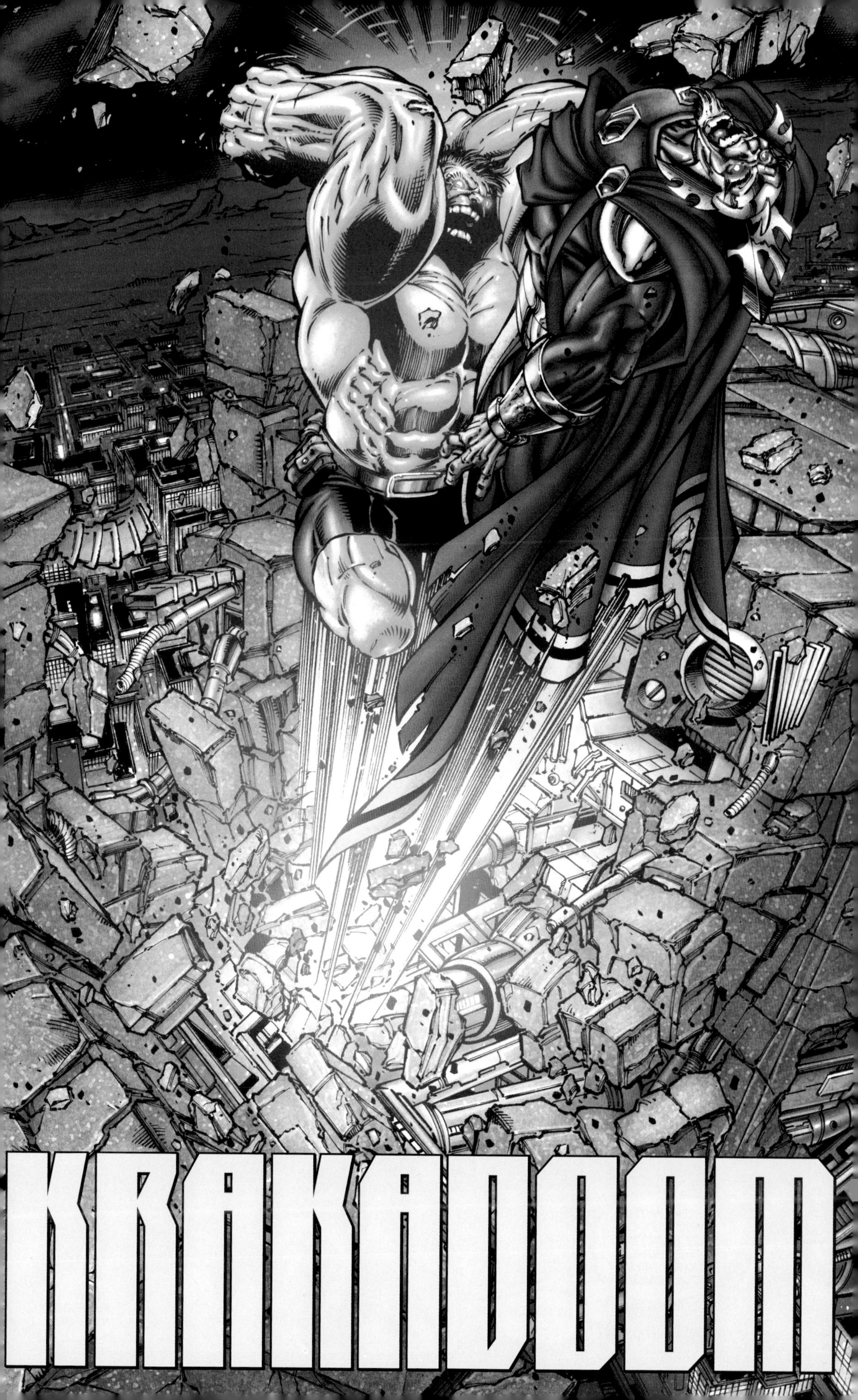
KRAKADOOM

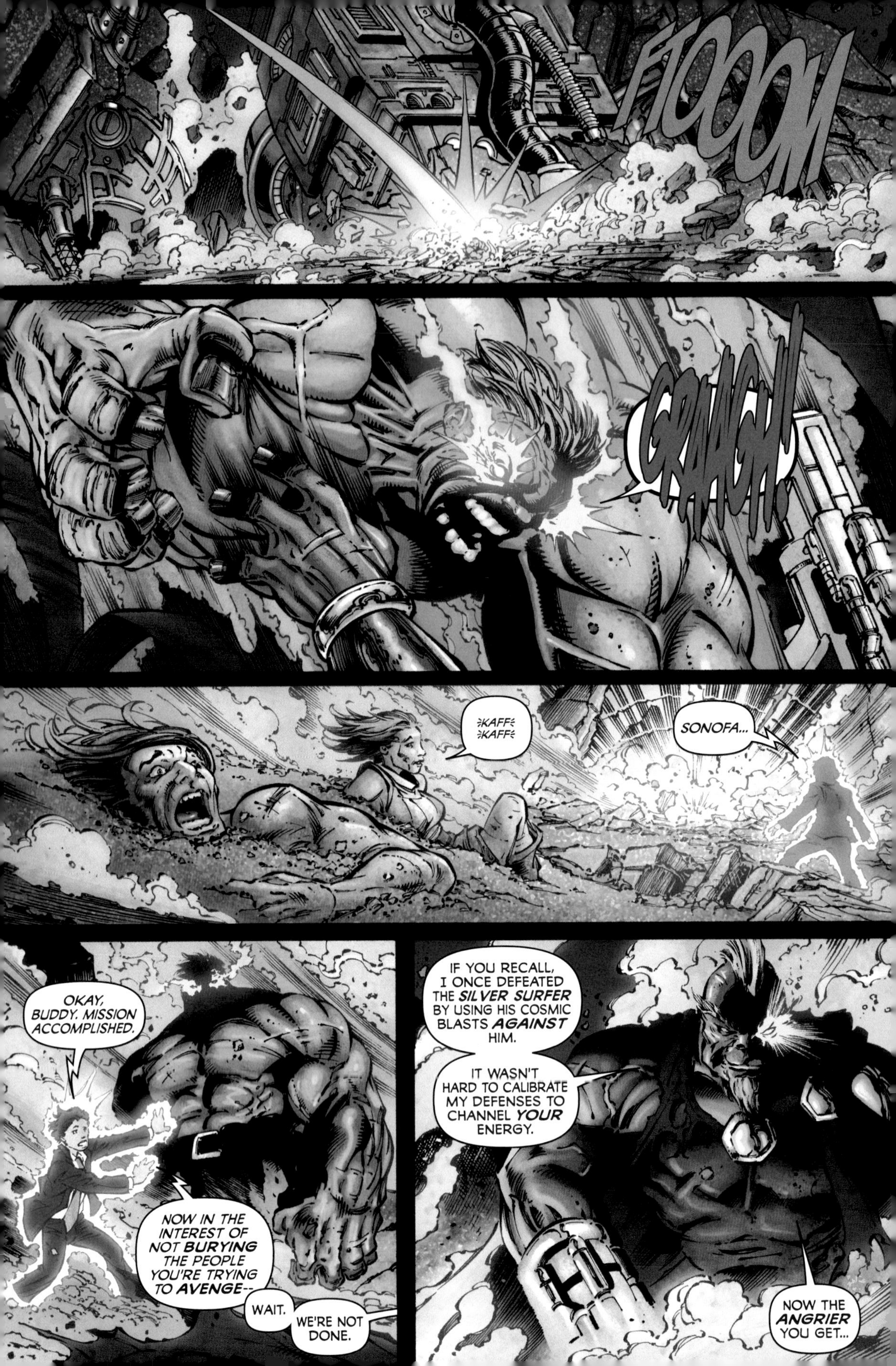
FTOOOM
GRAAGH!!
≠KAFF≠ ≠KAFF≠
SONOFA...
OKAY, BUDDY. MISSION ACCOMPLISHED.
NOW IN THE INTEREST OF NOT BURYING THE PEOPLE YOU'RE TRYING TO AVENGE--
WAIT.
WE'RE NOT DONE.
IF YOU RECALL, I ONCE DEFEATED THE SILVER SURFER BY USING HIS COSMIC BLASTS AGAINST HIM.
IT WASN'T HARD TO CALIBRATE MY DEFENSES TO CHANNEL YOUR ENERGY.
NOW THE ANGRIER YOU GET...

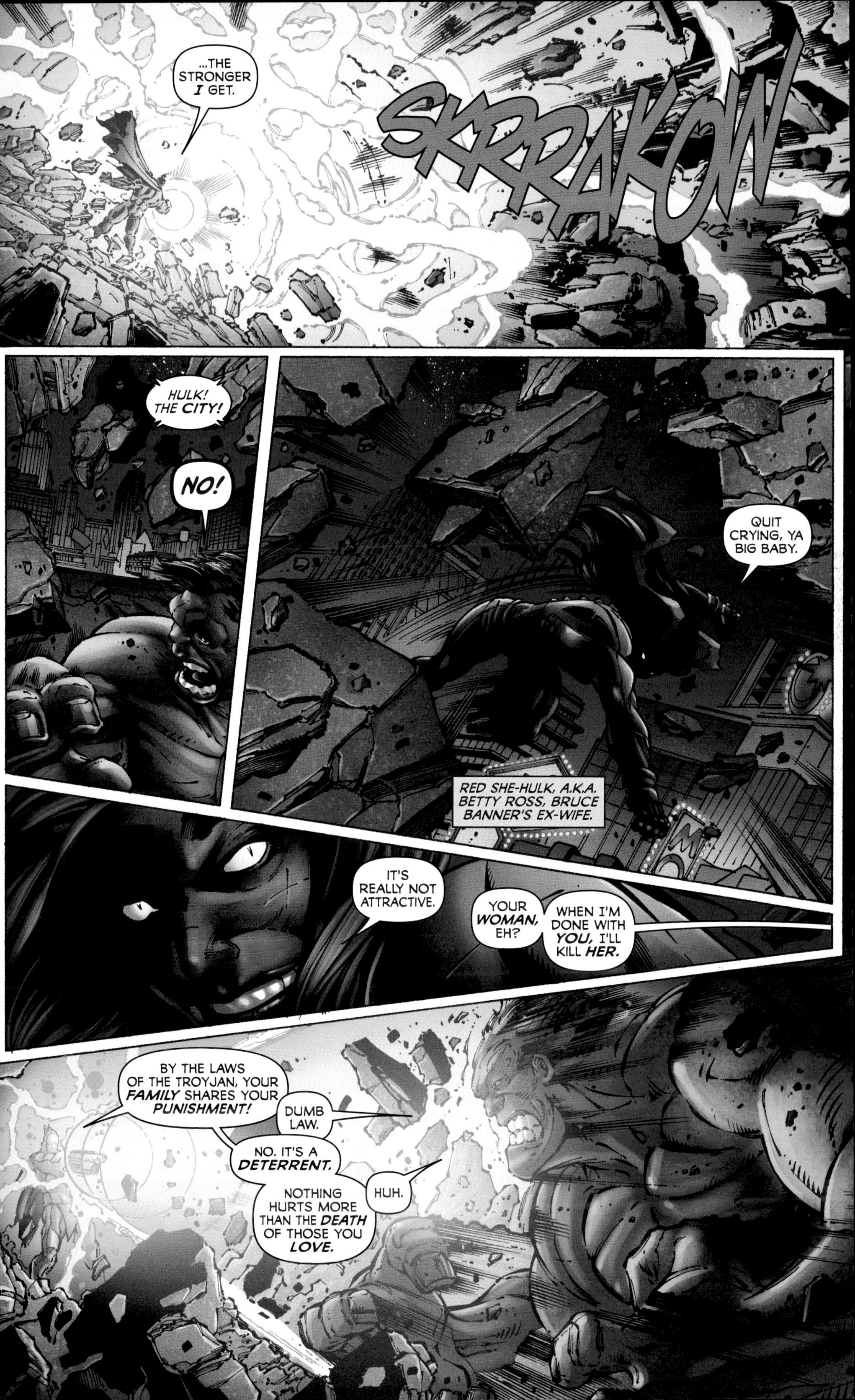
...THE STRONGER *I* GET.
SKRRAKOW
HULK! THE *CITY!*
NO!
QUIT CRYING, YA BIG BABY.
RED SHE-HULK, A.K.A. BETTY ROSS, BRUCE BANNER'S EX-WIFE.
IT'S REALLY NOT ATTRACTIVE.
YOUR ***WOMAN,*** EH?
WHEN I'M DONE WITH ***YOU,*** I'LL KILL ***HER.***
BY THE LAWS OF THE TROYJAN, YOUR ***FAMILY*** SHARES YOUR ***PUNISHMENT!***
DUMB LAW.
NO. IT'S A ***DETERRENT.***
HUH.
NOTHING HURTS MORE THAN THE ***DEATH*** OF THOSE YOU ***LOVE.***

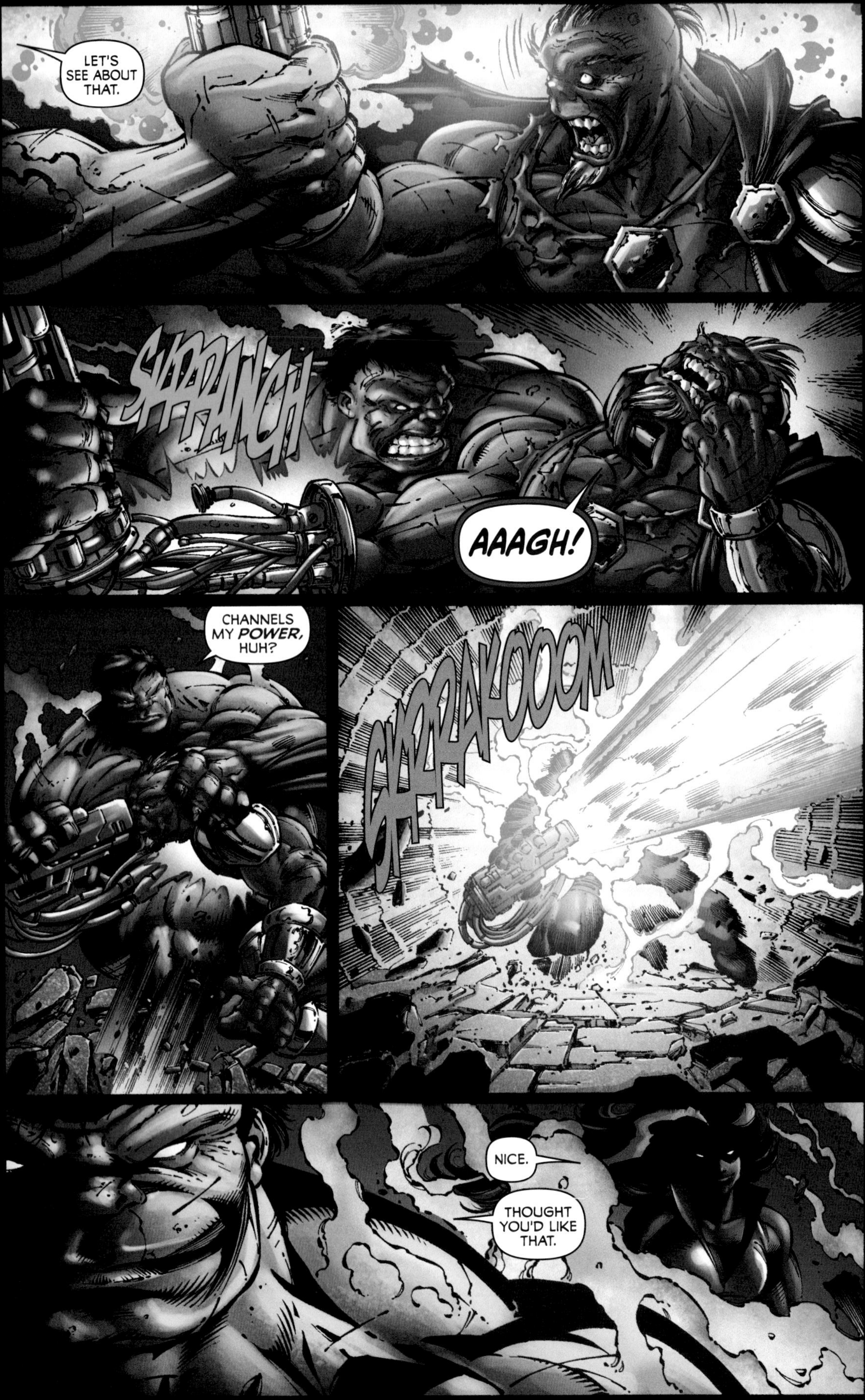
LET'S SEE ABOUT THAT.
SKRRANCH
AAAGH!
CHANNELS MY *POWER,* HUH?
SKRRAKOOOM
NICE.
THOUGHT YOU'D LIKE THAT.

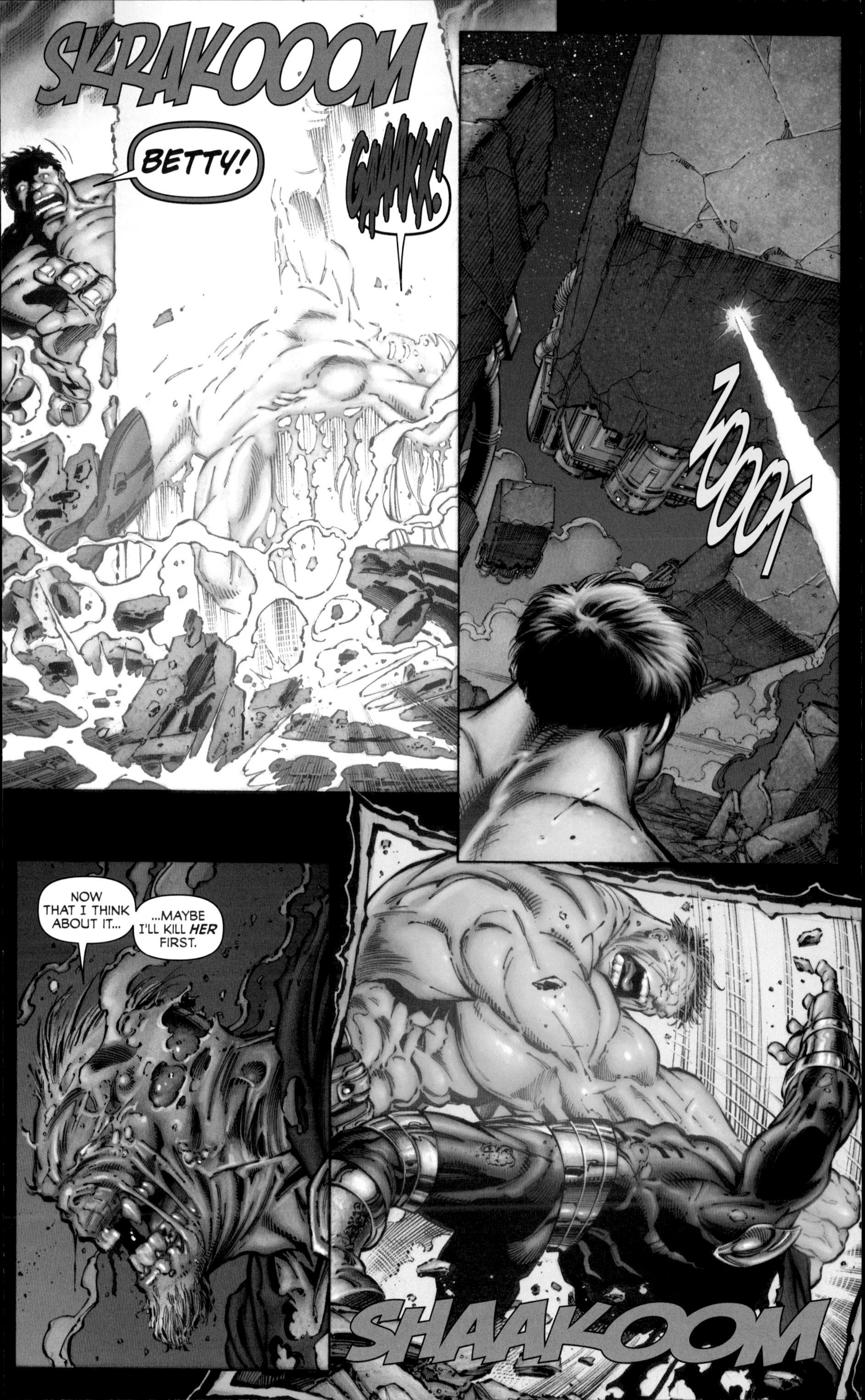
SKRAKOOOM
BETTY!
GAAAKK!
ZOOOK
NOW THAT I THINK ABOUT IT...
...MAYBE I'LL KILL HER FIRST.
SHAAKOOM

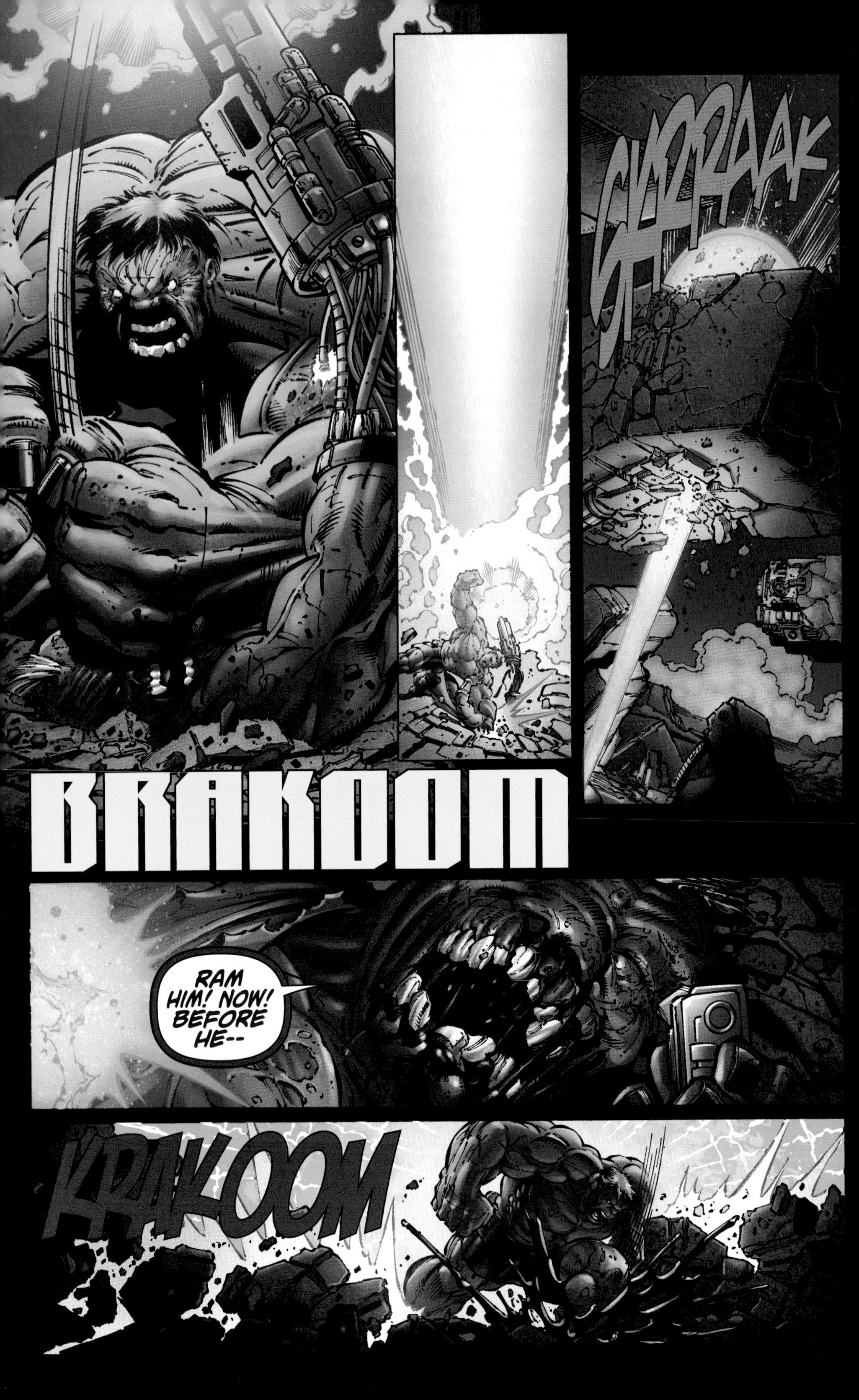
GKRRAAK
BRAKOOM
RAM HIM! NOW! BEFORE HE--
KRAKOOM

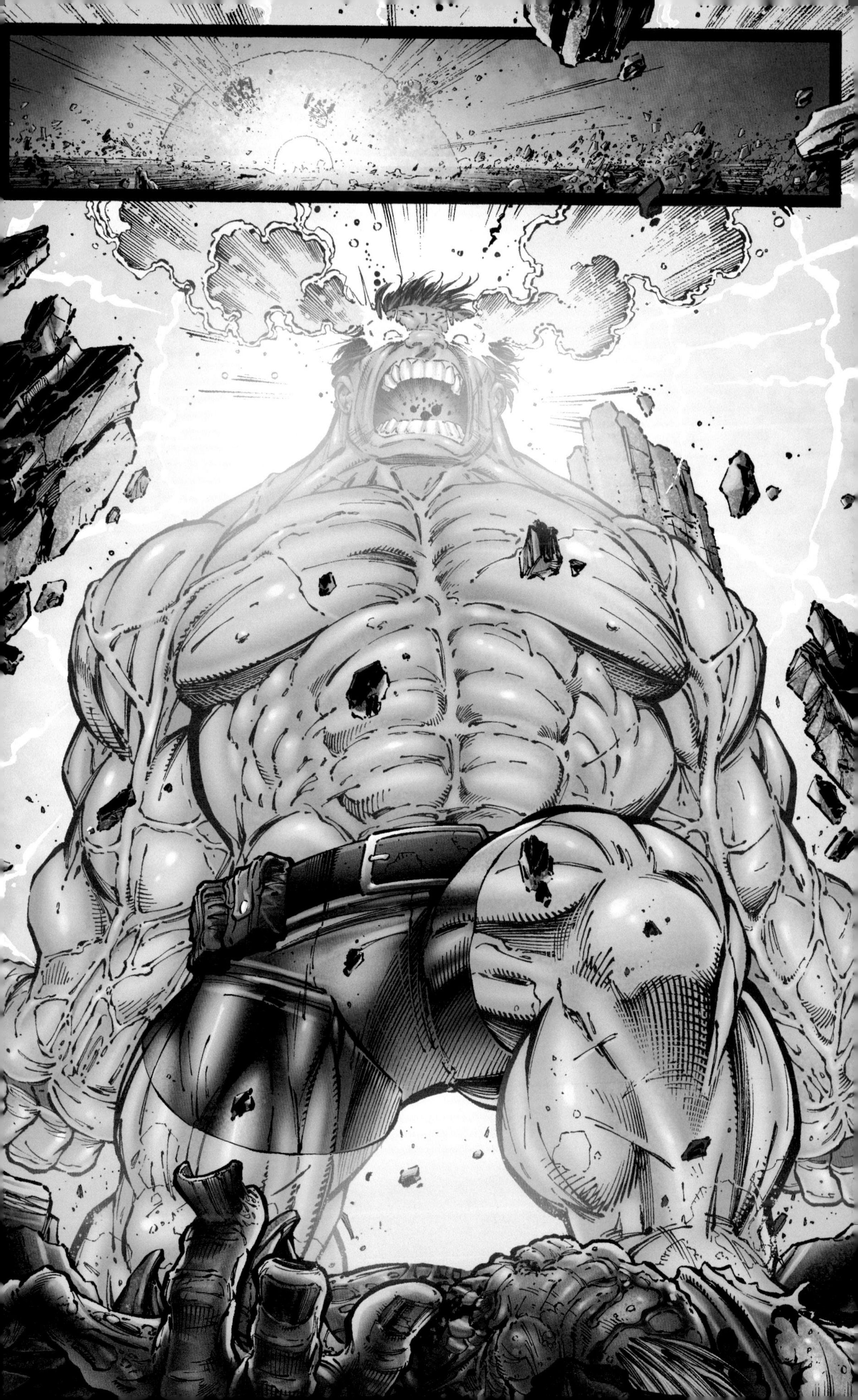

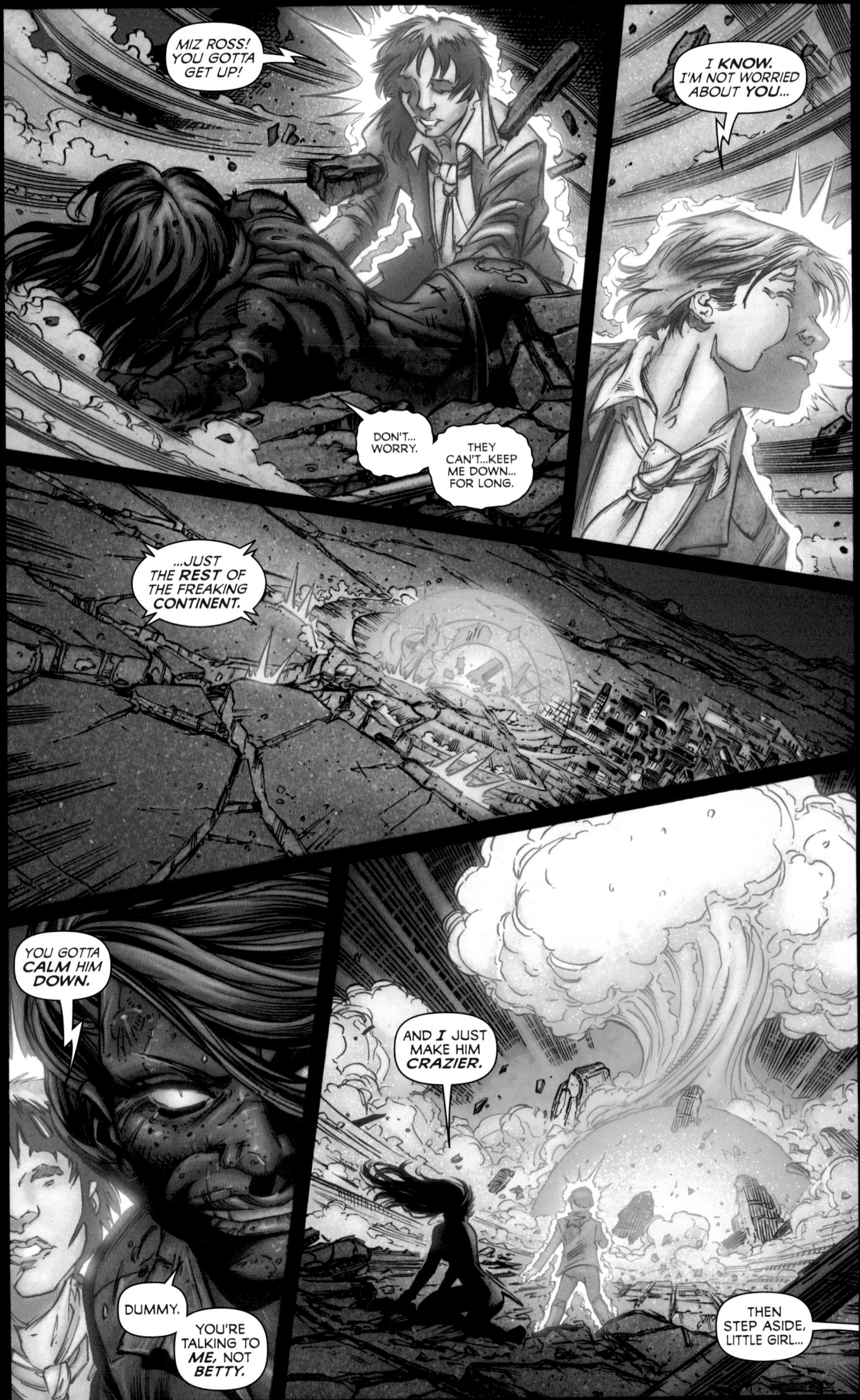
MIZ ROSS! YOU GOTTA GET UP!
I KNOW. I'M NOT WORRIED ABOUT YOU...
DON'T... WORRY.
THEY CAN'T...KEEP ME DOWN... FOR LONG.
...JUST THE REST OF THE FREAKING CONTINENT.
YOU GOTTA CALM HIM DOWN.
DUMMY.
YOU'RE TALKING TO ME, NOT BETTY.
AND I JUST MAKE HIM CRAZIER.
THEN STEP ASIDE, LITTLE GIRL...

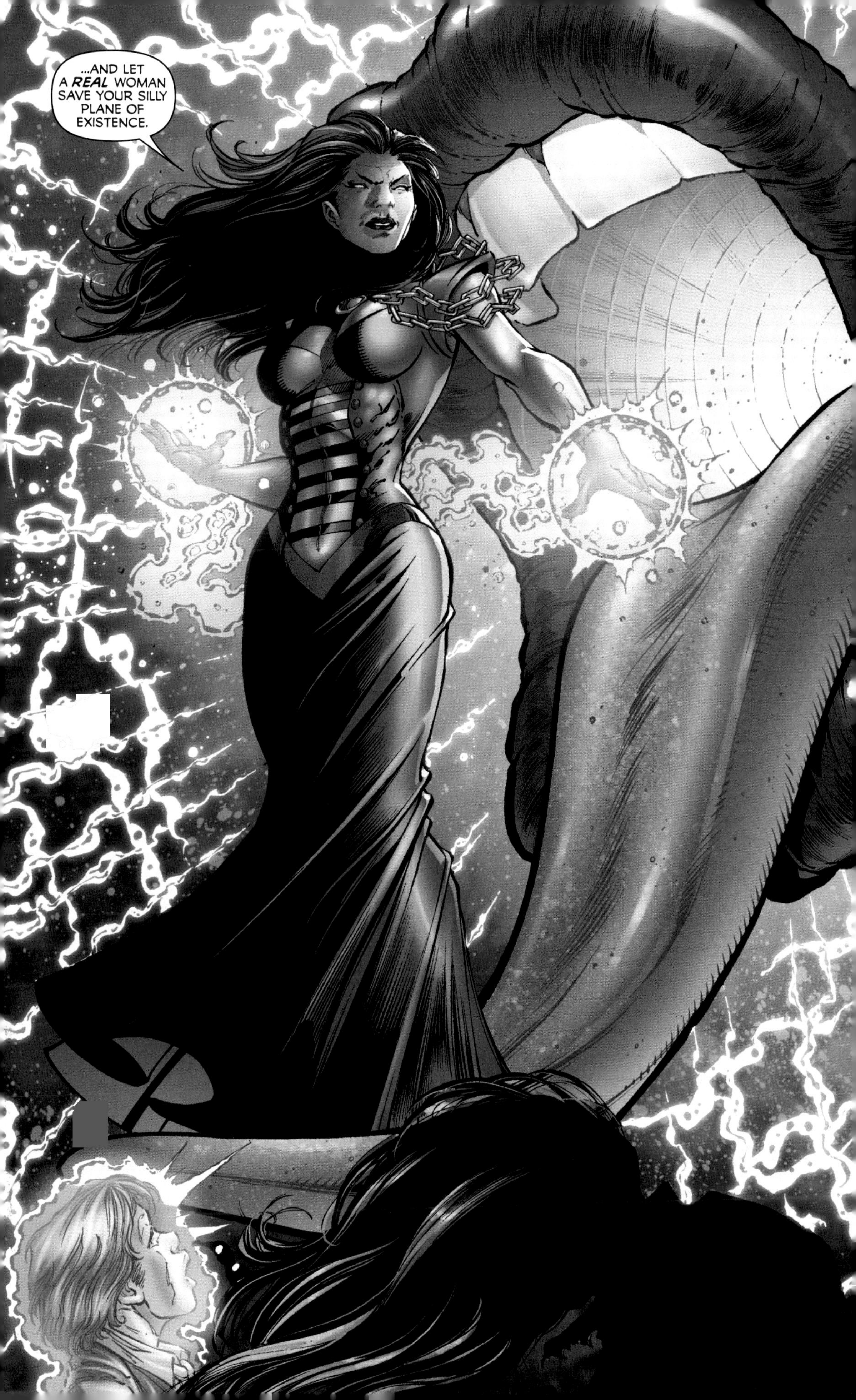
...AND LET A *REAL* WOMAN SAVE YOUR SILLY PLANE OF EXISTENCE.

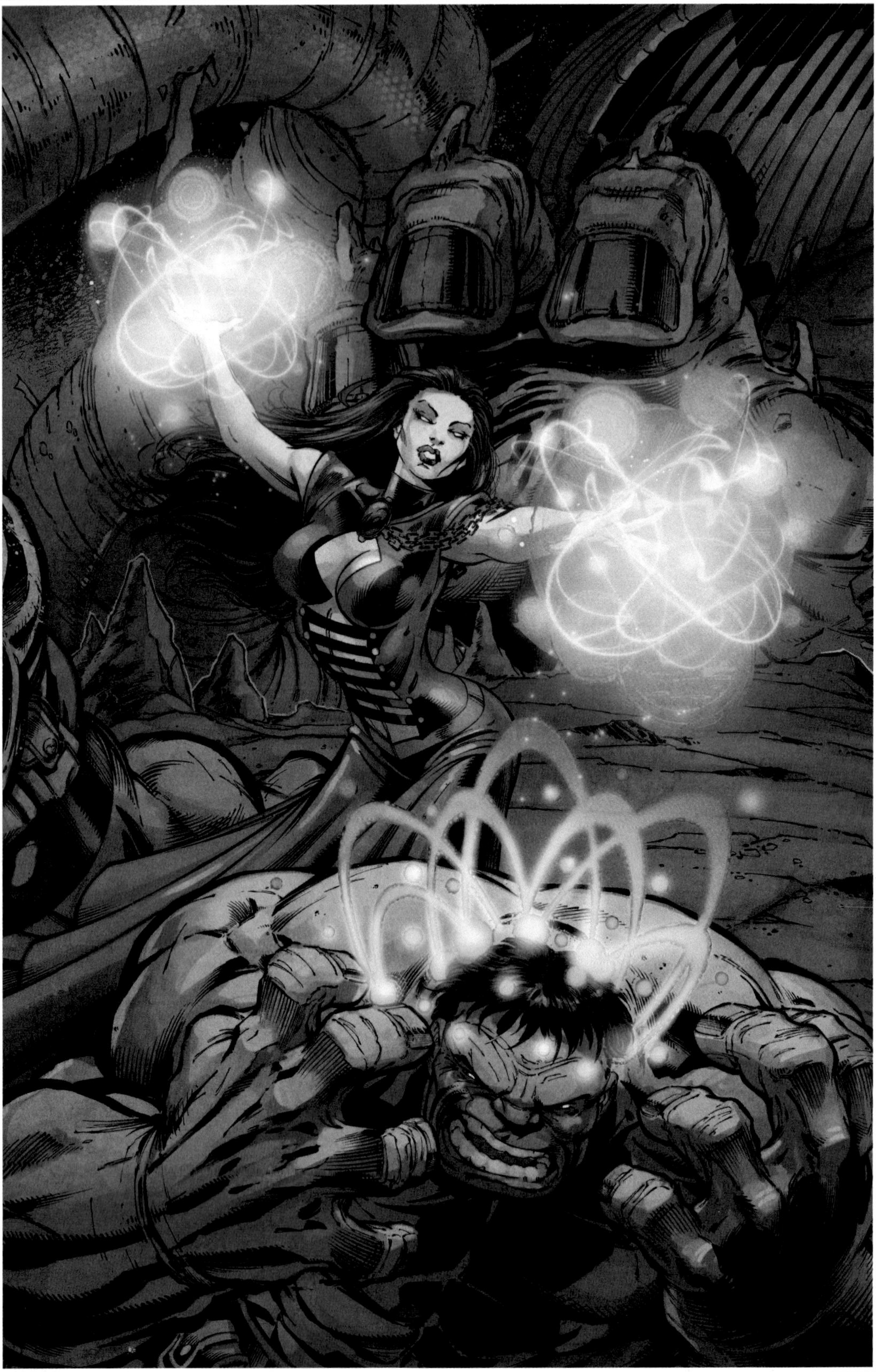

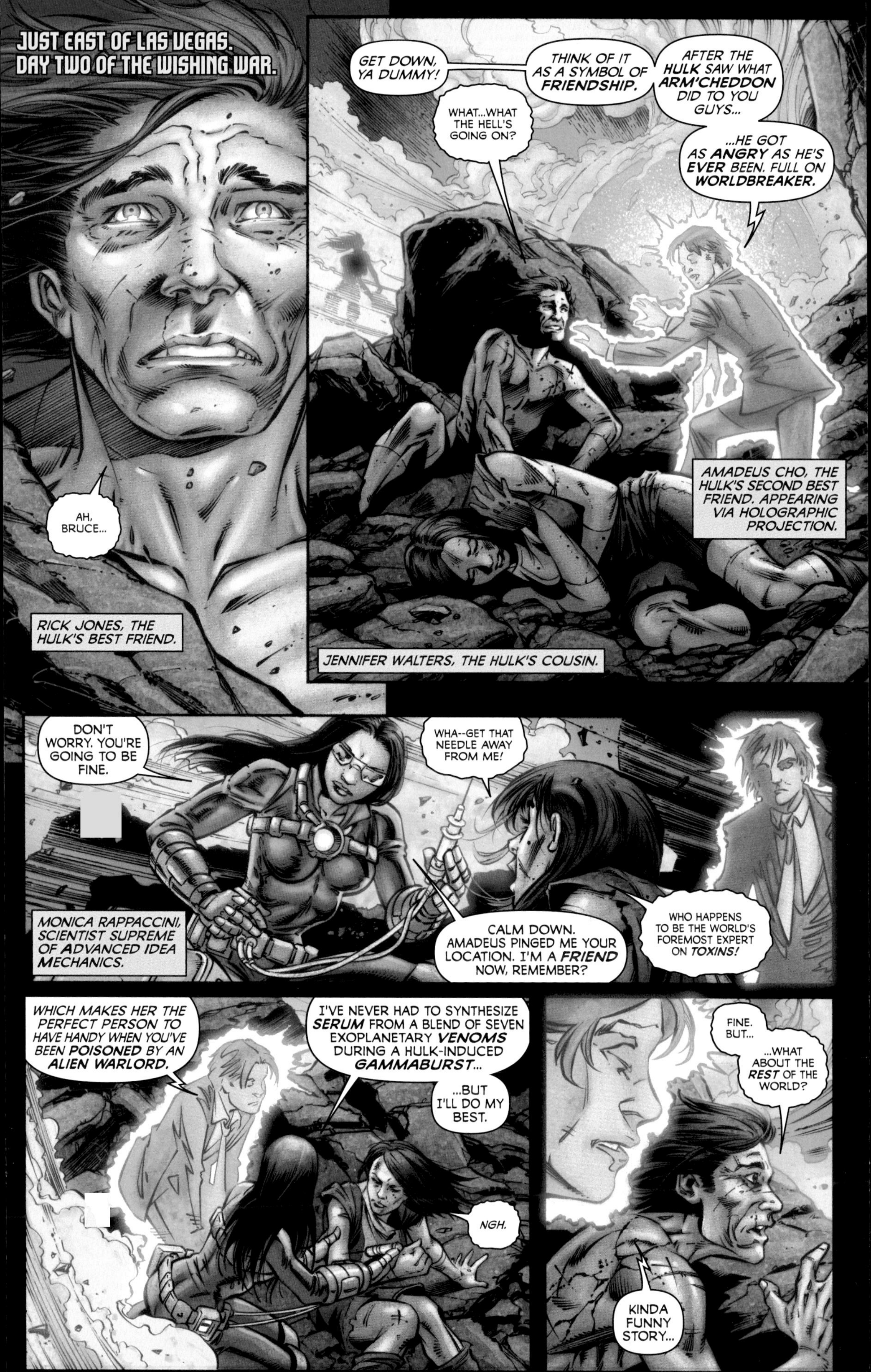
JUST EAST OF LAS VEGAS. DAY TWO OF THE WISHING WAR.
AH, BRUCE...
RICK JONES, THE HULK'S BEST FRIEND.
GET DOWN, YA DUMMY!
THINK OF IT AS A SYMBOL OF FRIENDSHIP.
AFTER THE HULK SAW WHAT ARM'CHEDDON DID TO YOU GUYS...
WHAT...WHAT THE HELL'S GOING ON?
...HE GOT AS ANGRY AS HE'S EVER BEEN. FULL ON WORLDBREAKER.
AMADEUS CHO, THE HULK'S SECOND BEST FRIEND. APPEARING VIA HOLOGRAPHIC PROJECTION.
JENNIFER WALTERS, THE HULK'S COUSIN.
DON'T WORRY. YOU'RE GOING TO BE FINE.
WHA--GET THAT NEEDLE AWAY FROM ME!
MONICA RAPPACCINI, SCIENTIST SUPREME OF ADVANCED IDEA MECHANICS.
CALM DOWN. AMADEUS PINGED ME YOUR LOCATION. I'M A FRIEND NOW, REMEMBER?
WHO HAPPENS TO BE THE WORLD'S FOREMOST EXPERT ON TOXINS!
WHICH MAKES HER THE PERFECT PERSON TO HAVE HANDY WHEN YOU'VE BEEN POISONED BY AN ALIEN WARLORD.
I'VE NEVER HAD TO SYNTHESIZE SERUM FROM A BLEND OF SEVEN EXOPLANETARY VENOMS DURING A HULK-INDUCED GAMMABURST...
...BUT I'LL DO MY BEST.
NGH.
FINE. BUT...
...WHAT ABOUT THE REST OF THE WORLD?
KINDA FUNNY STORY...

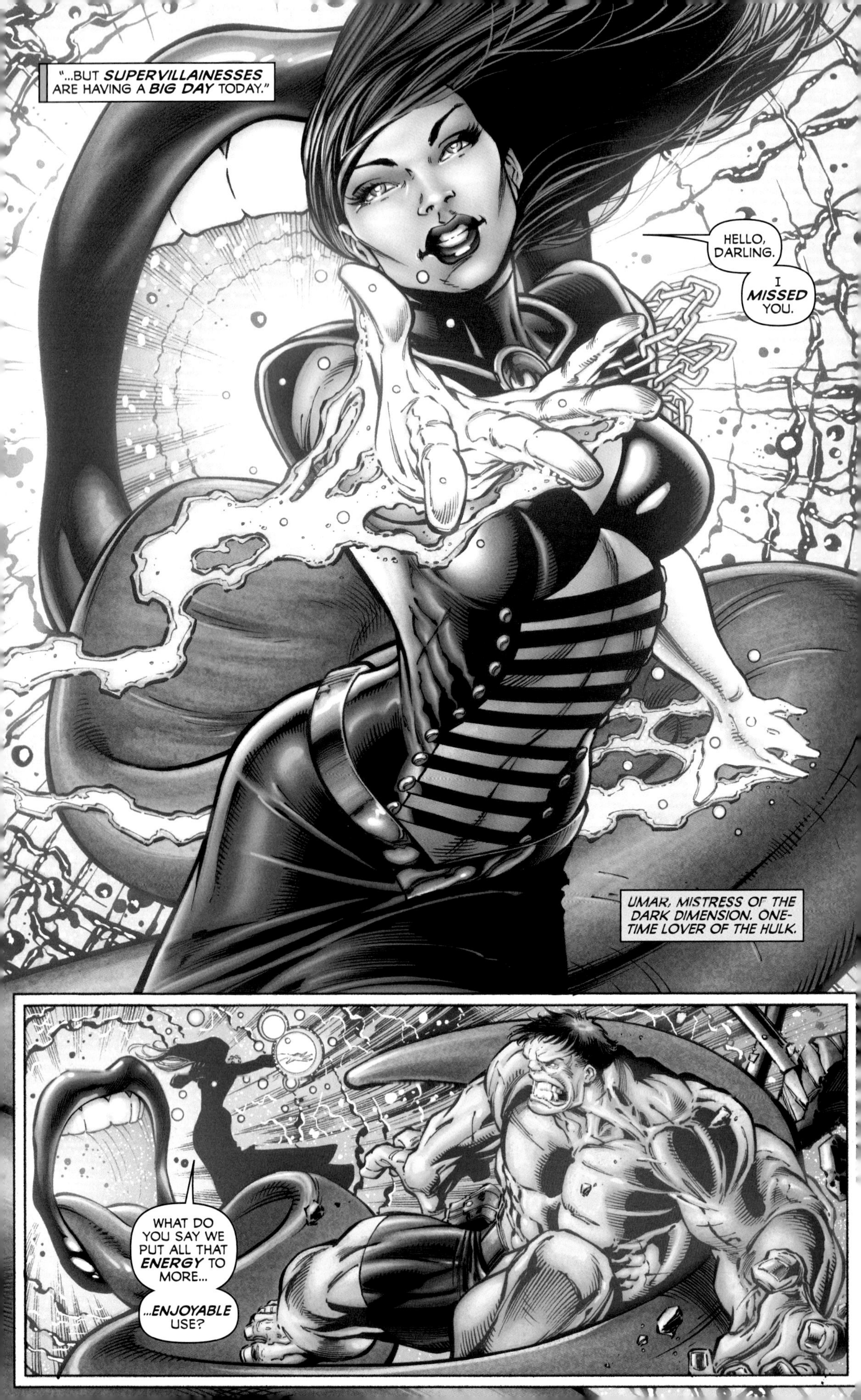
"...BUT SUPERVILLAINESSES ARE HAVING A BIG DAY TODAY."
HELLO, DARLING.
I MISSED YOU.
UMAR, MISTRESS OF THE DARK DIMENSION. ONE-TIME LOVER OF THE HULK.
WHAT DO YOU SAY WE PUT ALL THAT ENERGY TO MORE...
...ENJOYABLE USE?

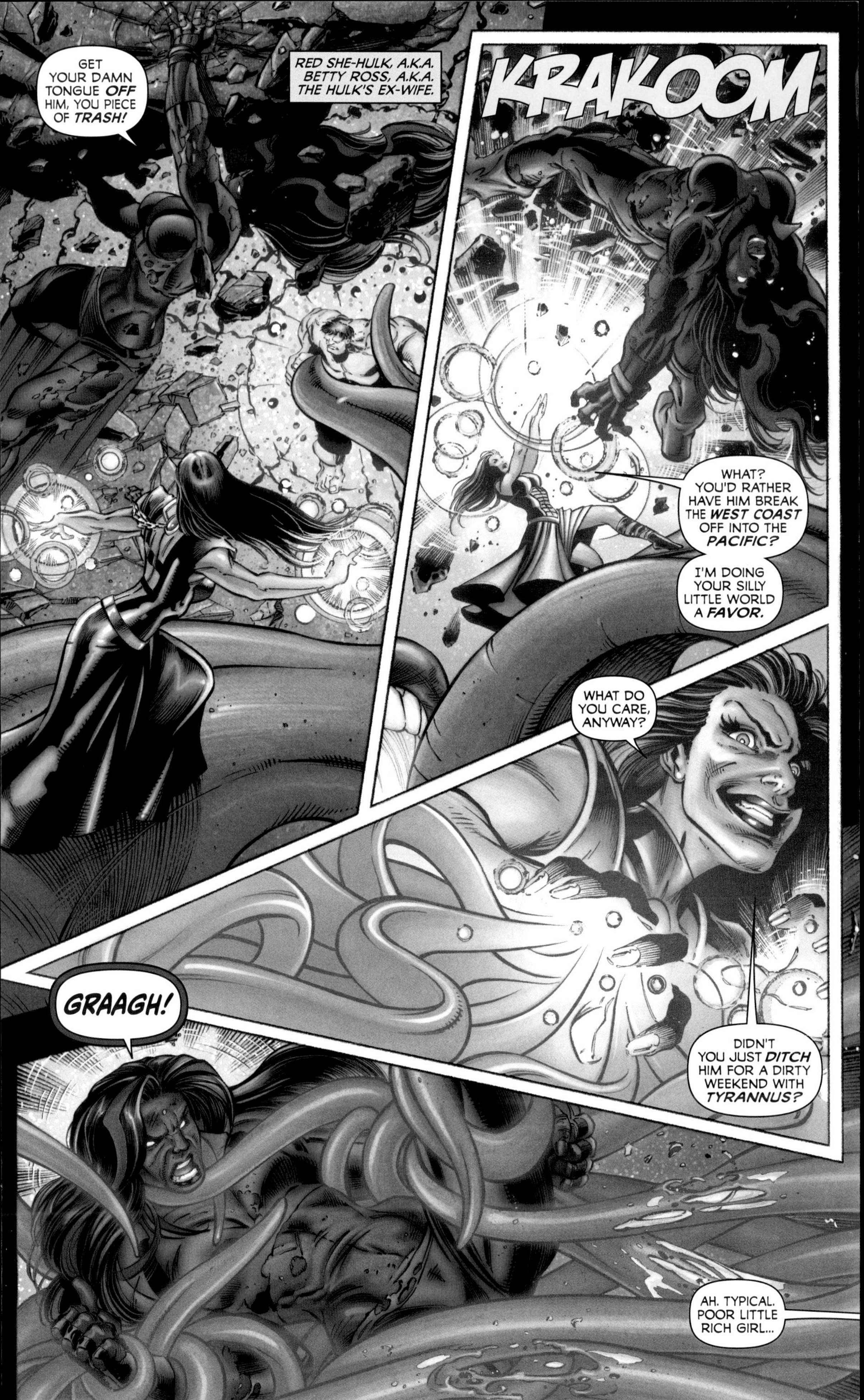
GET YOUR DAMN TONGUE OFF HIM, YOU PIECE OF TRASH!
RED SHE-HULK, A.K.A. BETTY ROSS, A.K.A. THE HULK'S EX-WIFE.
KRAKOOM
WHAT? YOU'D RATHER HAVE HIM BREAK THE WEST COAST OFF INTO THE PACIFIC?
I'M DOING YOUR SILLY LITTLE WORLD A FAVOR.
WHAT DO YOU CARE, ANYWAY?
DIDN'T YOU JUST DITCH HIM FOR A DIRTY WEEKEND WITH TYRANNUS?
GRAAGH!
AH. TYPICAL. POOR LITTLE RICH GIRL...

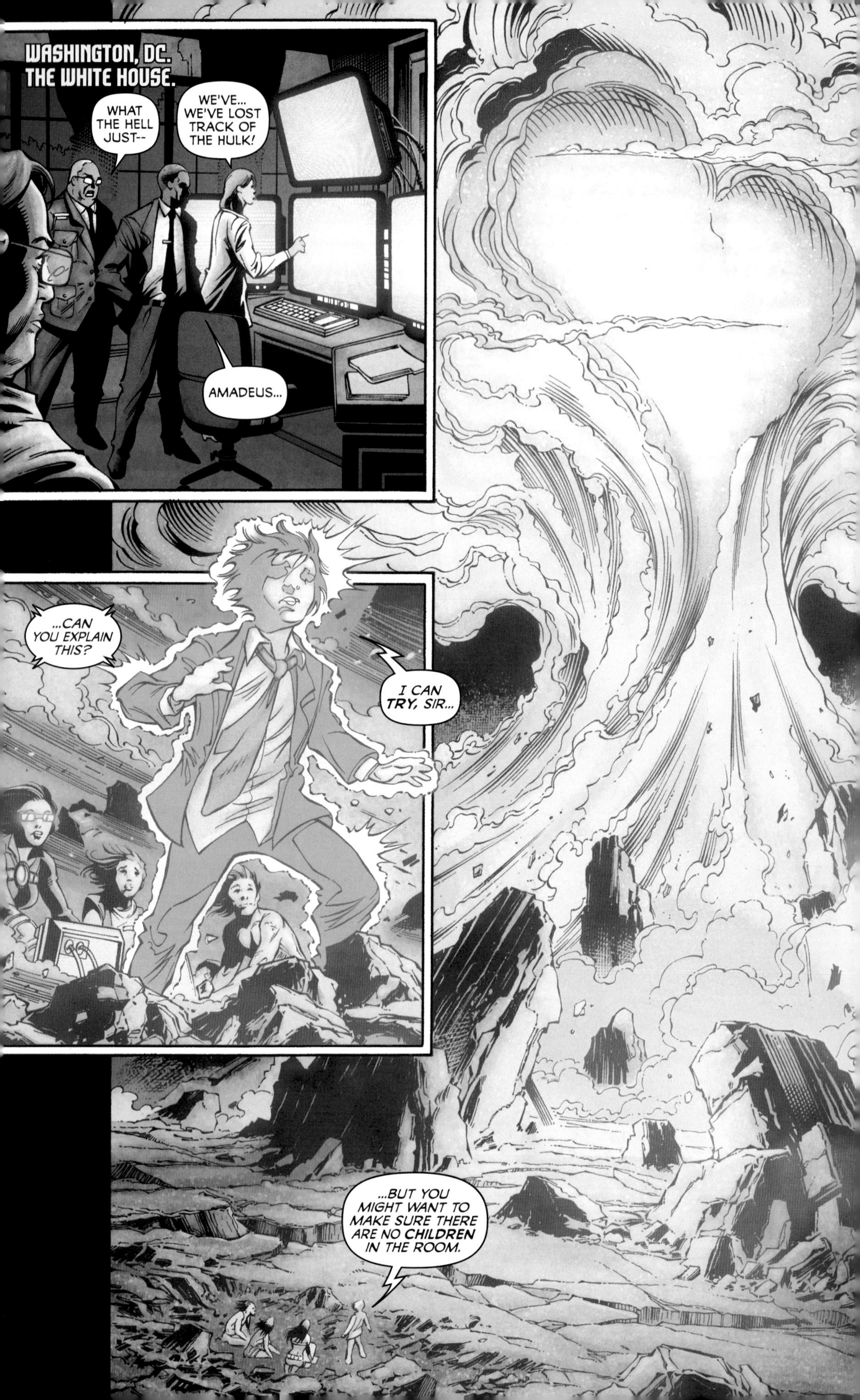
WASHINGTON, DC.
THE WHITE HOUSE.
WHAT THE HELL JUST--
WE'VE... WE'VE LOST TRACK OF THE HULK!
AMADEUS...
...CAN YOU EXPLAIN THIS?
I CAN TRY, SIR...
...BUT YOU MIGHT WANT TO MAKE SURE THERE ARE NO CHILDREN IN THE ROOM.

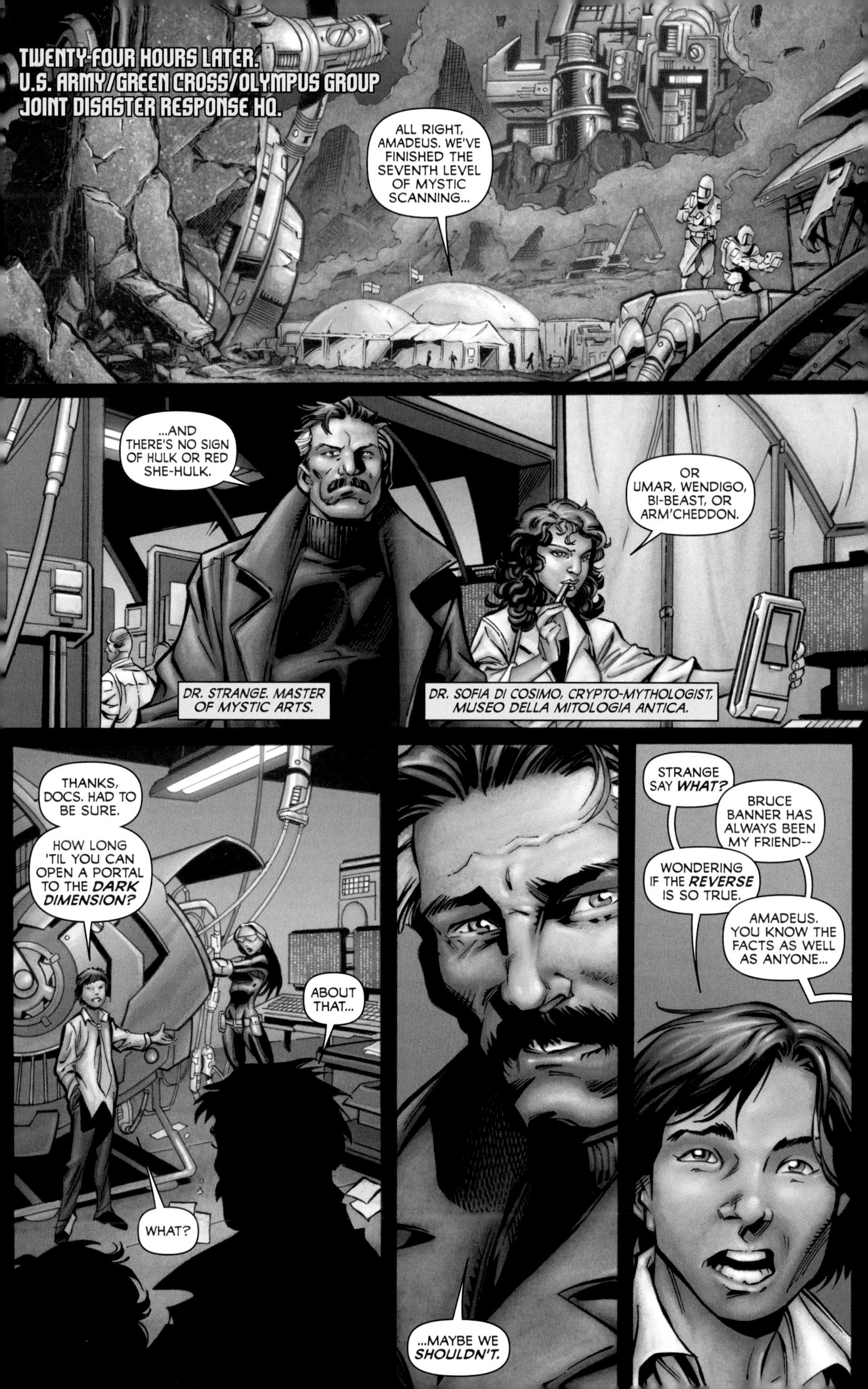
TWENTY-FOUR HOURS LATER. U.S. ARMY/GREEN CROSS/OLYMPUS GROUP JOINT DISASTER RESPONSE HQ.
ALL RIGHT, AMADEUS. WE'VE FINISHED THE SEVENTH LEVEL OF MYSTIC SCANNING...
...AND THERE'S NO SIGN OF HULK OR RED SHE-HULK.
OR UMAR, WENDIGO, BI-BEAST, OR ARM'CHEDDON.
DR. STRANGE. MASTER OF MYSTIC ARTS.
DR. SOFIA DI COSIMO, CRYPTO-MYTHOLOGIST, MUSEO DELLA MITOLOGIA ANTICA.
THANKS, DOCS. HAD TO BE SURE.
HOW LONG 'TIL YOU CAN OPEN A PORTAL TO THE DARK DIMENSION?
ABOUT THAT...
WHAT?
...MAYBE WE SHOULDN'T.
STRANGE SAY WHAT?
BRUCE BANNER HAS ALWAYS BEEN MY FRIEND--
WONDERING IF THE REVERSE IS SO TRUE.
AMADEUS. YOU KNOW THE FACTS AS WELL AS ANYONE...

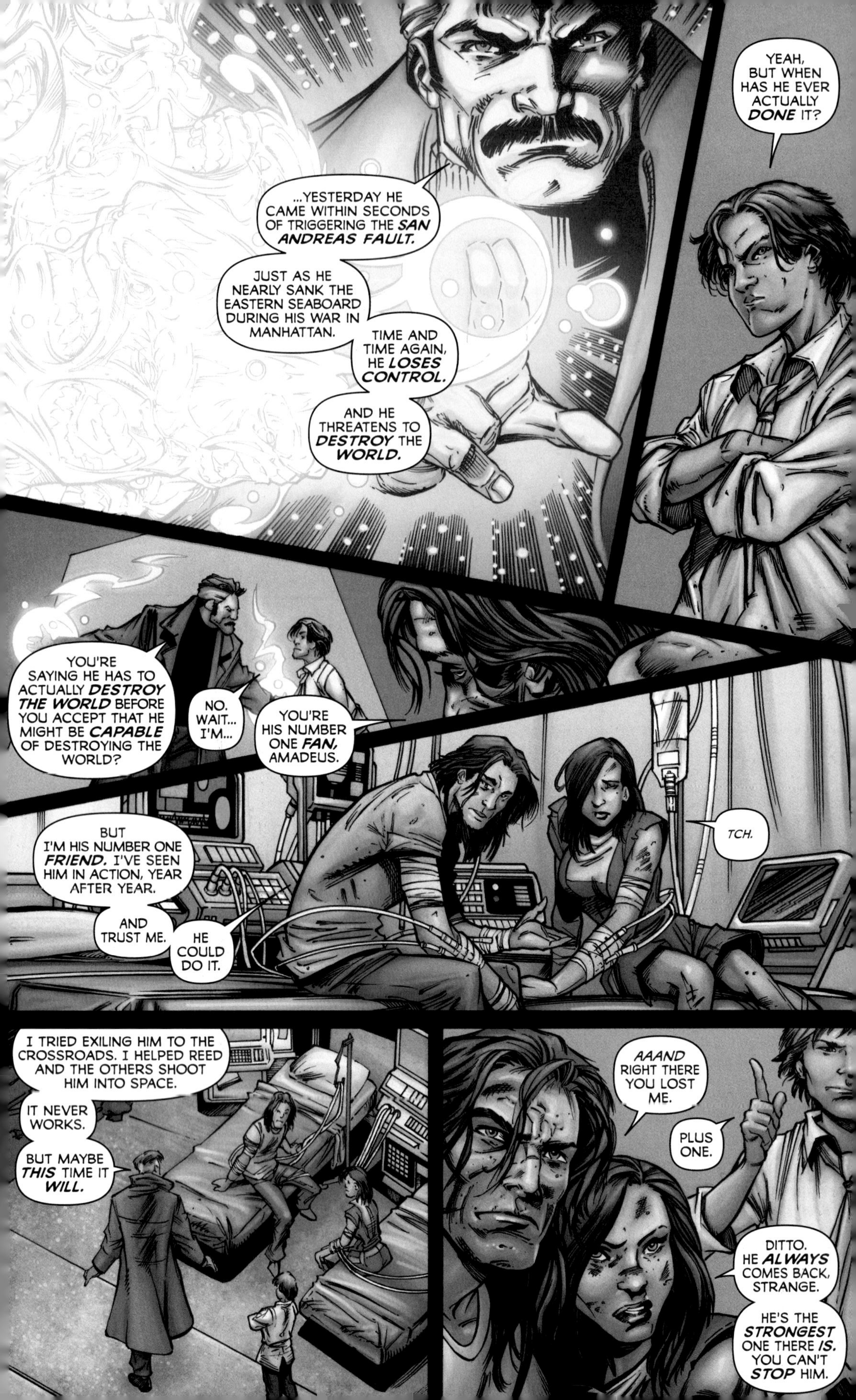
...YESTERDAY HE CAME WITHIN SECONDS OF TRIGGERING THE *SAN ANDREAS FAULT.*
JUST AS HE NEARLY SANK THE EASTERN SEABOARD DURING HIS WAR IN MANHATTAN.
TIME AND TIME AGAIN, HE *LOSES CONTROL.*
AND HE THREATENS TO *DESTROY* THE *WORLD.*
YEAH, BUT WHEN HAS HE EVER ACTUALLY *DONE* IT?
YOU'RE SAYING HE HAS TO ACTUALLY *DESTROY THE WORLD* BEFORE YOU ACCEPT THAT HE MIGHT BE *CAPABLE* OF DESTROYING THE WORLD?
NO. WAIT... I'M...
YOU'RE HIS NUMBER ONE *FAN,* AMADEUS.
BUT I'M HIS NUMBER ONE *FRIEND.* I'VE SEEN HIM IN ACTION, YEAR AFTER YEAR.
TCH.
AND TRUST ME.
HE COULD DO IT.
I TRIED EXILING HIM TO THE CROSSROADS. I HELPED REED AND THE OTHERS SHOOT HIM INTO SPACE.
IT NEVER WORKS.
BUT MAYBE *THIS* TIME IT *WILL.*
AAAND RIGHT THERE YOU LOST ME.
PLUS ONE.
DITTO. HE *ALWAYS* COMES BACK, STRANGE.
HE'S THE *STRONGEST* ONE THERE *IS.* YOU CAN'T *STOP* HIM.

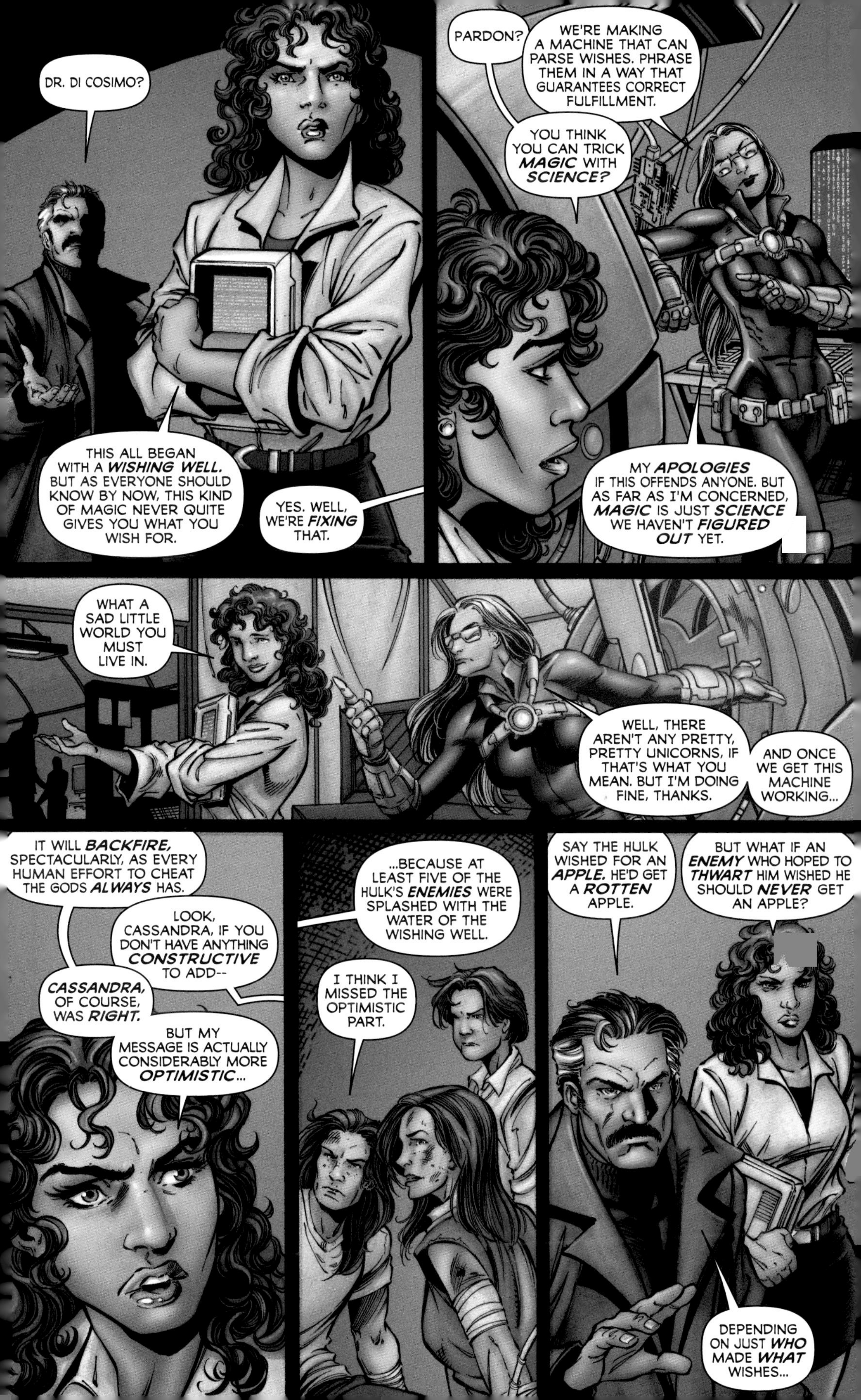
DR. DI COSIMO?
THIS ALL BEGAN WITH A WISHING WELL. BUT AS EVERYONE SHOULD KNOW BY NOW, THIS KIND OF MAGIC NEVER QUITE GIVES YOU WHAT YOU WISH FOR.
YES. WELL, WE'RE FIXING THAT.
PARDON?
WE'RE MAKING A MACHINE THAT CAN PARSE WISHES. PHRASE THEM IN A WAY THAT GUARANTEES CORRECT FULFILLMENT.
YOU THINK YOU CAN TRICK MAGIC WITH SCIENCE?
MY APOLOGIES IF THIS OFFENDS ANYONE. BUT AS FAR AS I'M CONCERNED, MAGIC IS JUST SCIENCE WE HAVEN'T FIGURED OUT YET.
WHAT A SAD LITTLE WORLD YOU MUST LIVE IN.
WELL, THERE AREN'T ANY PRETTY, PRETTY UNICORNS, IF THAT'S WHAT YOU MEAN. BUT I'M DOING FINE, THANKS.
AND ONCE WE GET THIS MACHINE WORKING...
IT WILL BACKFIRE, SPECTACULARLY, AS EVERY HUMAN EFFORT TO CHEAT THE GODS ALWAYS HAS.
LOOK, CASSANDRA, IF YOU DON'T HAVE ANYTHING CONSTRUCTIVE TO ADD--
CASSANDRA, OF COURSE, WAS RIGHT.
BUT MY MESSAGE IS ACTUALLY CONSIDERABLY MORE OPTIMISTIC...
...BECAUSE AT LEAST FIVE OF THE HULK'S ENEMIES WERE SPLASHED WITH THE WATER OF THE WISHING WELL.
I THINK I MISSED THE OPTIMISTIC PART.
SAY THE HULK WISHED FOR AN APPLE. HE'D GET A ROTTEN APPLE.
BUT WHAT IF AN ENEMY WHO HOPED TO THWART HIM WISHED HE SHOULD NEVER GET AN APPLE?
DEPENDING ON JUST WHO MADE WHAT WISHES...

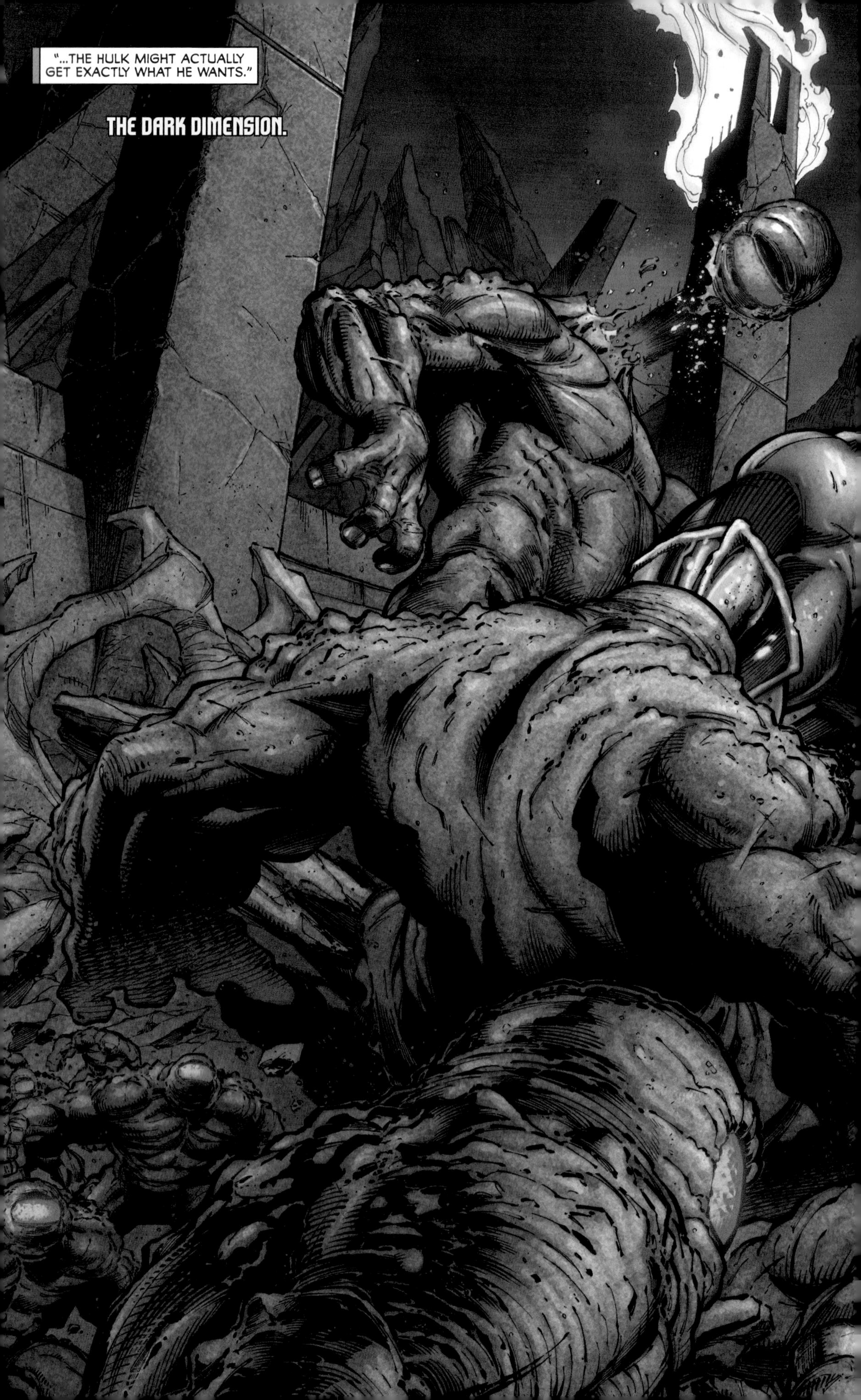
"...THE HULK MIGHT ACTUALLY GET EXACTLY WHAT HE WANTS."
THE DARK DIMENSION.

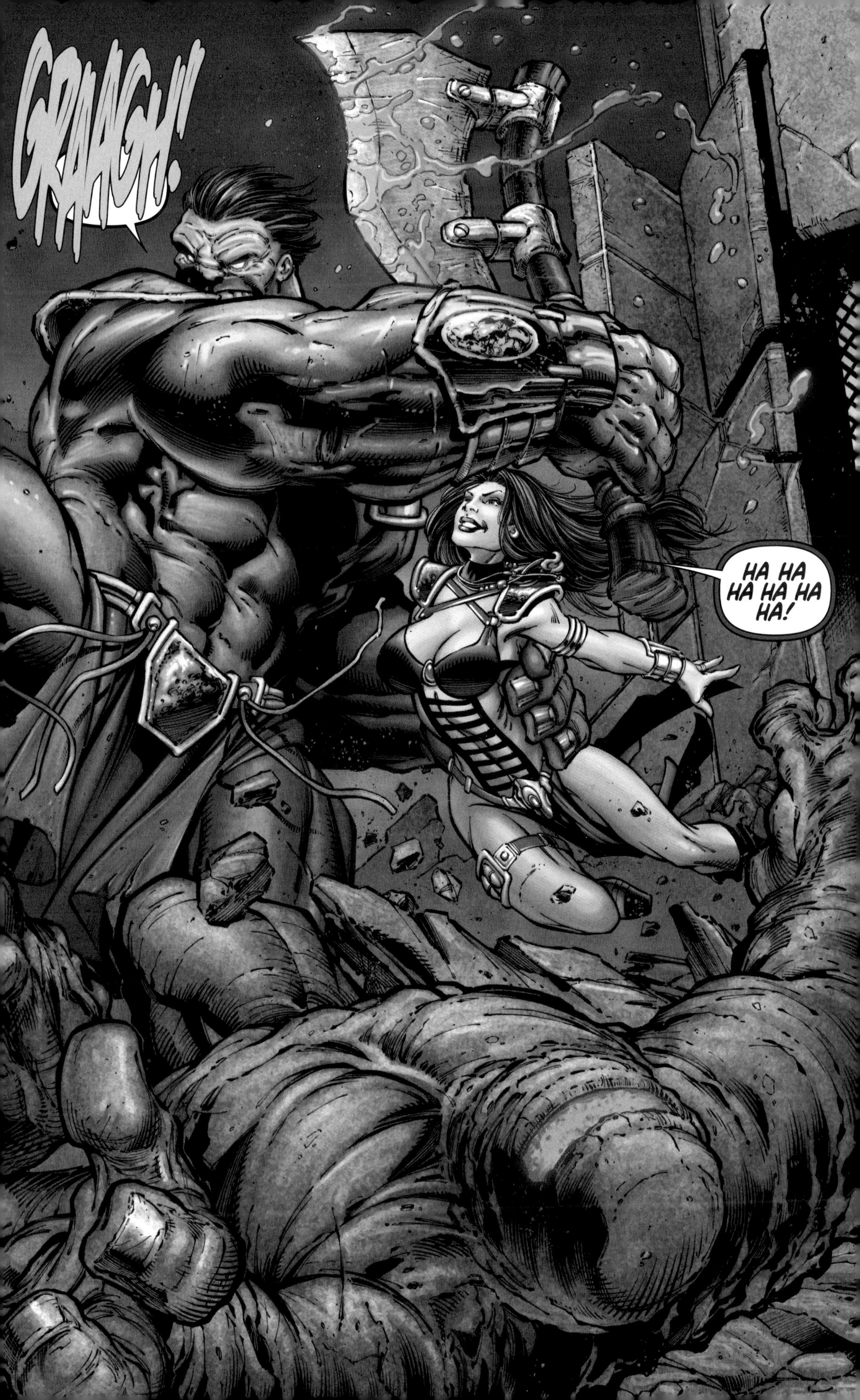
GRAAGH!!
HA HA HA HA HA HA!

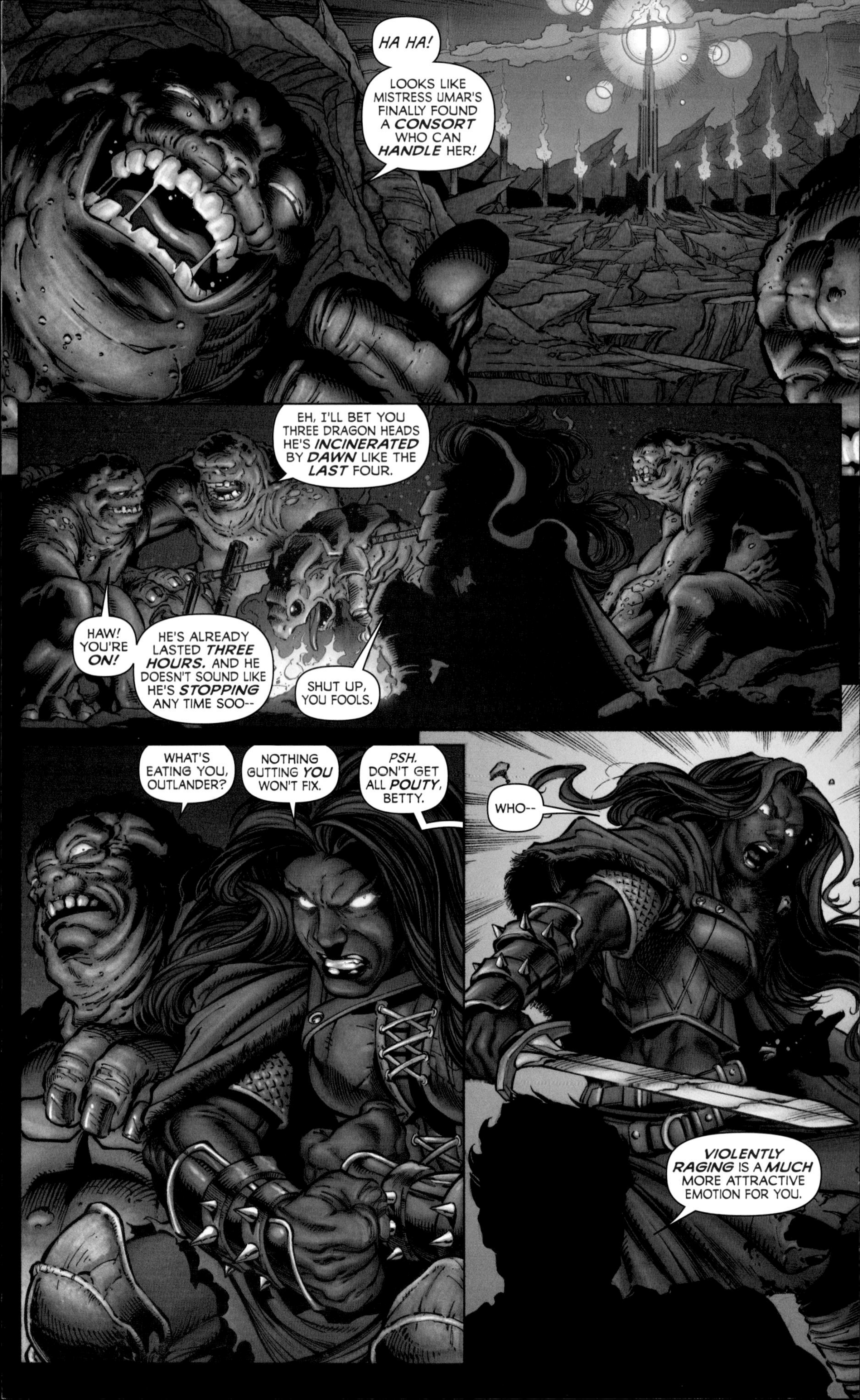
HA HA!
LOOKS LIKE MISTRESS UMAR'S FINALLY FOUND A CONSORT WHO CAN HANDLE HER!
EH, I'LL BET YOU THREE DRAGON HEADS HE'S INCINERATED BY DAWN LIKE THE LAST FOUR.
HAW! YOU'RE ON!
HE'S ALREADY LASTED THREE HOURS. AND HE DOESN'T SOUND LIKE HE'S STOPPING ANY TIME SOO--
SHUT UP, YOU FOOLS.
WHAT'S EATING YOU, OUTLANDER?
NOTHING GUTTING YOU WON'T FIX.
PSH. DON'T GET ALL POUTY, BETTY.
WHO--
VIOLENTLY RAGING IS A MUCH MORE ATTRACTIVE EMOTION FOR YOU.

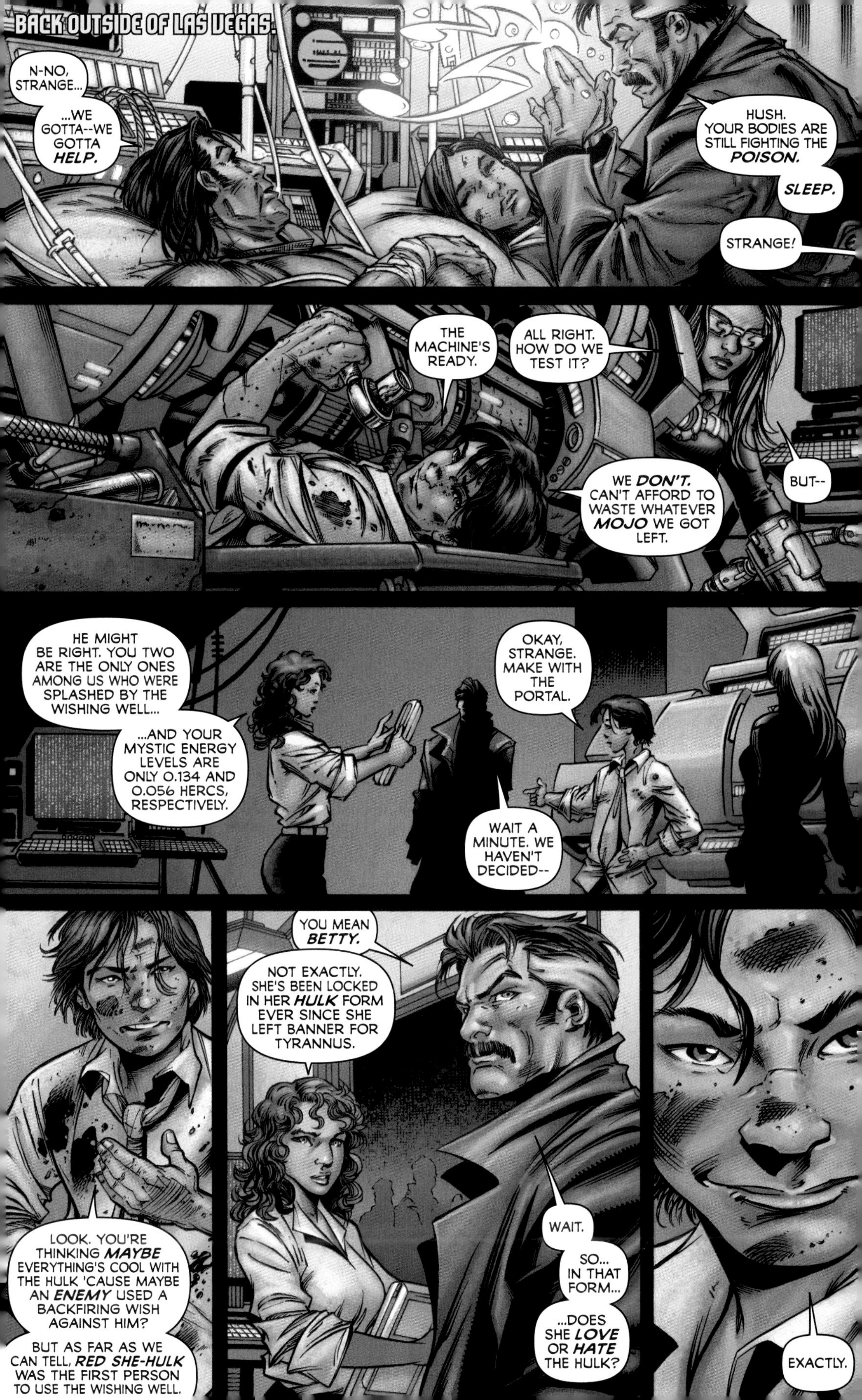
BACK OUTSIDE OF LAS VEGAS.
N-NO, STRANGE...
...WE GOTTA--WE GOTTA HELP.
HUSH. YOUR BODIES ARE STILL FIGHTING THE POISON.
SLEEP.
STRANGE!
THE MACHINE'S READY.
ALL RIGHT. HOW DO WE TEST IT?
WE DON'T. CAN'T AFFORD TO WASTE WHATEVER MOJO WE GOT LEFT.
BUT--
HE MIGHT BE RIGHT. YOU TWO ARE THE ONLY ONES AMONG US WHO WERE SPLASHED BY THE WISHING WELL...
...AND YOUR MYSTIC ENERGY LEVELS ARE ONLY 0.134 AND 0.056 HERCS, RESPECTIVELY.
OKAY, STRANGE. MAKE WITH THE PORTAL.
WAIT A MINUTE. WE HAVEN'T DECIDED--
LOOK. YOU'RE THINKING MAYBE EVERYTHING'S COOL WITH THE HULK 'CAUSE MAYBE AN ENEMY USED A BACKFIRING WISH AGAINST HIM?
BUT AS FAR AS WE CAN TELL, RED SHE-HULK WAS THE FIRST PERSON TO USE THE WISHING WELL.
YOU MEAN BETTY.
NOT EXACTLY. SHE'S BEEN LOCKED IN HER HULK FORM EVER SINCE SHE LEFT BANNER FOR TYRANNUS.
WAIT.
SO... IN THAT FORM...
...DOES SHE LOVE OR HATE THE HULK?
EXACTLY.

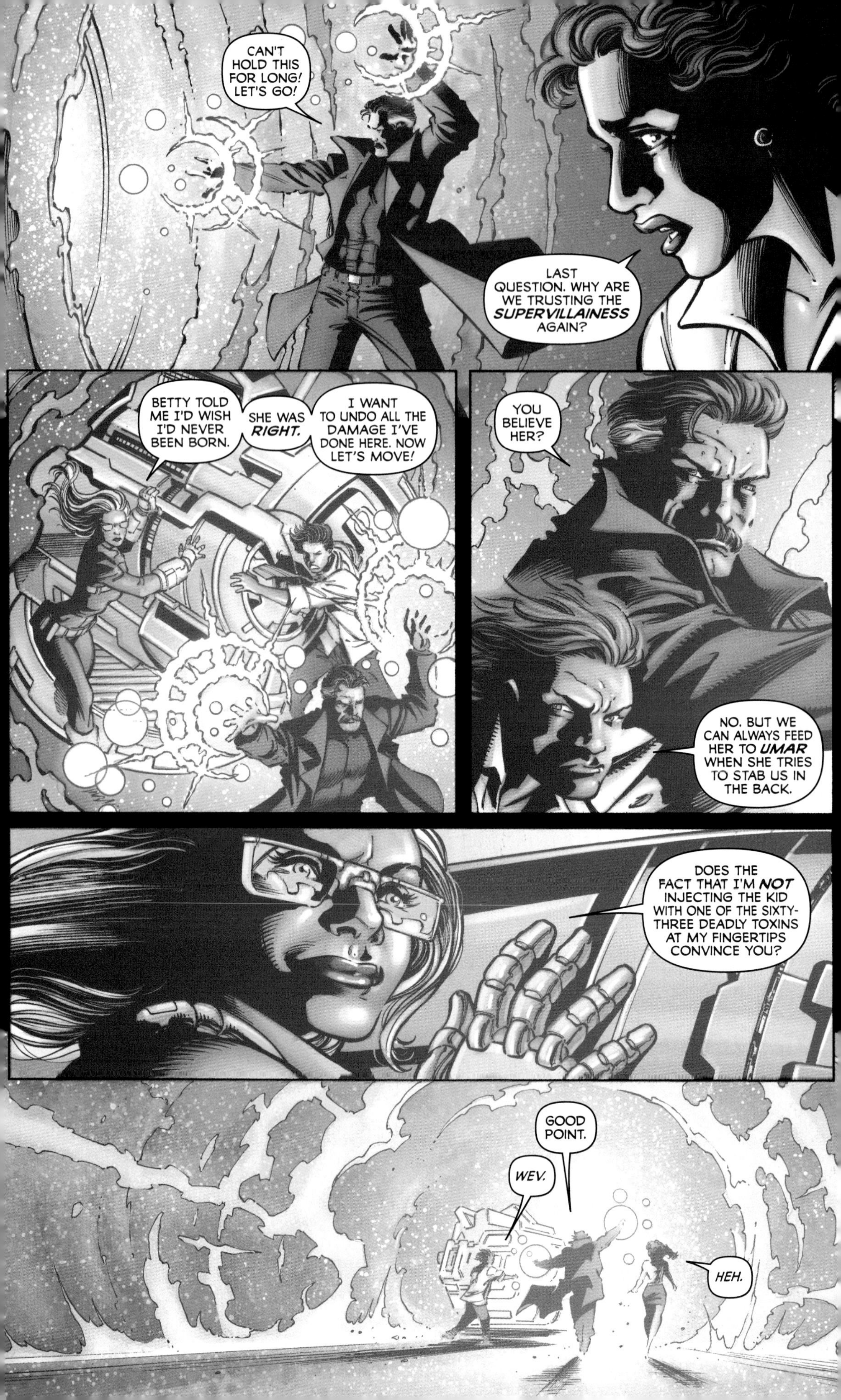
CAN'T HOLD THIS FOR LONG! LET'S GO!
LAST QUESTION. WHY ARE WE TRUSTING THE *SUPERVILLAINESS* AGAIN?
BETTY TOLD ME I'D WISH I'D NEVER BEEN BORN.
SHE WAS *RIGHT.*
I WANT TO UNDO ALL THE DAMAGE I'VE DONE HERE. NOW LET'S MOVE!
YOU BELIEVE HER?
NO. BUT WE CAN ALWAYS FEED HER TO *UMAR* WHEN SHE TRIES TO STAB US IN THE BACK.
DOES THE FACT THAT I'M *NOT* INJECTING THE KID WITH ONE OF THE SIXTY-THREE DEADLY TOXINS AT MY FINGERTIPS CONVINCE YOU?
GOOD POINT.
WEV.
HEH.

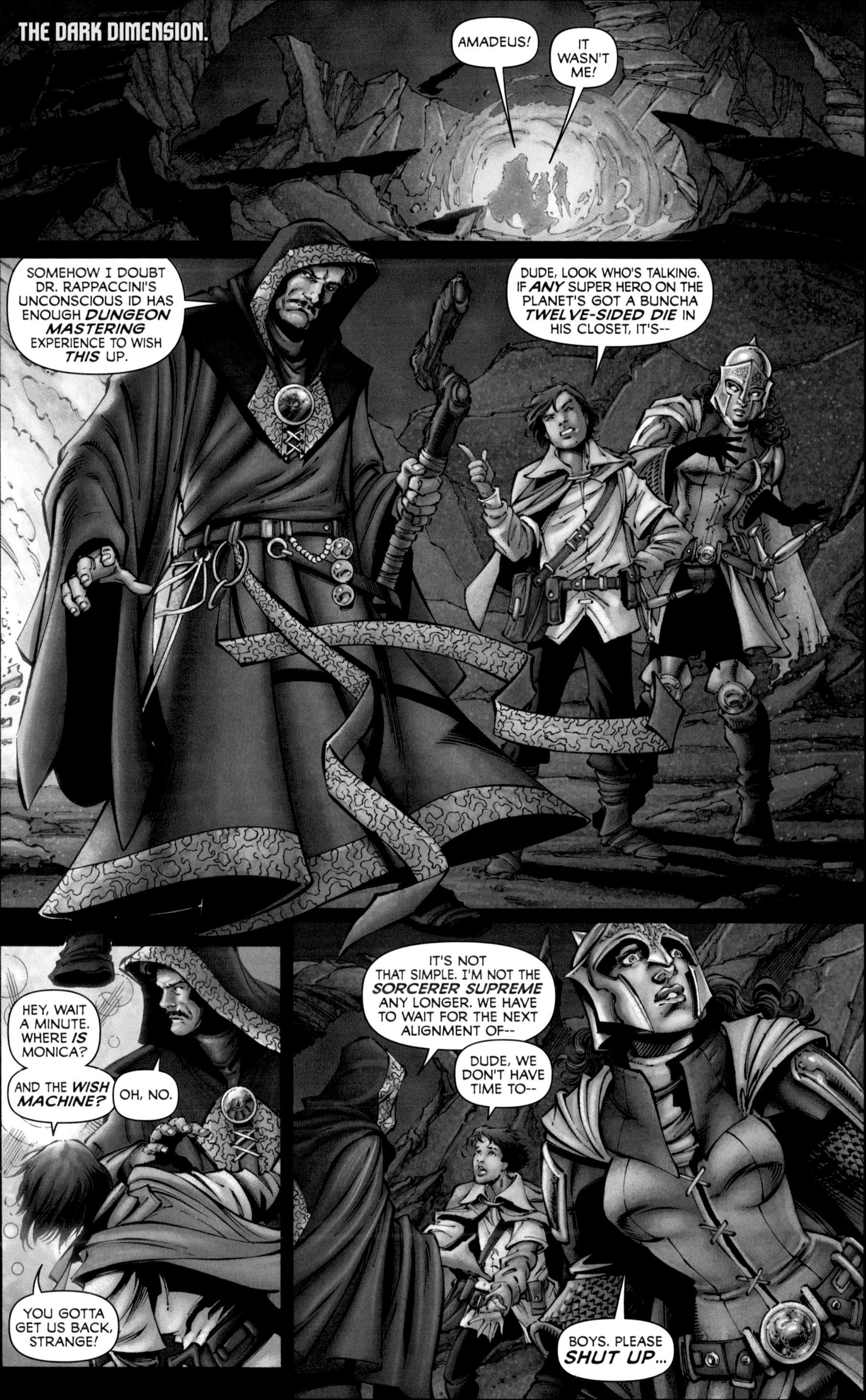
THE DARK DIMENSION.
AMADEUS!
IT WASN'T ME!
SOMEHOW I DOUBT DR. RAPPACCINI'S UNCONSCIOUS ID HAS ENOUGH DUNGEON MASTERING EXPERIENCE TO WISH THIS UP.
DUDE, LOOK WHO'S TALKING. IF ANY SUPER HERO ON THE PLANET'S GOT A BUNCHA TWELVE-SIDED DIE IN HIS CLOSET, IT'S--
HEY, WAIT A MINUTE. WHERE IS MONICA?
AND THE WISH MACHINE?
OH, NO.
YOU GOTTA GET US BACK, STRANGE!
IT'S NOT THAT SIMPLE. I'M NOT THE SORCERER SUPREME ANY LONGER. WE HAVE TO WAIT FOR THE NEXT ALIGNMENT OF--
DUDE, WE DON'T HAVE TIME TO--
BOYS. PLEASE SHUT UP...

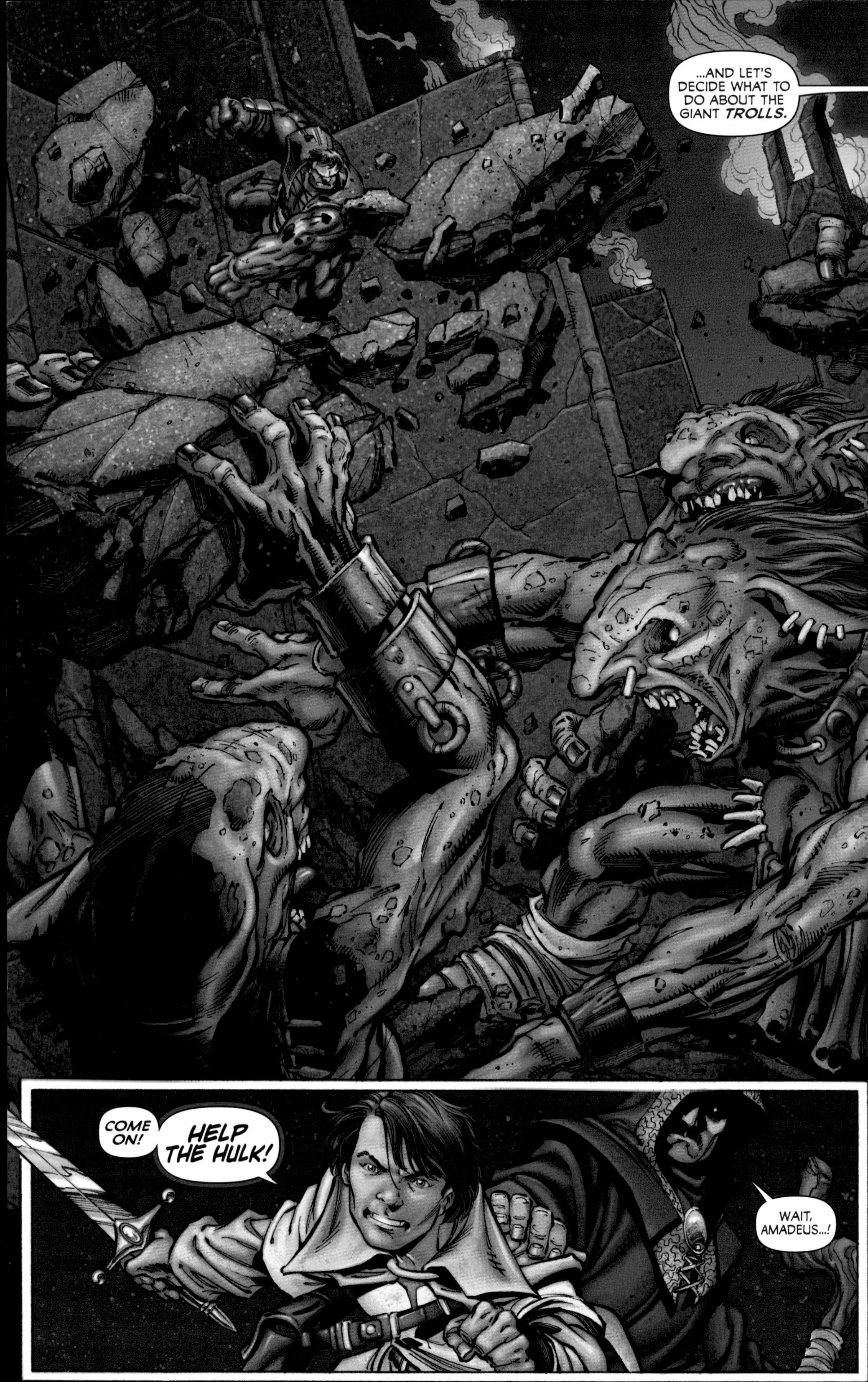
...AND LET'S DECIDE WHAT TO DO ABOUT THE GIANT TROLLS.
COME ON!
HELP THE HULK!
WAIT, AMADEUS...!

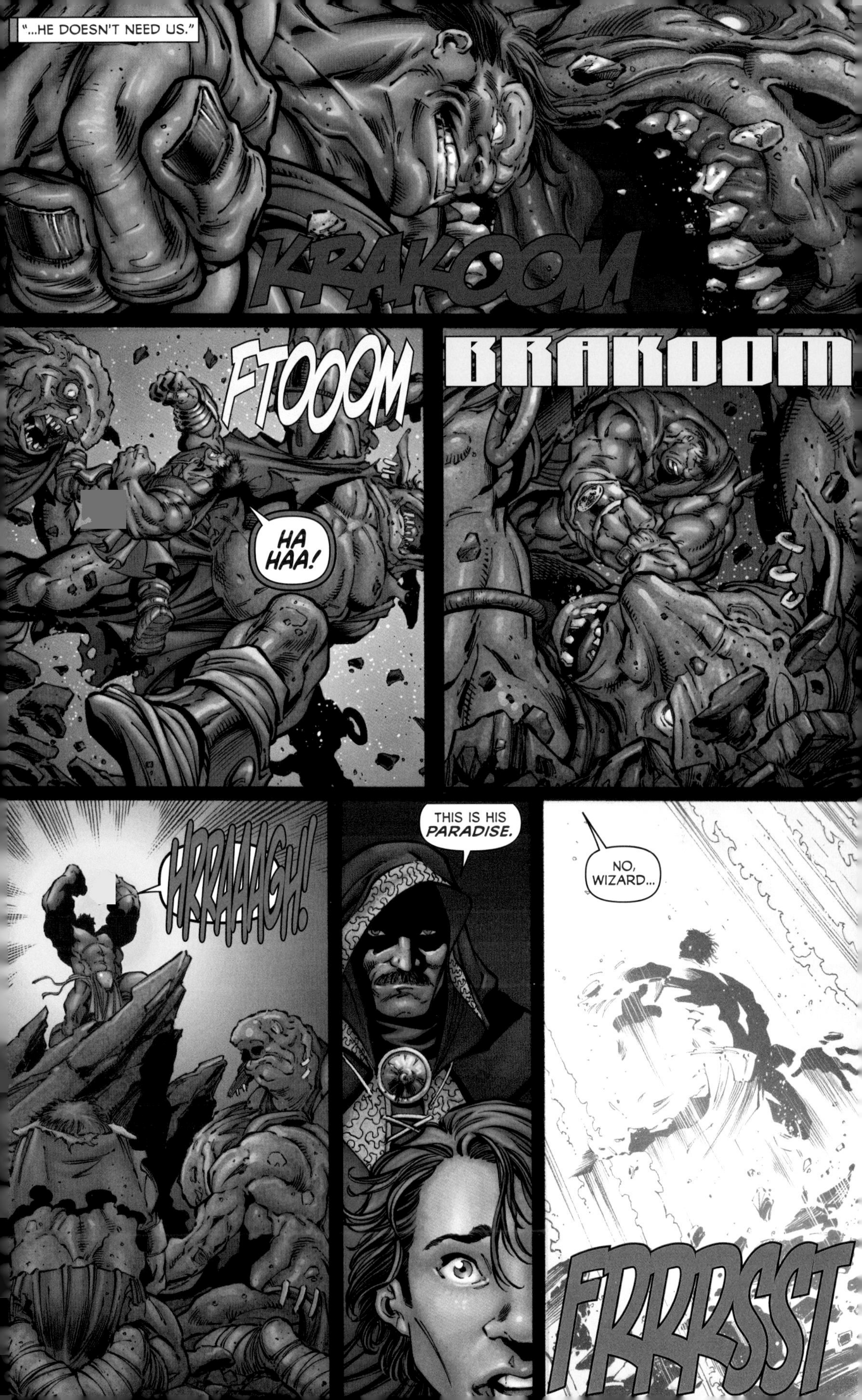
"...HE DOESN'T NEED US."
KRAKOOM
FTOOOM
HA HAA!
BRAKOOM
HRAAAGH!
THIS IS HIS *PARADISE.*
NO, WIZARD...
FRRRSST

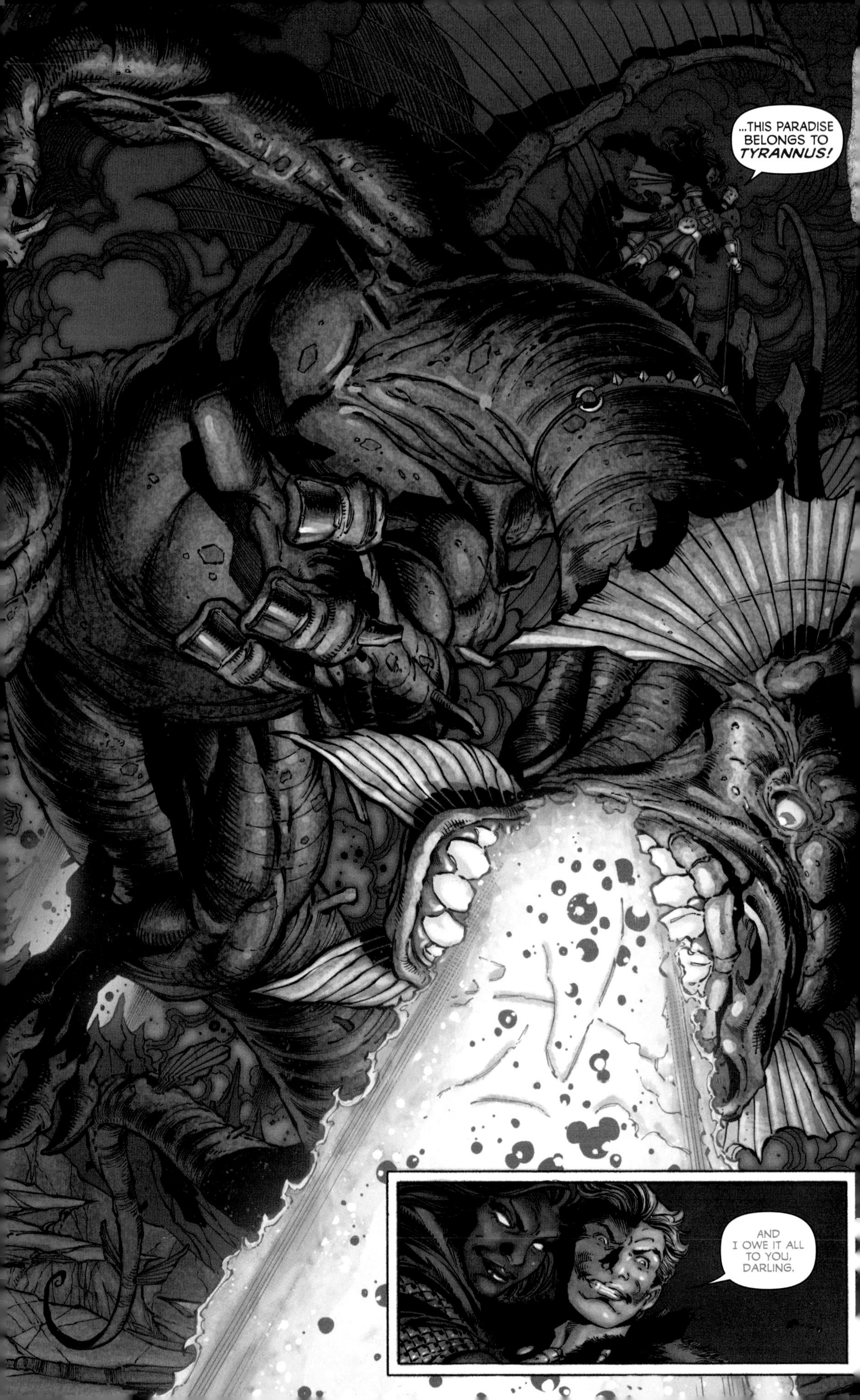
...THIS PARADISE BELONGS TO TYRANNUS!
AND I OWE IT ALL TO YOU, DARLING.

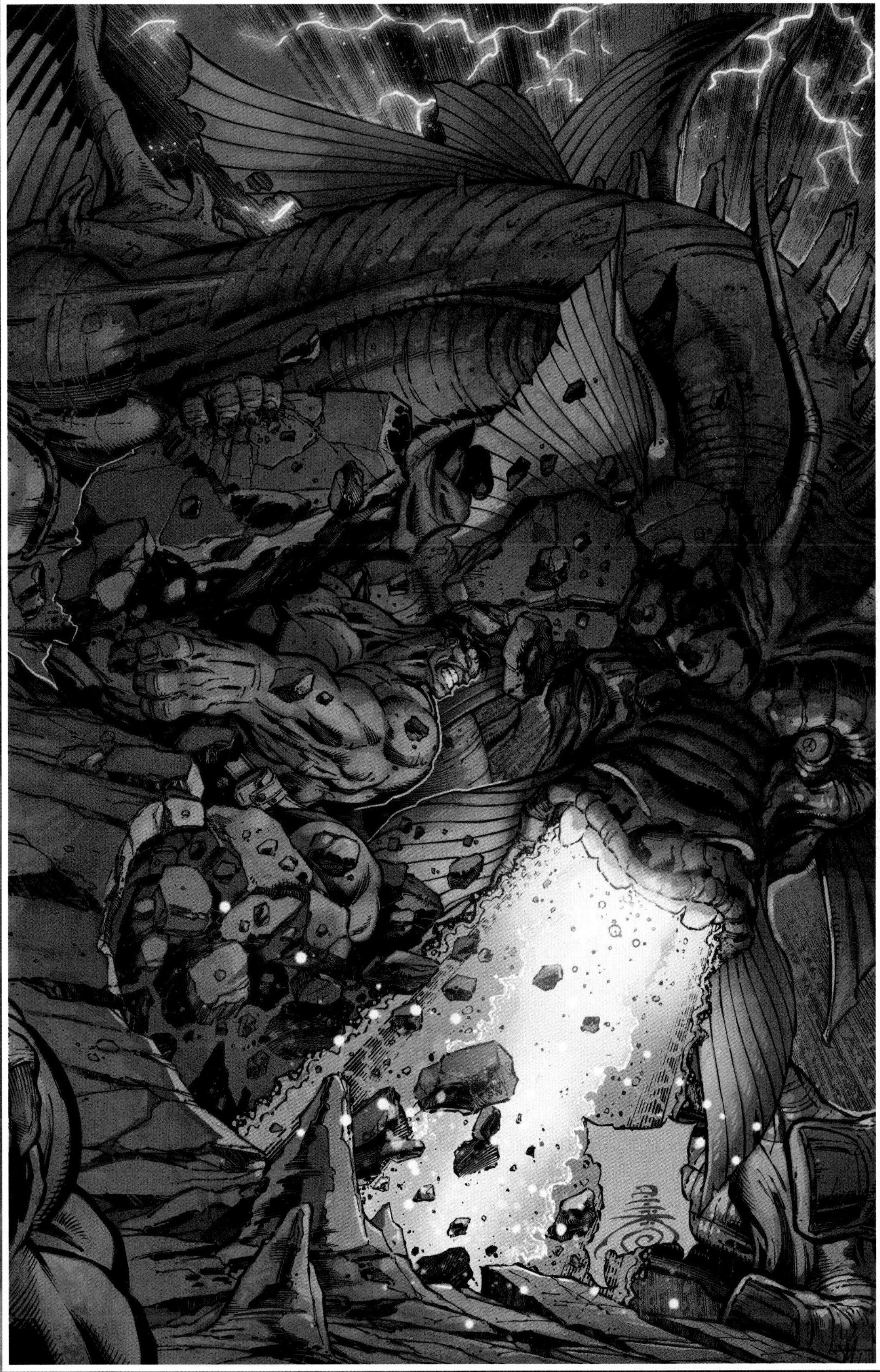

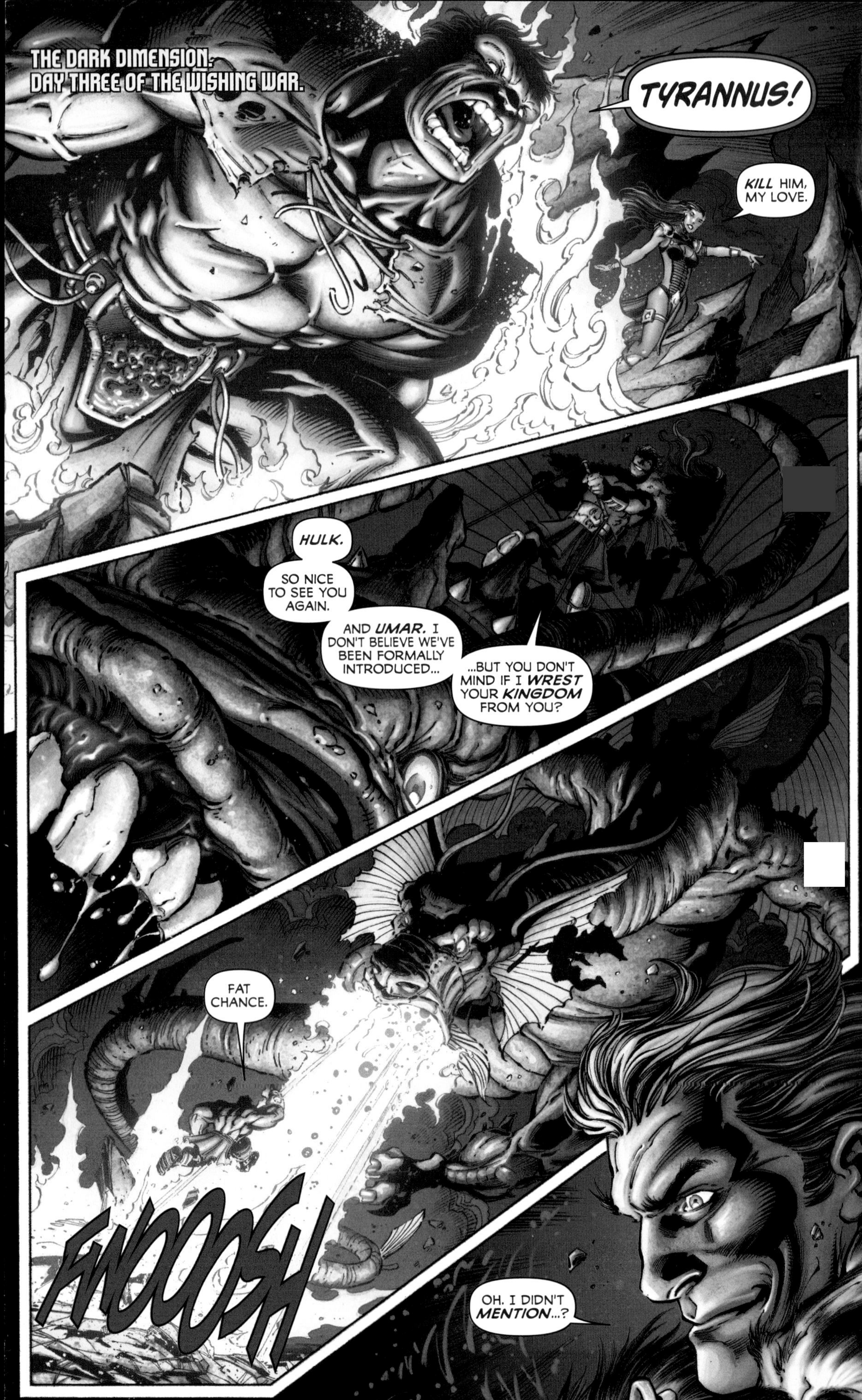
THE DARK DIMENSION:
DAY THREE OF THE WISHING WAR.
TYRANNUS!
KILL HIM, MY LOVE.
HULK.
SO NICE TO SEE YOU AGAIN.
AND UMAR. I DON'T BELIEVE WE'VE BEEN FORMALLY INTRODUCED...
...BUT YOU DON'T MIND IF I WREST YOUR KINGDOM FROM YOU?
FAT CHANCE.
FWOOOSH
OH. I DIDN'T MENTION...?

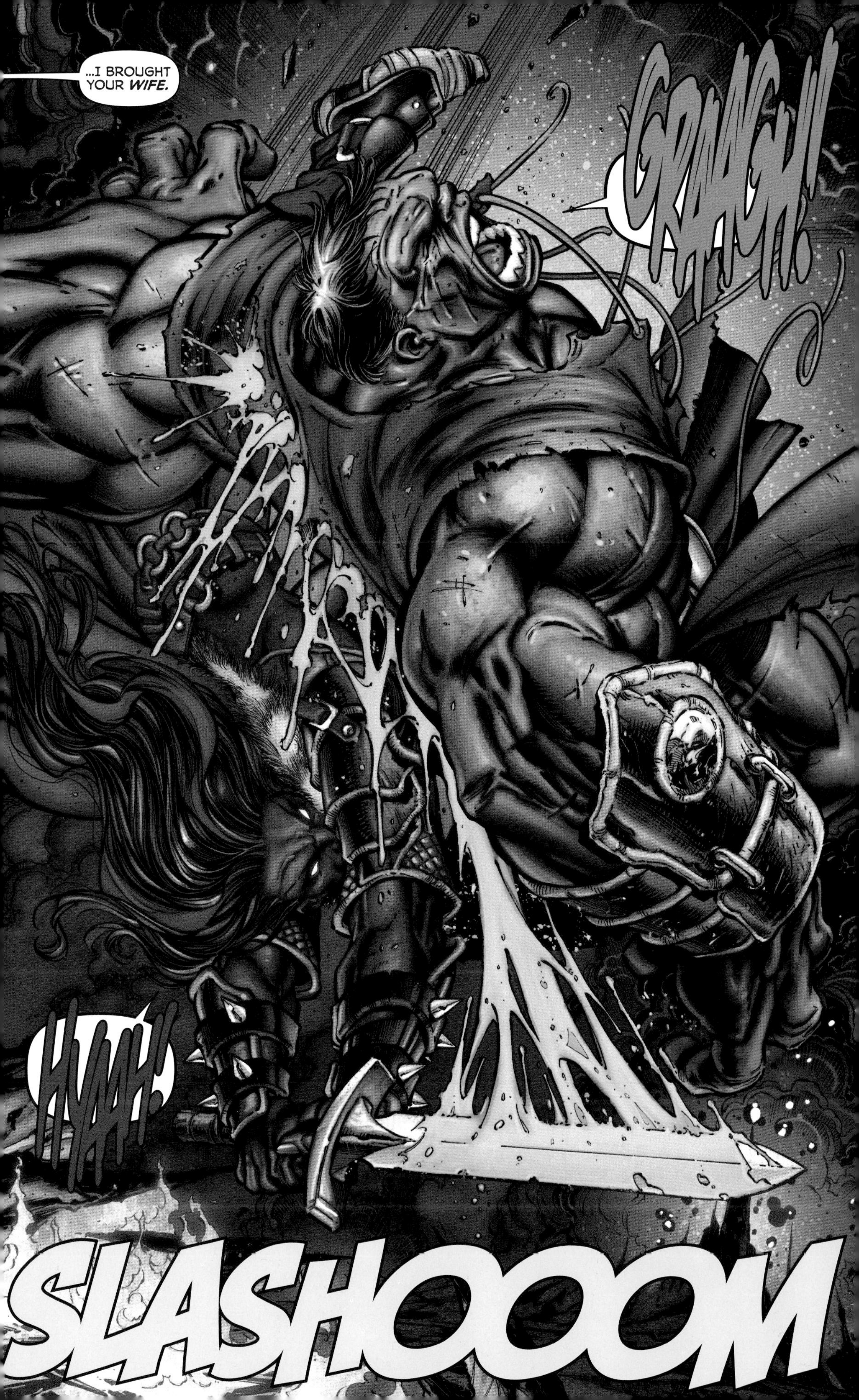
...I BROUGHT YOUR *WIFE.*
GRAAAGH!!
HYAAH!
SLASHOOOM

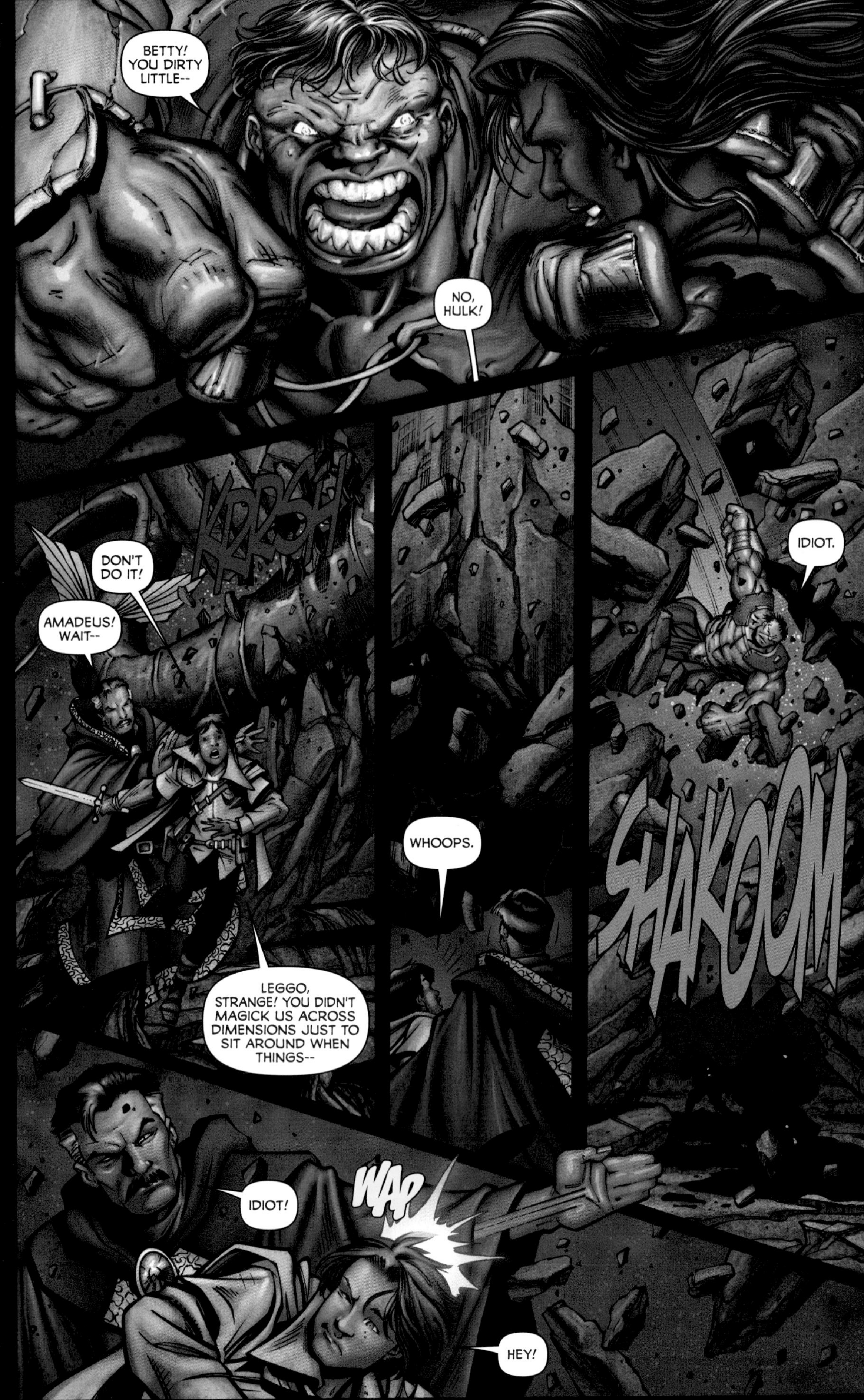
BETTY! YOU DIRTY LITTLE--
NO, HULK!
KRASH
DON'T DO IT!
AMADEUS! WAIT--
LEGGO, STRANGE! YOU DIDN'T MAGICK US ACROSS DIMENSIONS JUST TO SIT AROUND WHEN THINGS--
WHOOPS.
IDIOT.
SHAKOOM
IDIOT!
WAP
HEY!

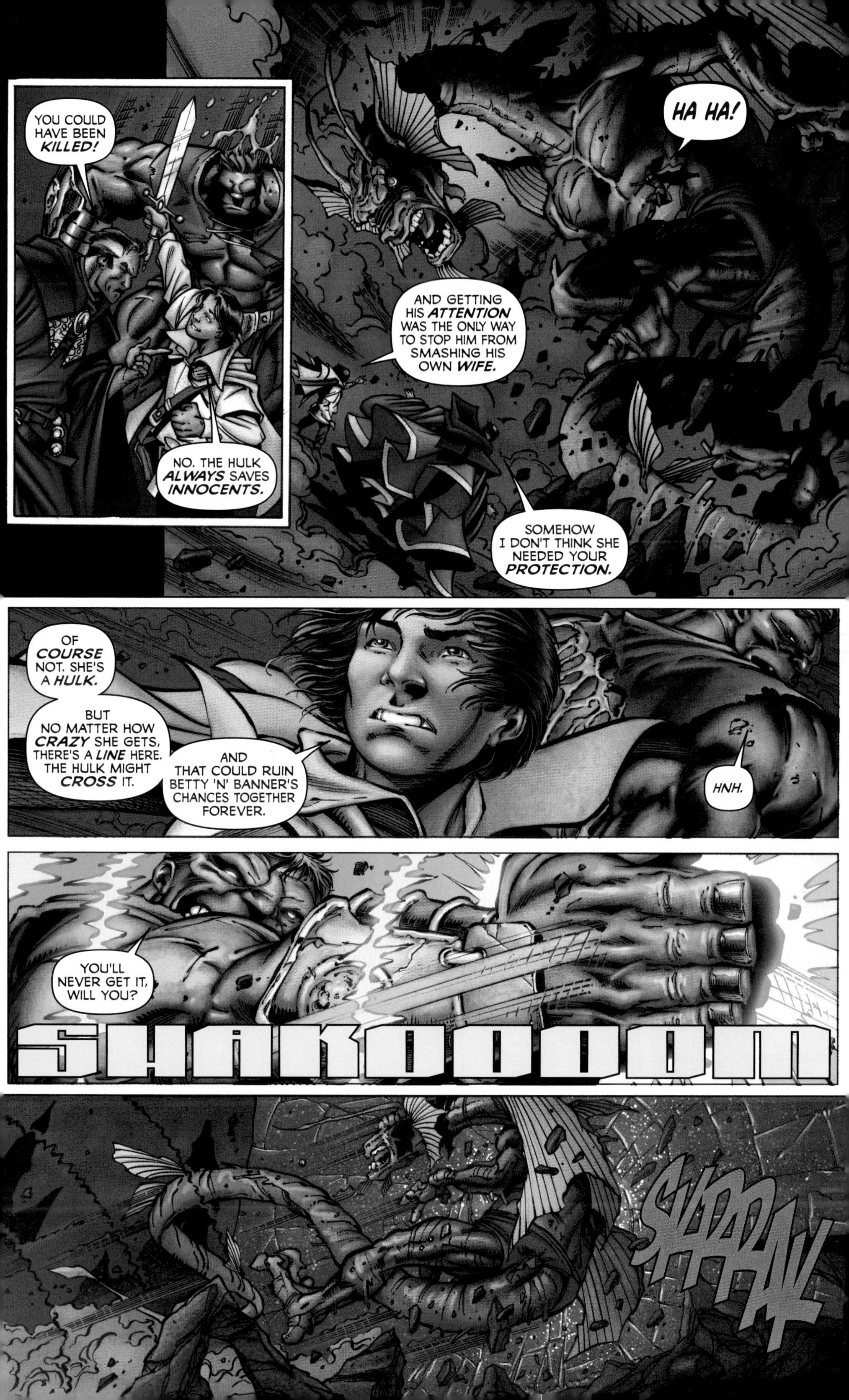
YOU COULD HAVE BEEN KILLED!
NO. THE HULK ALWAYS SAVES INNOCENTS.
HA HA!
AND GETTING HIS ATTENTION WAS THE ONLY WAY TO STOP HIM FROM SMASHING HIS OWN WIFE.
SOMEHOW I DON'T THINK SHE NEEDED YOUR PROTECTION.
OF COURSE NOT. SHE'S A HULK.
BUT NO MATTER HOW CRAZY SHE GETS, THERE'S A LINE HERE. THE HULK MIGHT CROSS IT.
AND THAT COULD RUIN BETTY 'N' BANNER'S CHANCES TOGETHER FOREVER.
HNH.
YOU'LL NEVER GET IT, WILL YOU?
SHAKOOOOM
SHRAAK

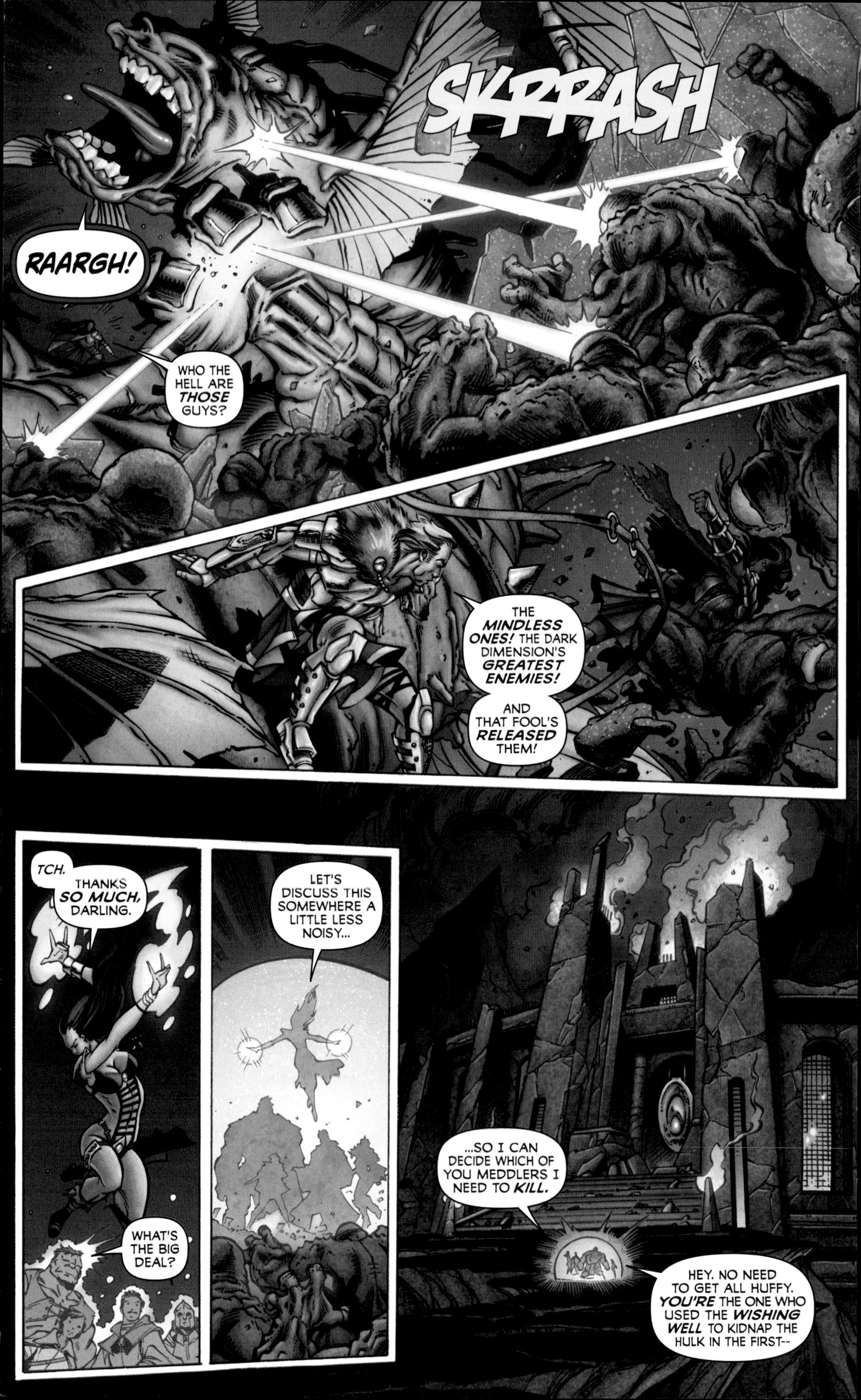
SKRRASH
RAARGH!
WHO THE HELL ARE THOSE GUYS?
THE MINDLESS ONES! THE DARK DIMENSION'S GREATEST ENEMIES!
AND THAT FOOL'S RELEASED THEM!
TCH.
THANKS SO MUCH, DARLING.
WHAT'S THE BIG DEAL?
LET'S DISCUSS THIS SOMEWHERE A LITTLE LESS NOISY...
...SO I CAN DECIDE WHICH OF YOU MEDDLERS I NEED TO KILL.
HEY. NO NEED TO GET ALL HUFFY. YOU'RE THE ONE WHO USED THE WISHING WELL TO KIDNAP THE HULK IN THE FIRST--

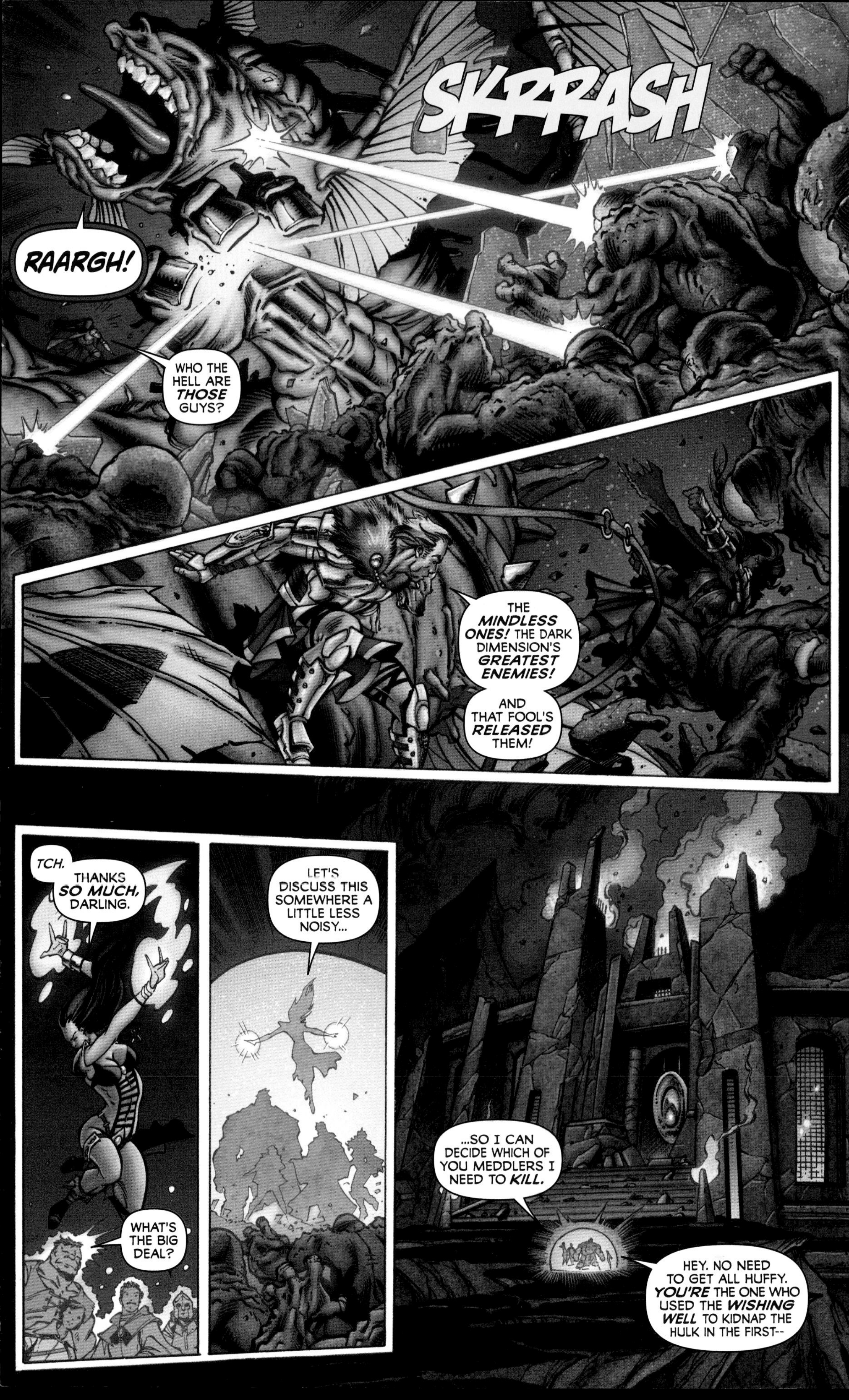
SKRRASH
RAARGH!
WHO THE HELL ARE *THOSE* GUYS?
THE *MINDLESS ONES!* THE DARK DIMENSION'S *GREATEST ENEMIES!*
AND THAT FOOL'S *RELEASED* THEM!
TCH.
THANKS *SO MUCH,* DARLING.
WHAT'S THE BIG DEAL?
LET'S DISCUSS THIS SOMEWHERE A LITTLE LESS NOISY...
...SO I CAN DECIDE WHICH OF YOU MEDDLERS I NEED TO *KILL.*
HEY. NO NEED TO GET ALL HUFFY. *YOU'RE* THE ONE WHO USED THE *WISHING WELL* TO KIDNAP THE HULK IN THE FIRST--

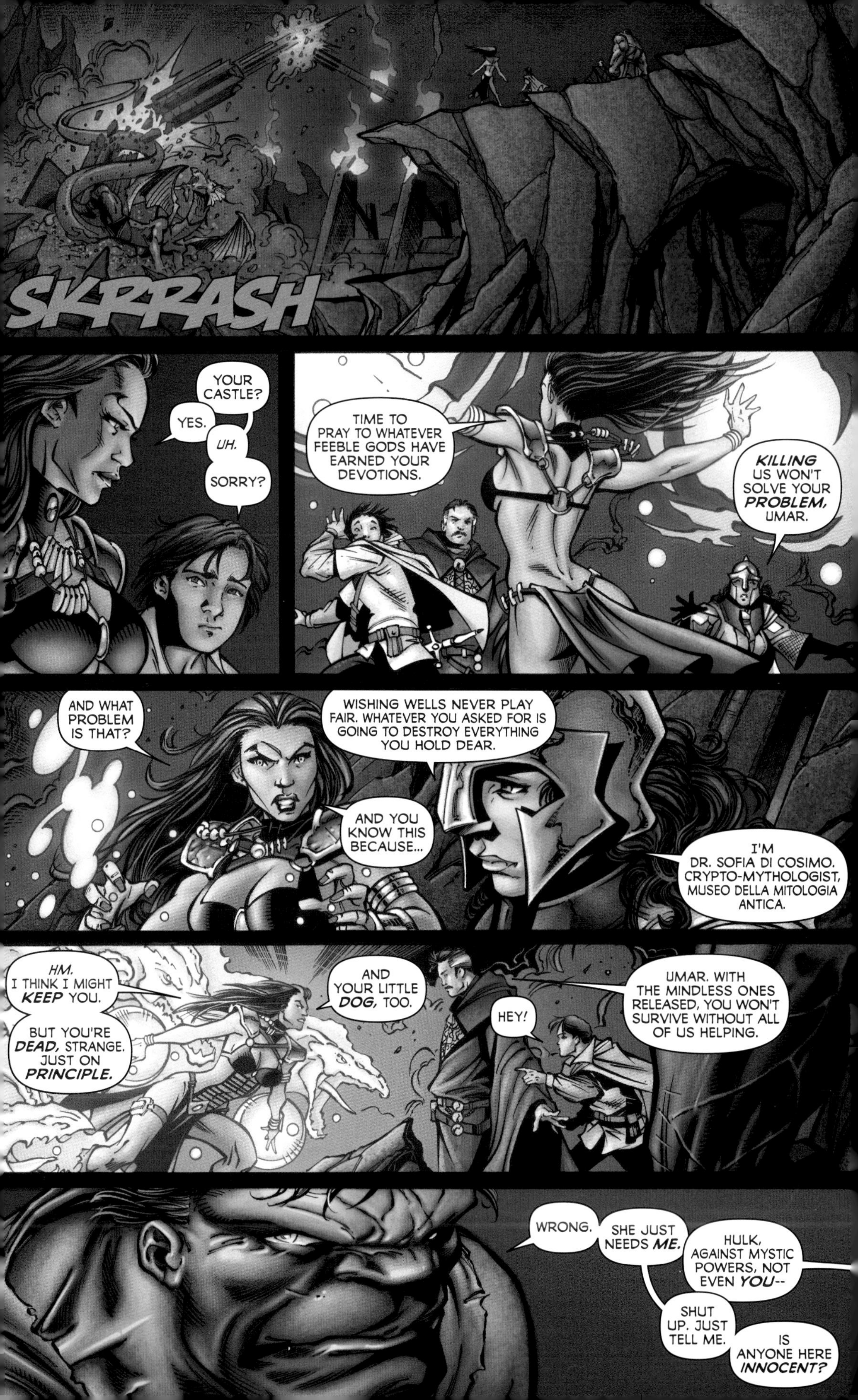
SKRRASH
YOUR CASTLE?
YES.
UH.
SORRY?
TIME TO PRAY TO WHATEVER FEEBLE GODS HAVE EARNED YOUR DEVOTIONS.
KILLING US WON'T SOLVE YOUR PROBLEM, UMAR.
AND WHAT PROBLEM IS THAT?
WISHING WELLS NEVER PLAY FAIR. WHATEVER YOU ASKED FOR IS GOING TO DESTROY EVERYTHING YOU HOLD DEAR.
AND YOU KNOW THIS BECAUSE...
I'M DR. SOFIA DI COSIMO. CRYPTO-MYTHOLOGIST, MUSEO DELLA MITOLOGIA ANTICA.
HM. I THINK I MIGHT KEEP YOU.
BUT YOU'RE DEAD, STRANGE. JUST ON PRINCIPLE.
AND YOUR LITTLE DOG, TOO.
HEY!
UMAR. WITH THE MINDLESS ONES RELEASED, YOU WON'T SURVIVE WITHOUT ALL OF US HELPING.
WRONG.
SHE JUST NEEDS ME.
HULK, AGAINST MYSTIC POWERS, NOT EVEN YOU--
SHUT UP. JUST TELL ME.
IS ANYONE HERE INNOCENT?

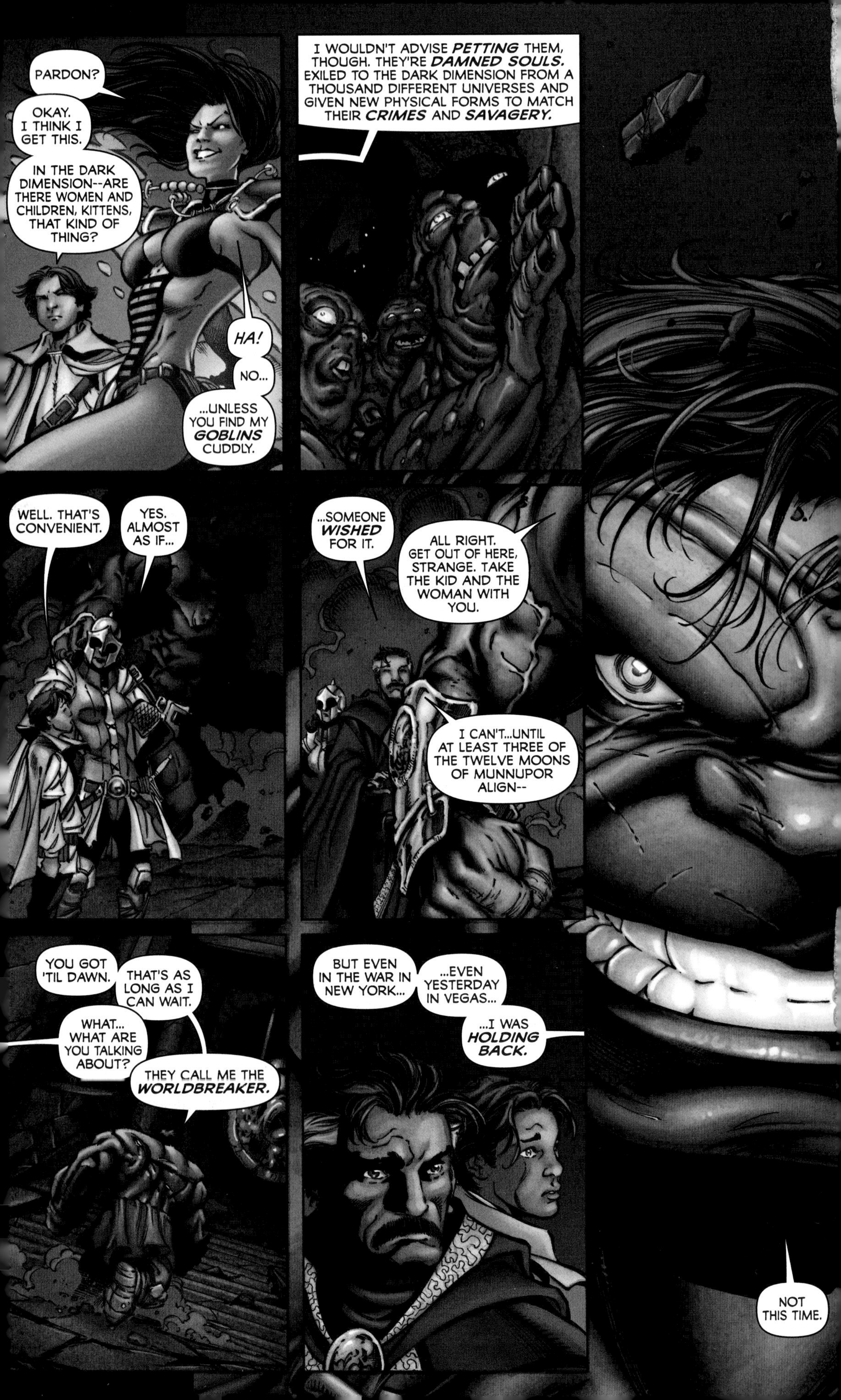
PARDON?
OKAY. I THINK I GET THIS.
IN THE DARK DIMENSION--ARE THERE WOMEN AND CHILDREN, KITTENS, THAT KIND OF THING?
HA!
NO...
...UNLESS YOU FIND MY GOBLINS CUDDLY.
I WOULDN'T ADVISE PETTING THEM, THOUGH. THEY'RE DAMNED SOULS. EXILED TO THE DARK DIMENSION FROM A THOUSAND DIFFERENT UNIVERSES AND GIVEN NEW PHYSICAL FORMS TO MATCH THEIR CRIMES AND SAVAGERY.
WELL. THAT'S CONVENIENT.
YES. ALMOST AS IF...
...SOMEONE WISHED FOR IT.
ALL RIGHT. GET OUT OF HERE, STRANGE. TAKE THE KID AND THE WOMAN WITH YOU.
I CAN'T...UNTIL AT LEAST THREE OF THE TWELVE MOONS OF MUNNUPOR ALIGN--
YOU GOT 'TIL DAWN.
THAT'S AS LONG AS I CAN WAIT.
WHAT... WHAT ARE YOU TALKING ABOUT?
THEY CALL ME THE WORLDBREAKER.
BUT EVEN IN THE WAR IN NEW YORK...
...EVEN YESTERDAY IN VEGAS...
...I WAS HOLDING BACK.
NOT THIS TIME.

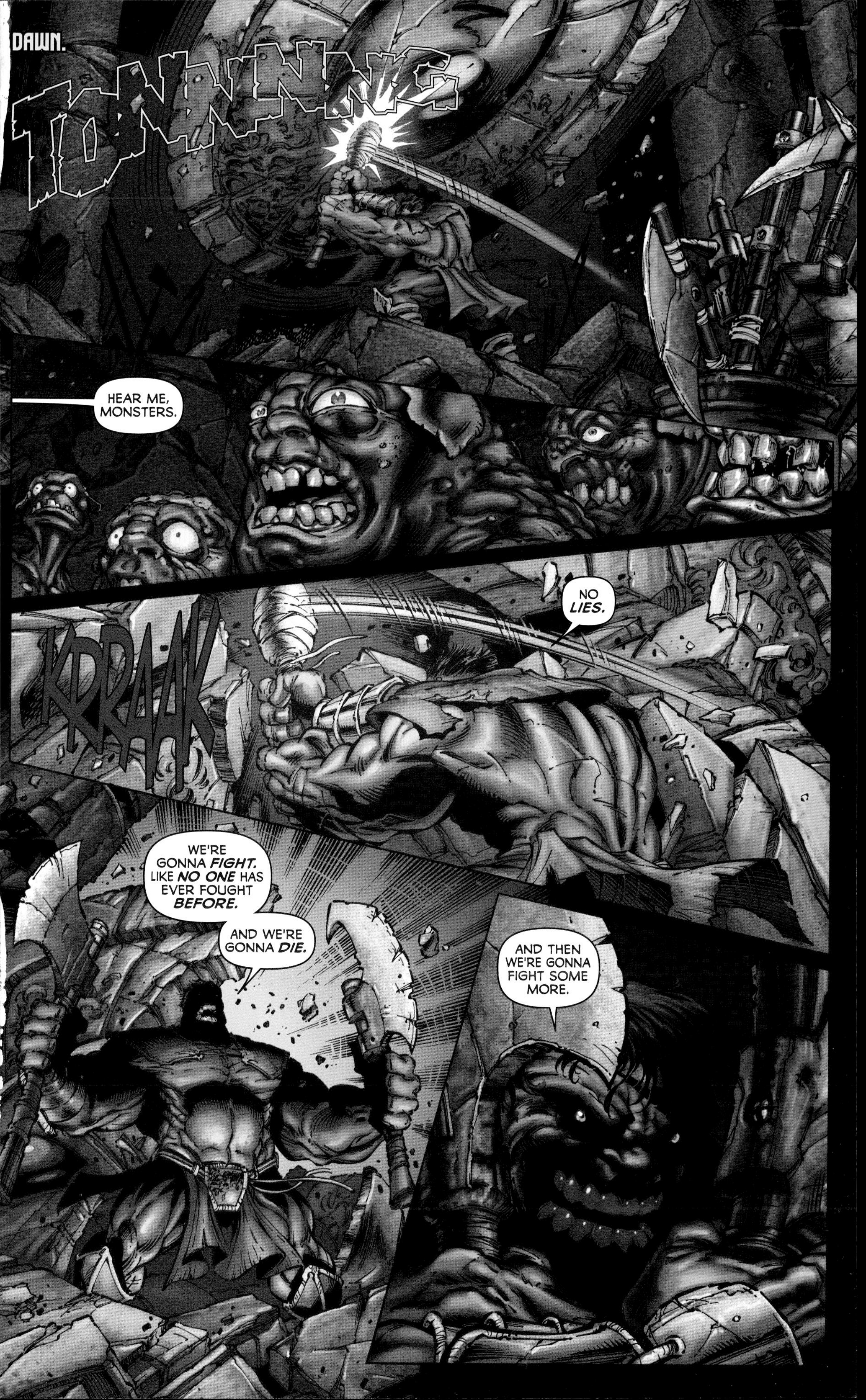
DAWN.
TOONNNNNG
HEAR ME, MONSTERS.
NO LIES.
KRRAAK
WE'RE GONNA FIGHT. LIKE NO ONE HAS EVER FOUGHT BEFORE.
AND WE'RE GONNA DIE.
AND THEN WE'RE GONNA FIGHT SOME MORE.

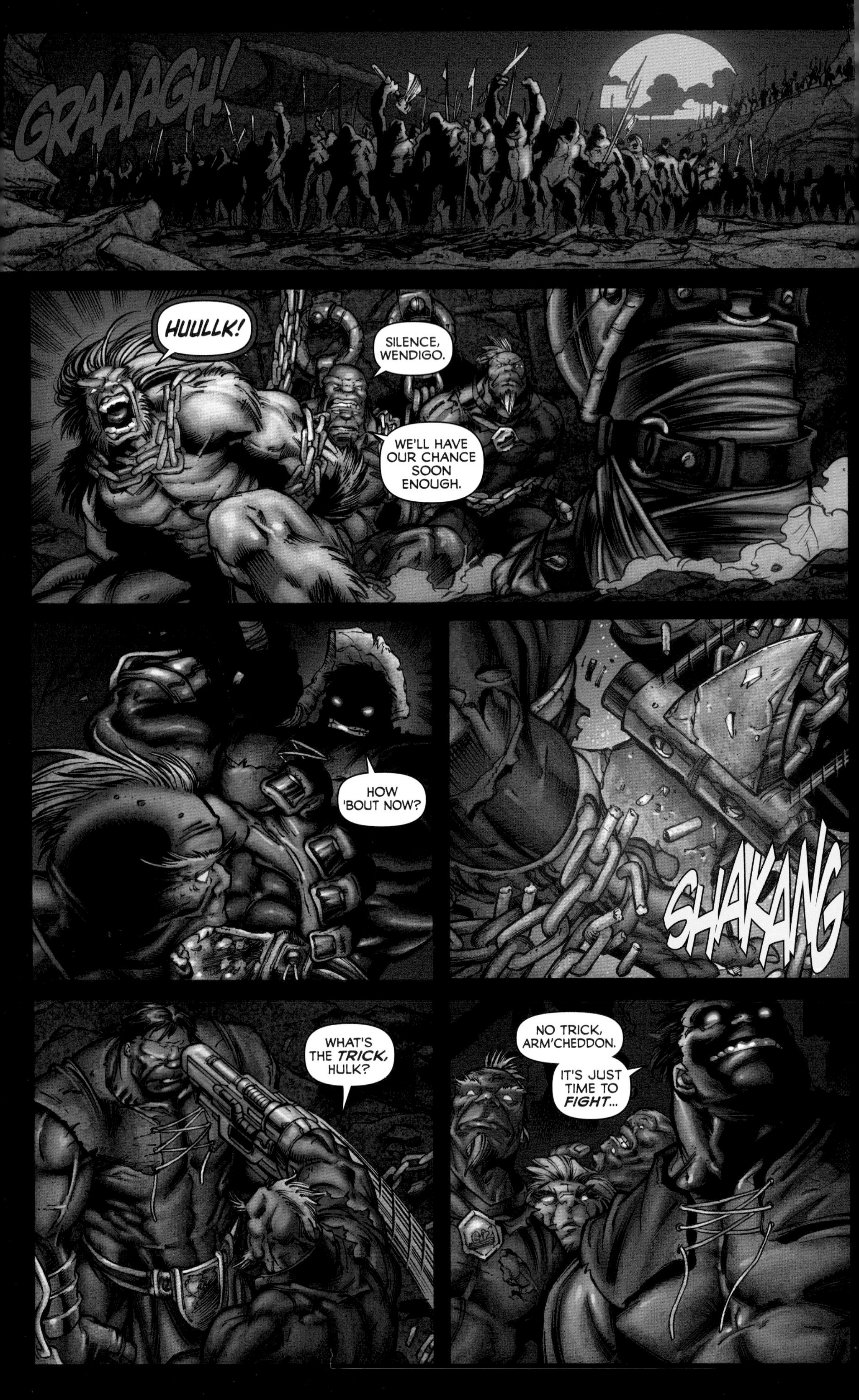
GRAAAGH!
HUULLK!
SILENCE, WENDIGO.
WE'LL HAVE OUR CHANCE SOON ENOUGH.
HOW 'BOUT NOW?
SHAKANG
WHAT'S THE *TRICK,* HULK?
NO TRICK, ARM'CHEDDON.
IT'S JUST TIME TO *FIGHT*...

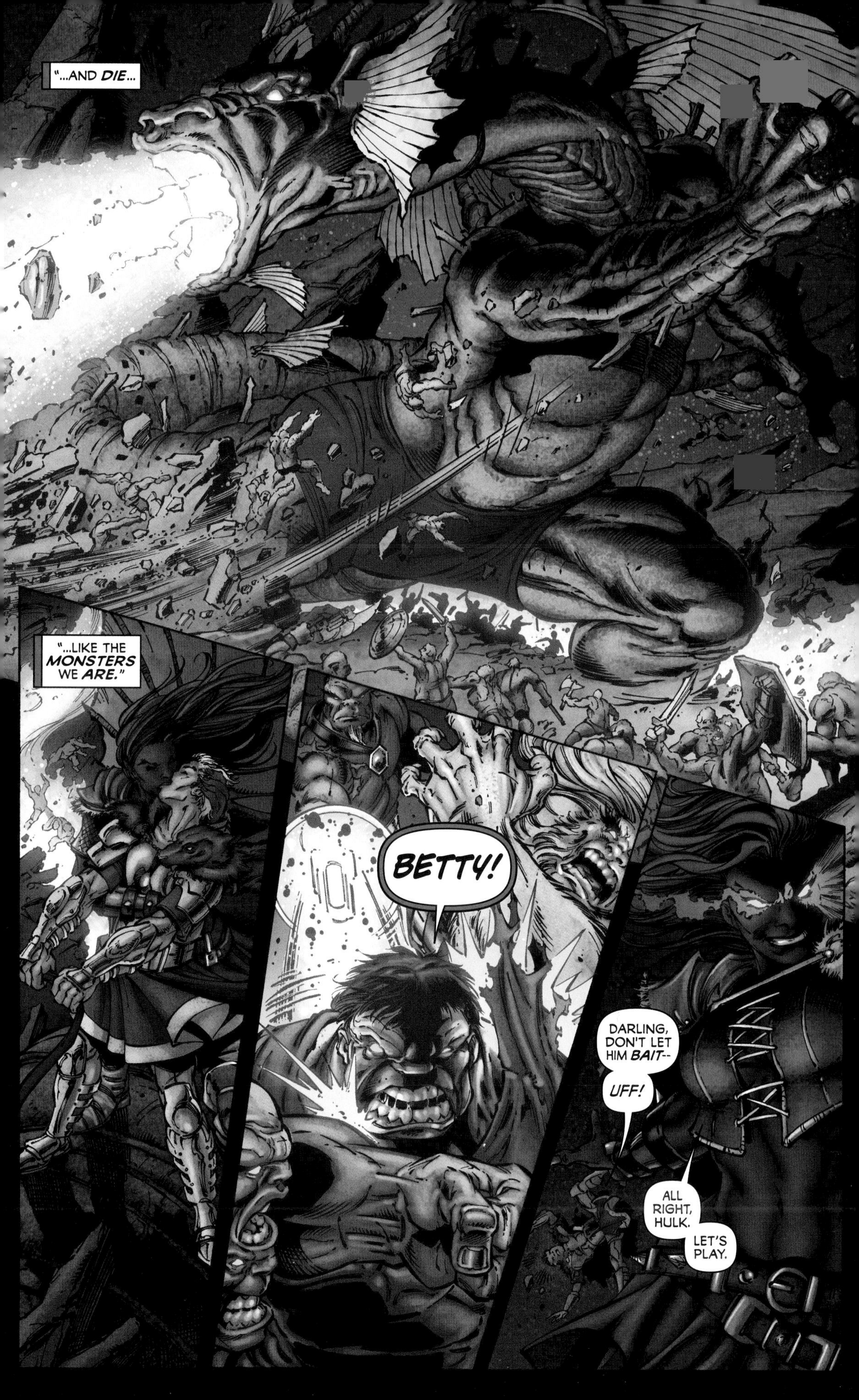
"...AND *DIE*...
"...LIKE THE *MONSTERS* WE *ARE*."
BETTY!
DARLING, DON'T LET HIM *BAIT*--
UFF!
ALL RIGHT, HULK.
LET'S PLAY.

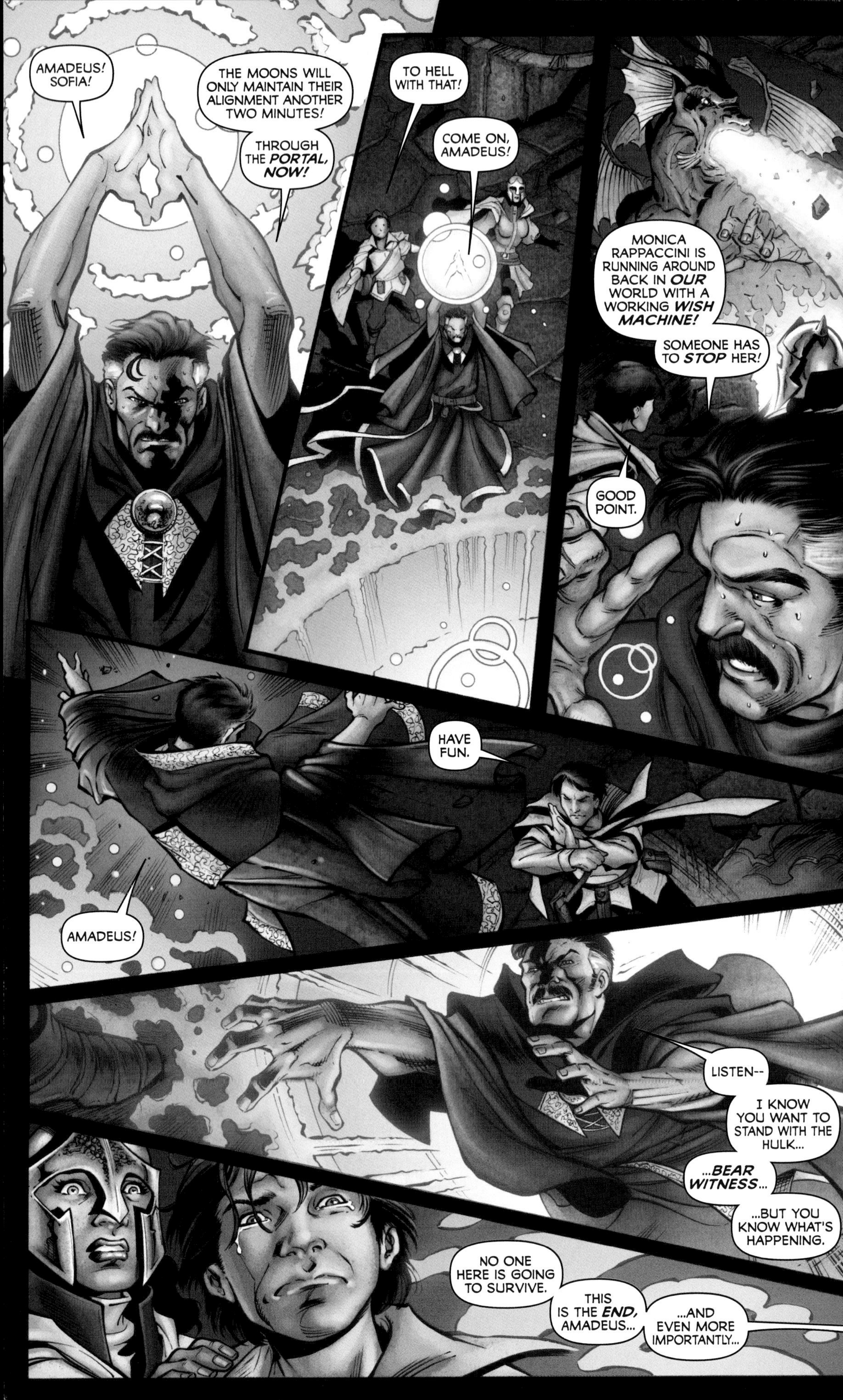
AMADEUS! SOFIA!
THE MOONS WILL ONLY MAINTAIN THEIR ALIGNMENT ANOTHER TWO MINUTES!
THROUGH THE PORTAL, NOW!
TO HELL WITH THAT!
COME ON, AMADEUS!
MONICA RAPPACCINI IS RUNNING AROUND BACK IN OUR WORLD WITH A WORKING WISH MACHINE!
SOMEONE HAS TO STOP HER!
GOOD POINT.
HAVE FUN.
AMADEUS!
LISTEN--
I KNOW YOU WANT TO STAND WITH THE HULK...
...BEAR WITNESS...
...BUT YOU KNOW WHAT'S HAPPENING.
NO ONE HERE IS GOING TO SURVIVE.
THIS IS THE END, AMADEUS...
...AND EVEN MORE IMPORTANTLY...

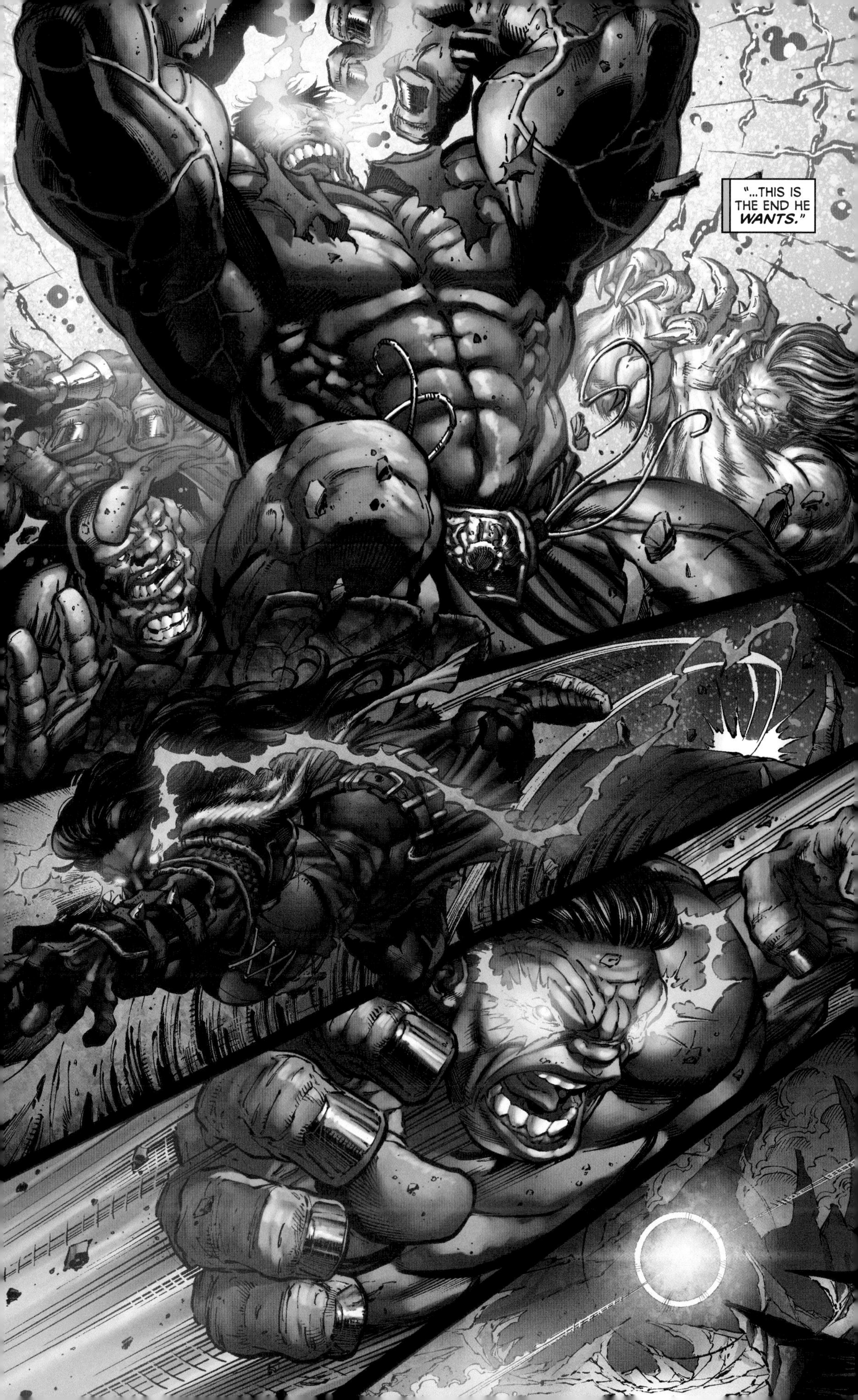
"...THIS IS THE END HE *WANTS.*"

WENDIGOOO--

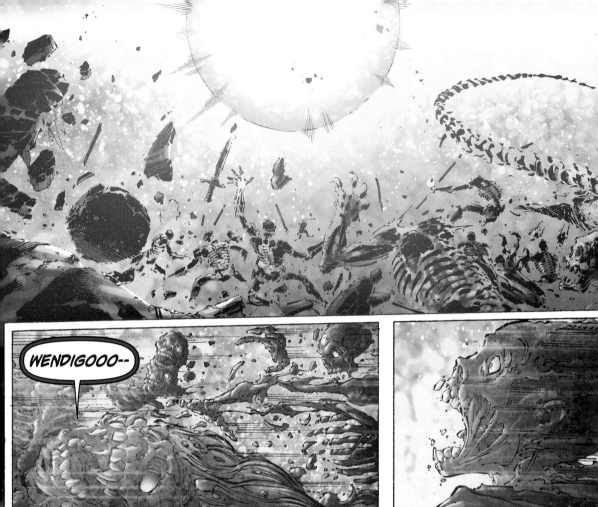

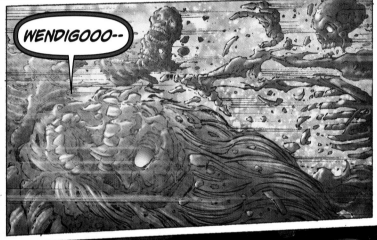

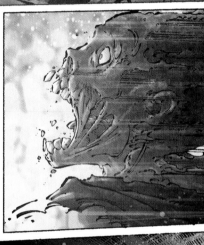

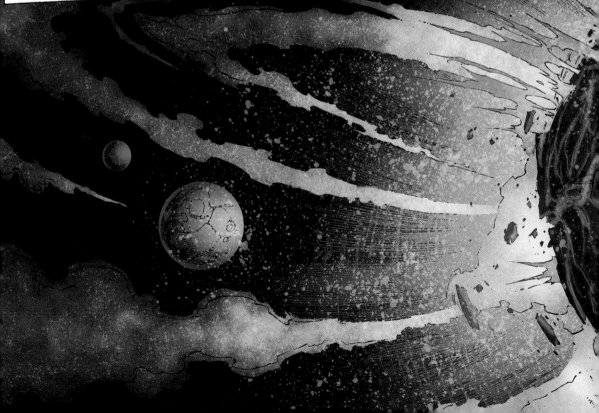

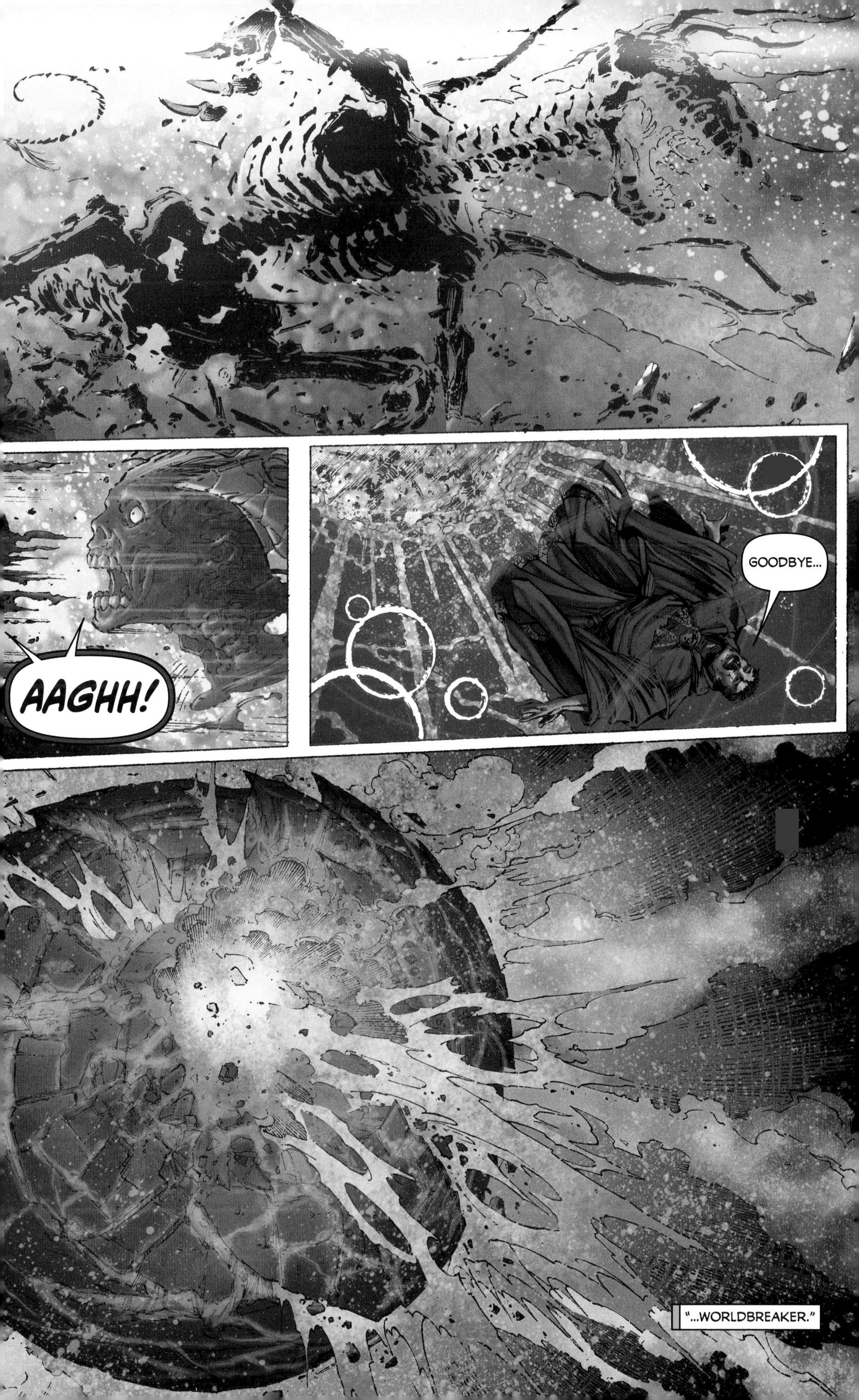
AAGHH!
GOODBYE...
"...WORLDBREAKER."

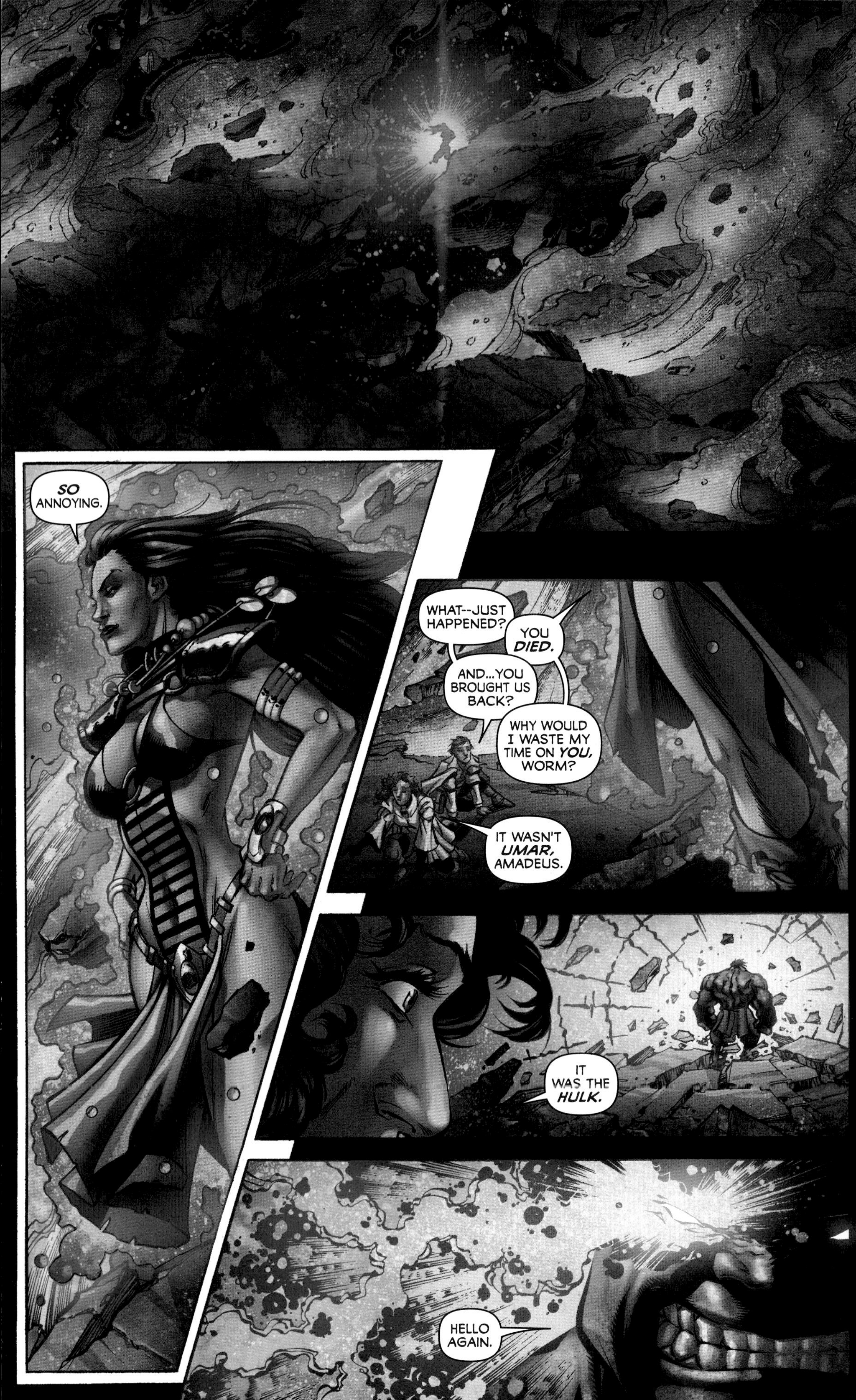
SO ANNOYING.
WHAT--JUST HAPPENED?
YOU DIED.
AND...YOU BROUGHT US BACK?
WHY WOULD I WASTE MY TIME ON YOU, WORM?
IT WASN'T UMAR, AMADEUS.
IT WAS THE HULK.
HELLO AGAIN.

AAGHH!

GOODBYE...

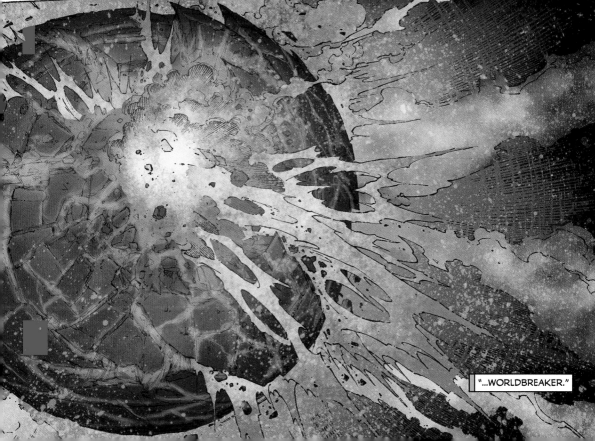

"...WORLDBREAKER."

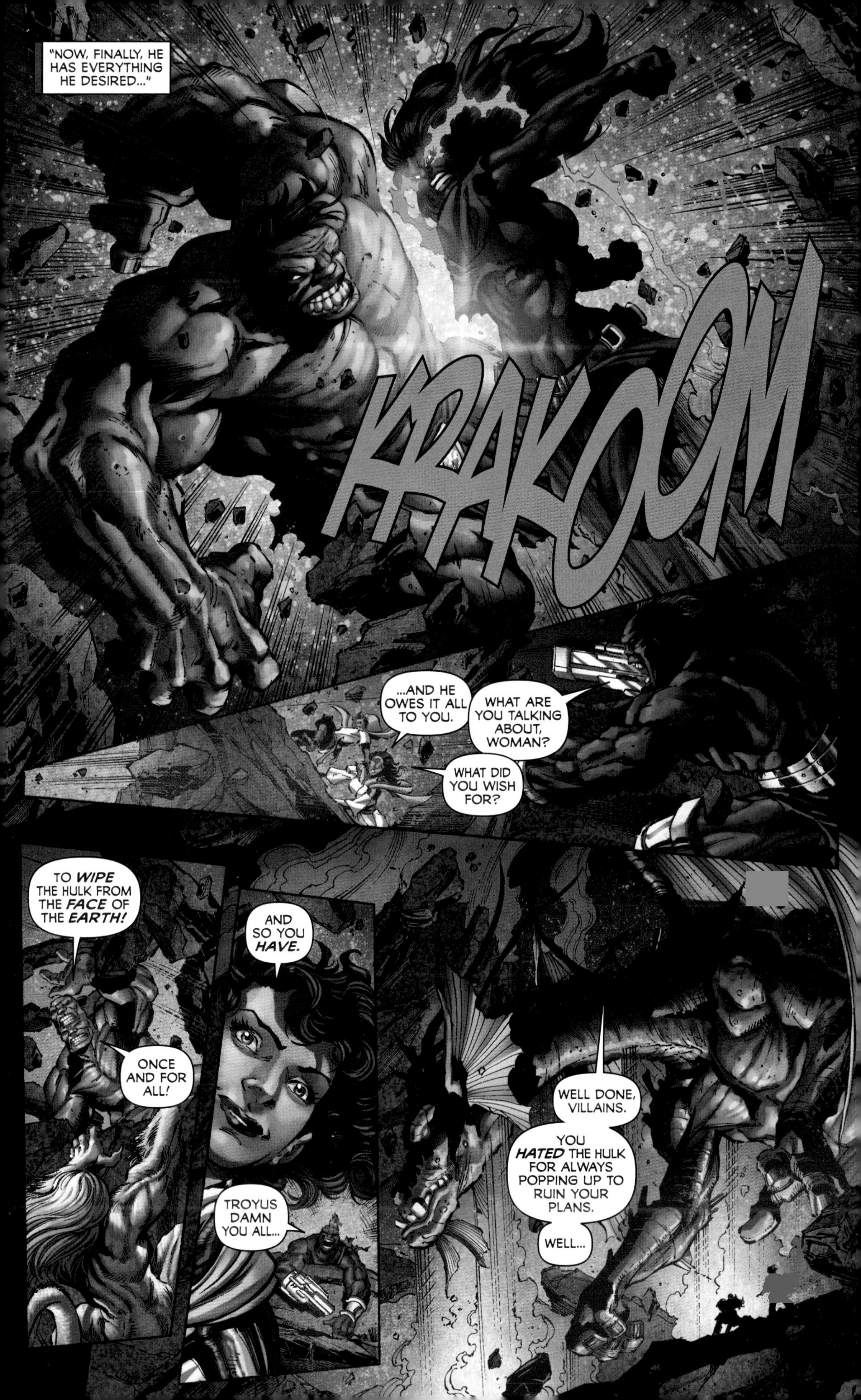
"NOW, FINALLY, HE HAS EVERYTHING HE DESIRED..."
KRAKOOM
...AND HE OWES IT ALL TO YOU.
WHAT ARE YOU TALKING ABOUT, WOMAN?
WHAT DID YOU WISH FOR?
TO WIPE THE HULK FROM THE FACE OF THE EARTH!
ONCE AND FOR ALL!
AND SO YOU HAVE.
TROYUS DAMN YOU ALL...
WELL DONE, VILLAINS.
YOU HATED THE HULK FOR ALWAYS POPPING UP TO RUIN YOUR PLANS.
WELL...

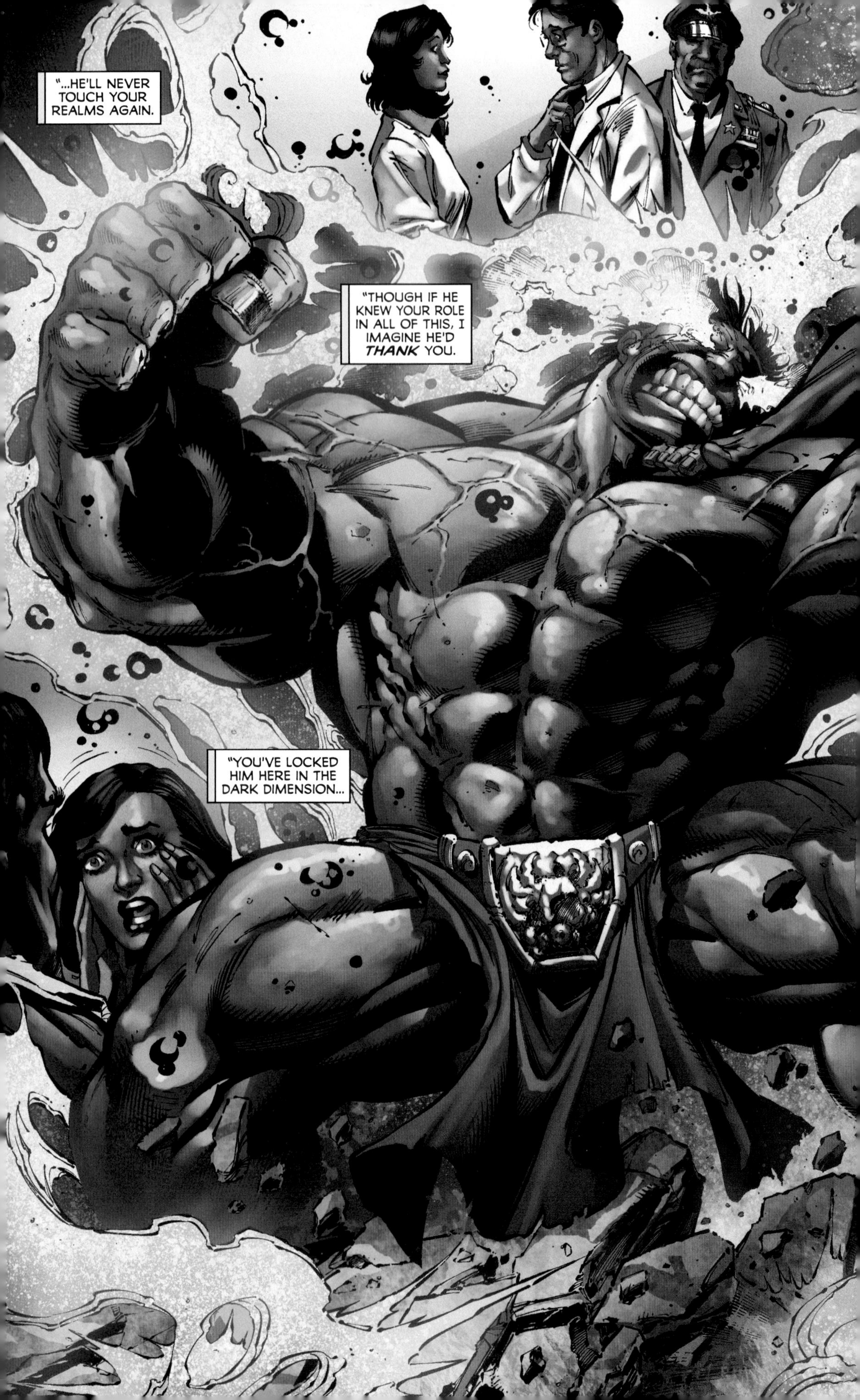
"...HE'LL NEVER TOUCH YOUR REALMS AGAIN.
"THOUGH IF HE KNEW YOUR ROLE IN ALL OF THIS, I IMAGINE HE'D *THANK* YOU.
"YOU'VE LOCKED HIM HERE IN THE DARK DIMENSION...

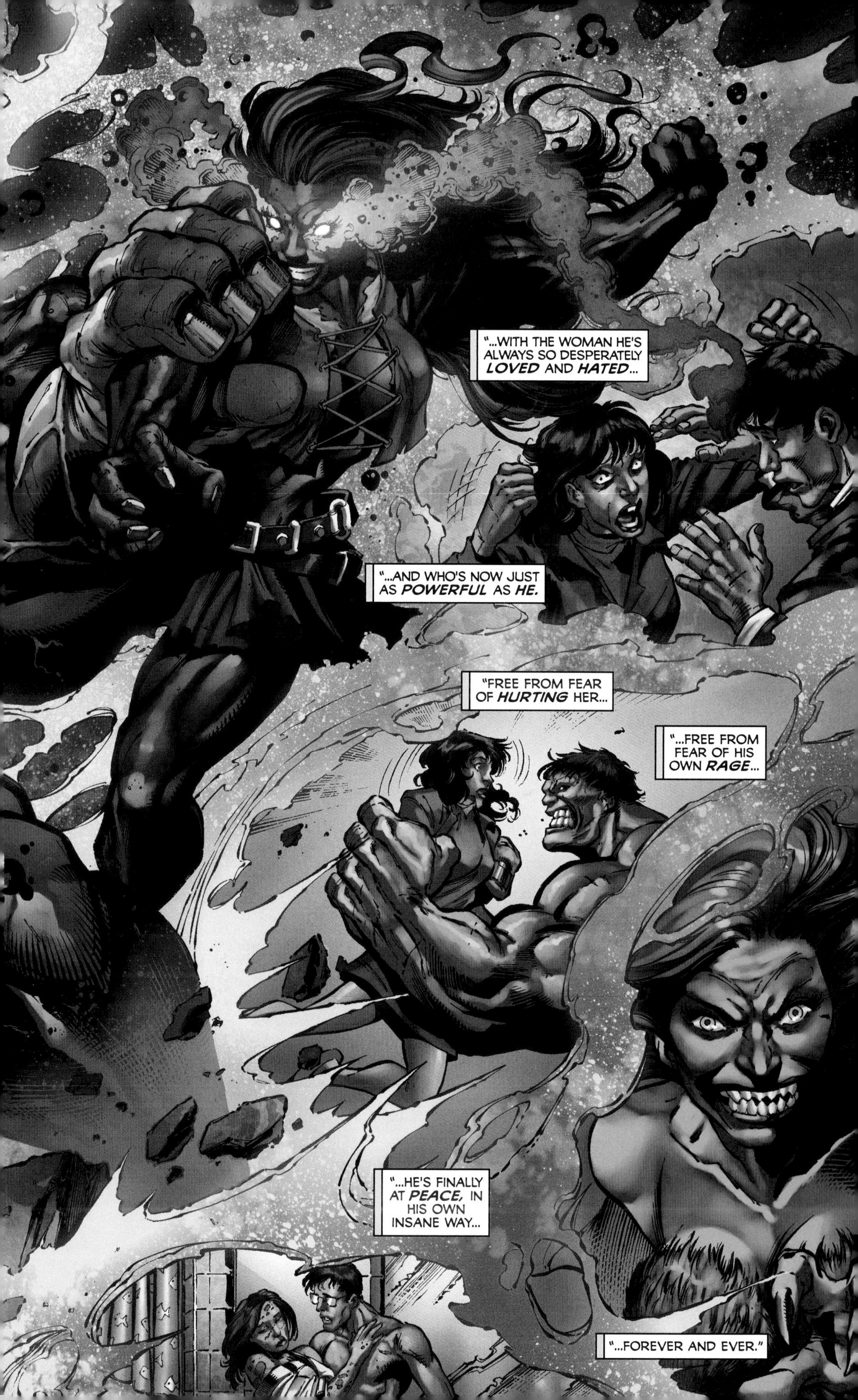
"...WITH THE WOMAN HE'S ALWAYS SO DESPERATELY *LOVED* AND *HATED*...
"...AND WHO'S NOW JUST AS *POWERFUL* AS *HE.*
"FREE FROM FEAR OF *HURTING* HER...
"...FREE FROM FEAR OF HIS OWN *RAGE*...
"...HE'S FINALLY AT *PEACE,* IN HIS OWN INSANE WAY...
"...FOREVER AND EVER."

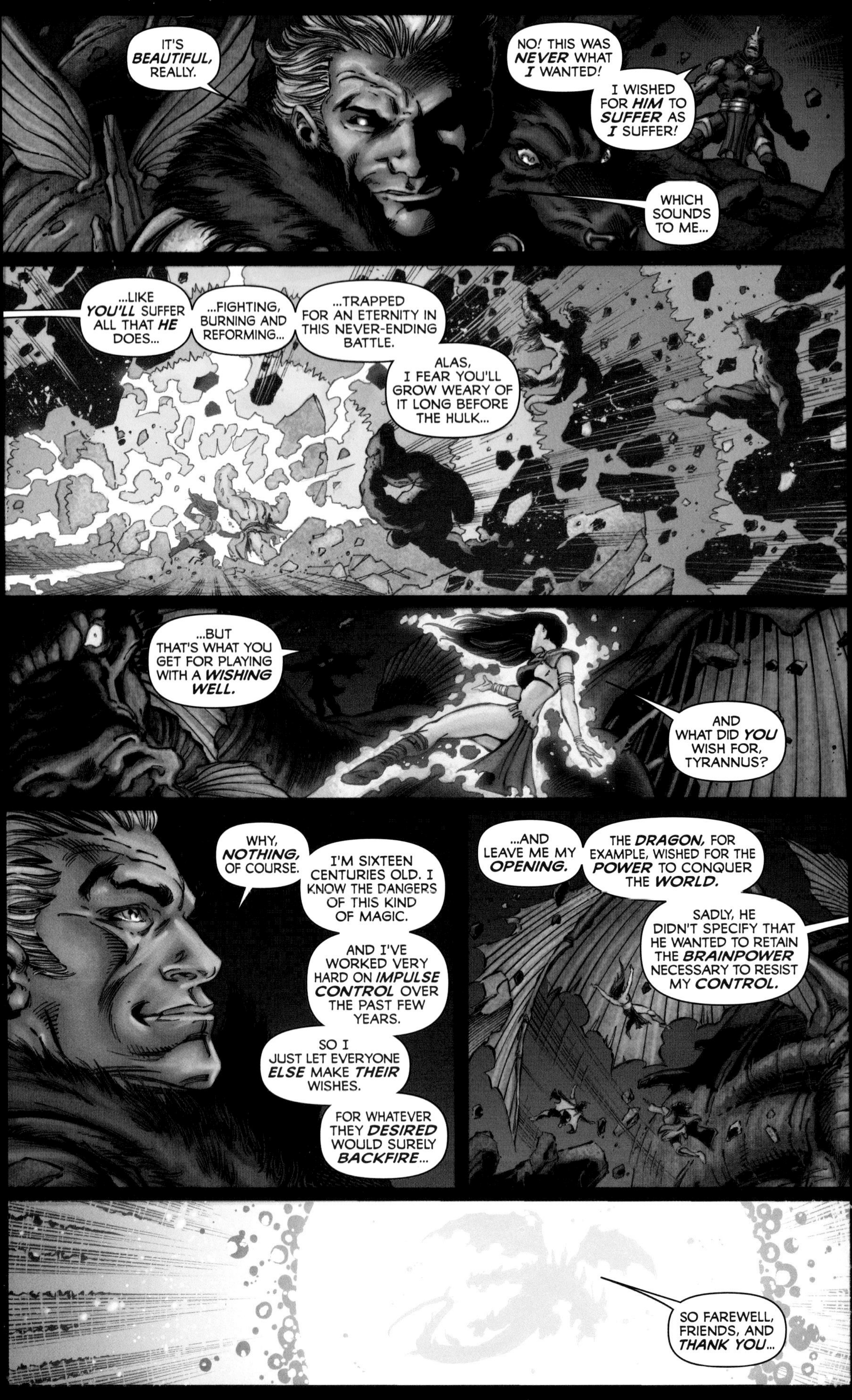
IT'S BEAUTIFUL, REALLY.
NO! THIS WAS NEVER WHAT I WANTED!
I WISHED FOR HIM TO SUFFER AS I SUFFER!
WHICH SOUNDS TO ME...
...LIKE YOU'LL SUFFER ALL THAT HE DOES...
...FIGHTING, BURNING AND REFORMING...
...TRAPPED FOR AN ETERNITY IN THIS NEVER-ENDING BATTLE.
ALAS, I FEAR YOU'LL GROW WEARY OF IT LONG BEFORE THE HULK...
...BUT THAT'S WHAT YOU GET FOR PLAYING WITH A WISHING WELL.
AND WHAT DID YOU WISH FOR, TYRANNUS?
WHY, NOTHING, OF COURSE.
I'M SIXTEEN CENTURIES OLD. I KNOW THE DANGERS OF THIS KIND OF MAGIC.
AND I'VE WORKED VERY HARD ON IMPULSE CONTROL OVER THE PAST FEW YEARS.
SO I JUST LET EVERYONE ELSE MAKE THEIR WISHES.
FOR WHATEVER THEY DESIRED WOULD SURELY BACKFIRE...
...AND LEAVE ME MY OPENING.
THE DRAGON, FOR EXAMPLE, WISHED FOR THE POWER TO CONQUER THE WORLD.
SADLY, HE DIDN'T SPECIFY THAT HE WANTED TO RETAIN THE BRAINPOWER NECESSARY TO RESIST MY CONTROL.
SO FAREWELL, FRIENDS, AND THANK YOU...

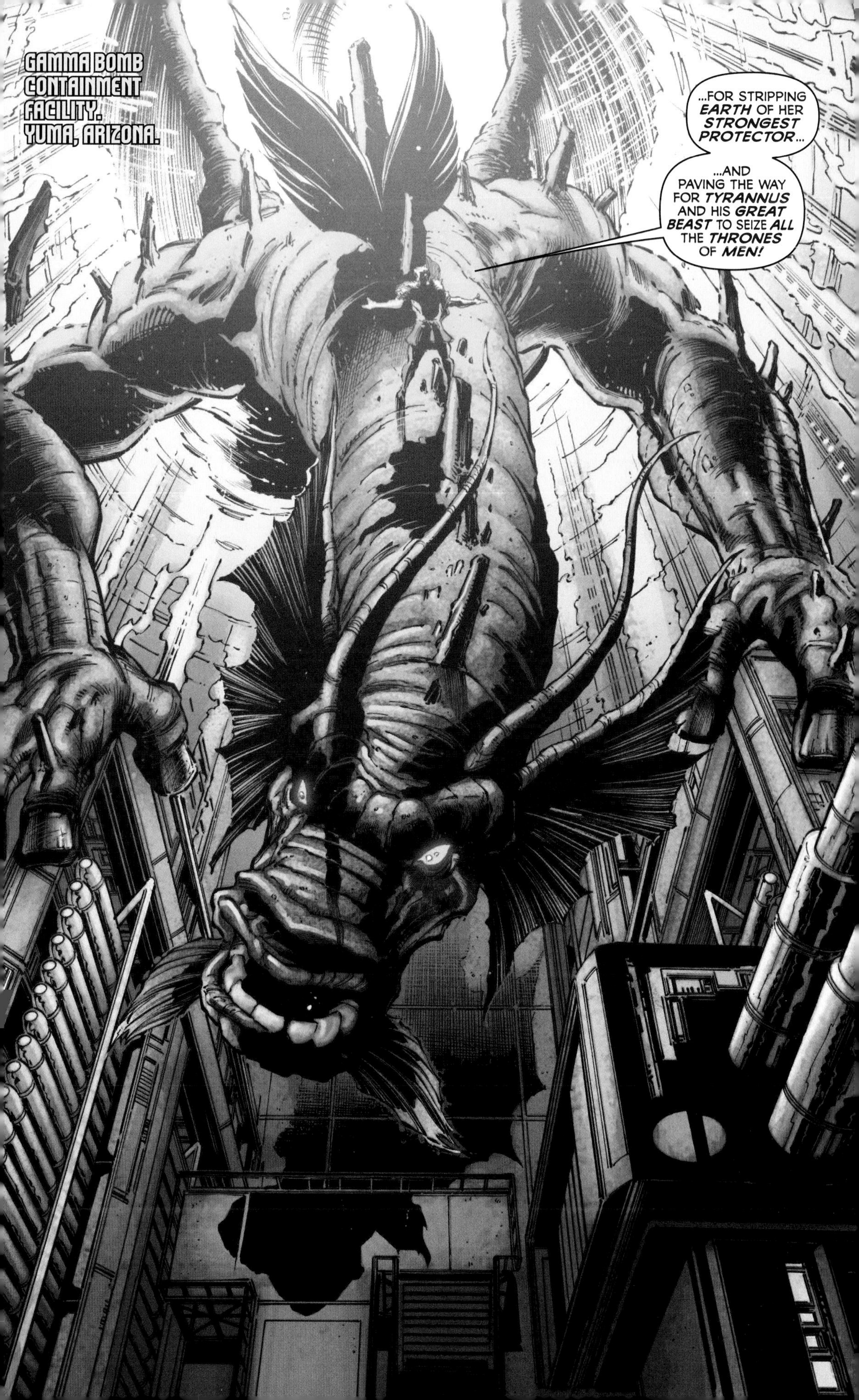
GAMMA BOMB CONTAINMENT FACILITY. YUMA, ARIZONA.
...FOR STRIPPING EARTH OF HER STRONGEST PROTECTOR...
...AND PAVING THE WAY FOR TYRANNUS AND HIS GREAT BEAST TO SEIZE ALL THE THRONES OF MEN!

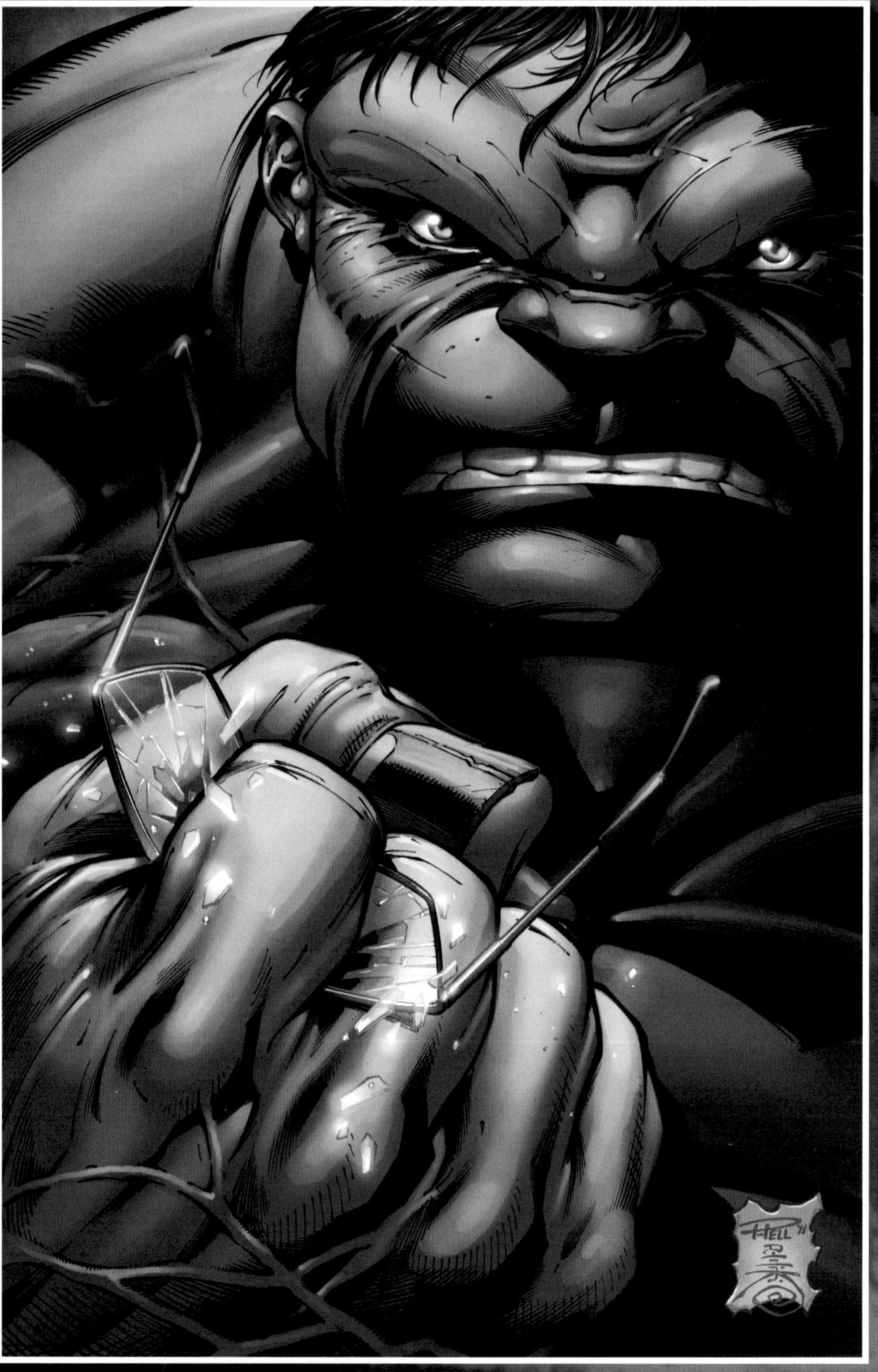

(635)

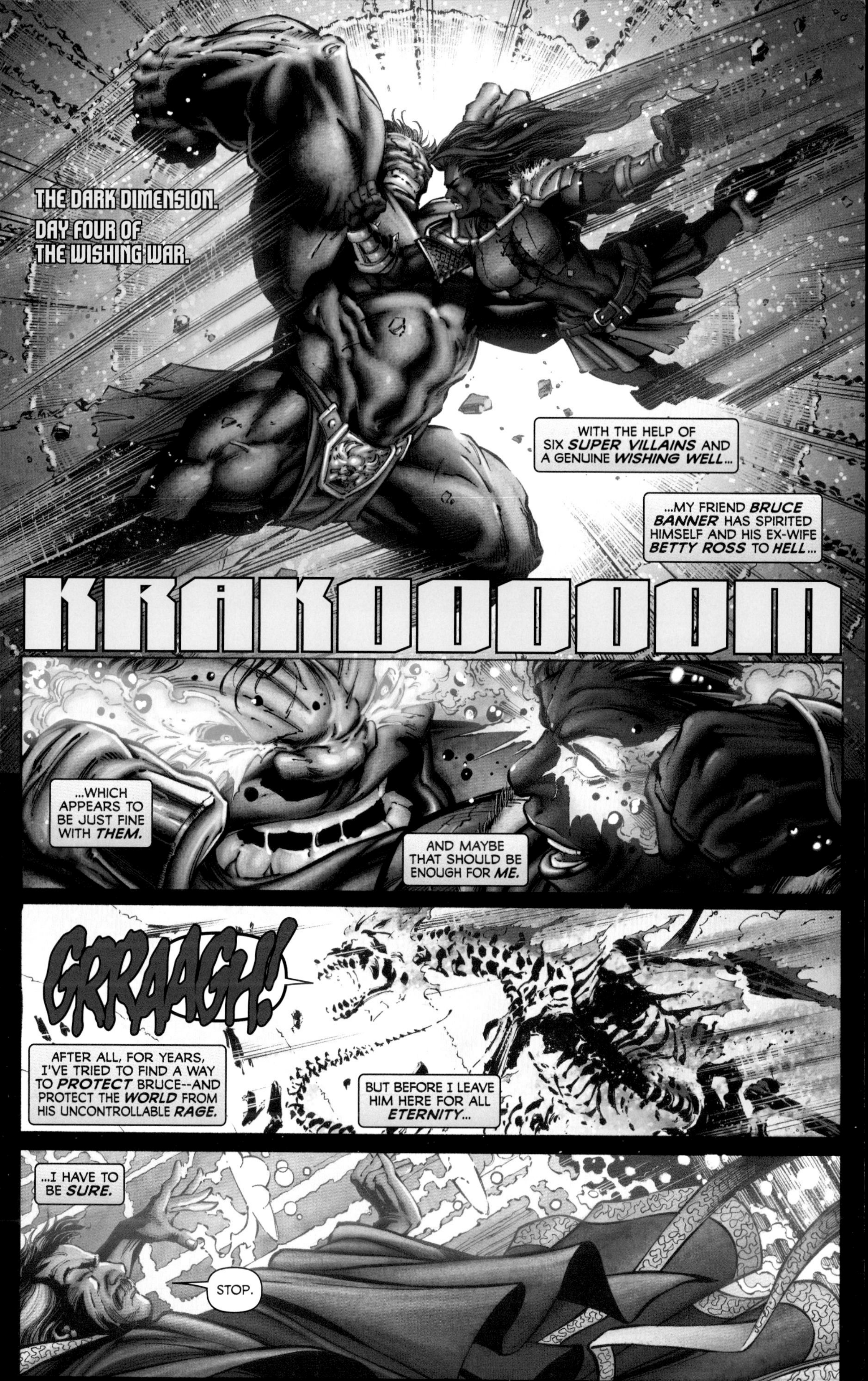
THE DARK DIMENSION.
DAY FOUR OF THE WISHING WAR.
WITH THE HELP OF SIX SUPER VILLAINS AND A GENUINE WISHING WELL...
...MY FRIEND BRUCE BANNER HAS SPIRITED HIMSELF AND HIS EX-WIFE BETTY ROSS TO HELL...
KRAKOOOOOM
...WHICH APPEARS TO BE JUST FINE WITH THEM.
AND MAYBE THAT SHOULD BE ENOUGH FOR ME.
GRRAAGH!
AFTER ALL, FOR YEARS, I'VE TRIED TO FIND A WAY TO PROTECT BRUCE--AND PROTECT THE WORLD FROM HIS UNCONTROLLABLE RAGE.
BUT BEFORE I LEAVE HIM HERE FOR ALL ETERNITY...
...I HAVE TO BE SURE.
STOP.

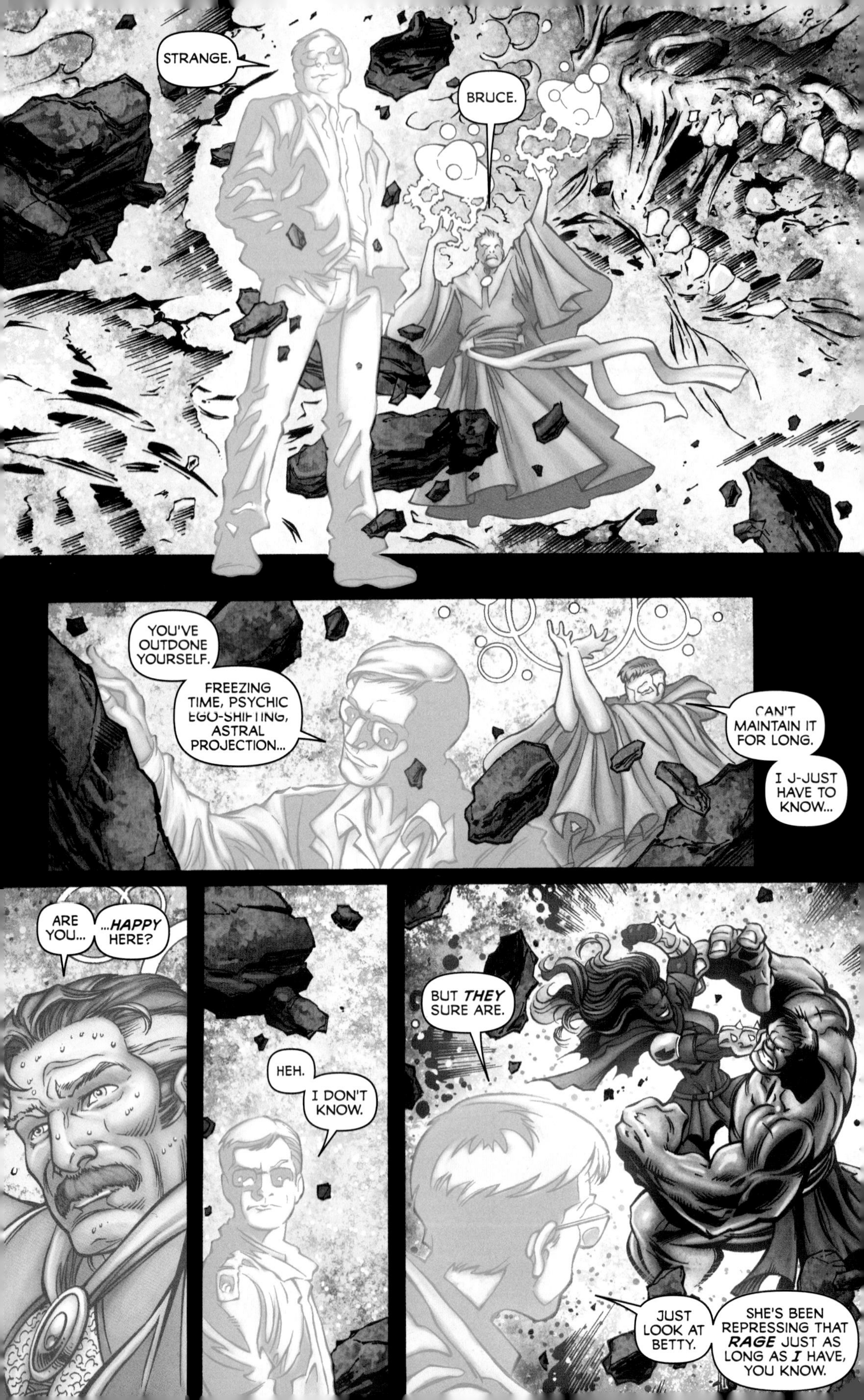
STRANGE.
BRUCE.
YOU'VE OUTDONE YOURSELF.
FREEZING TIME, PSYCHIC EGO-SHIFTING, ASTRAL PROJECTION...
CAN'T MAINTAIN IT FOR LONG.
I J-JUST HAVE TO KNOW...
ARE YOU...
...*HAPPY* HERE?
HEH.
I DON'T KNOW.
BUT *THEY* SURE ARE.
JUST LOOK AT BETTY.
SHE'S BEEN REPRESSING THAT *RAGE* JUST AS LONG AS *I* HAVE, YOU KNOW.

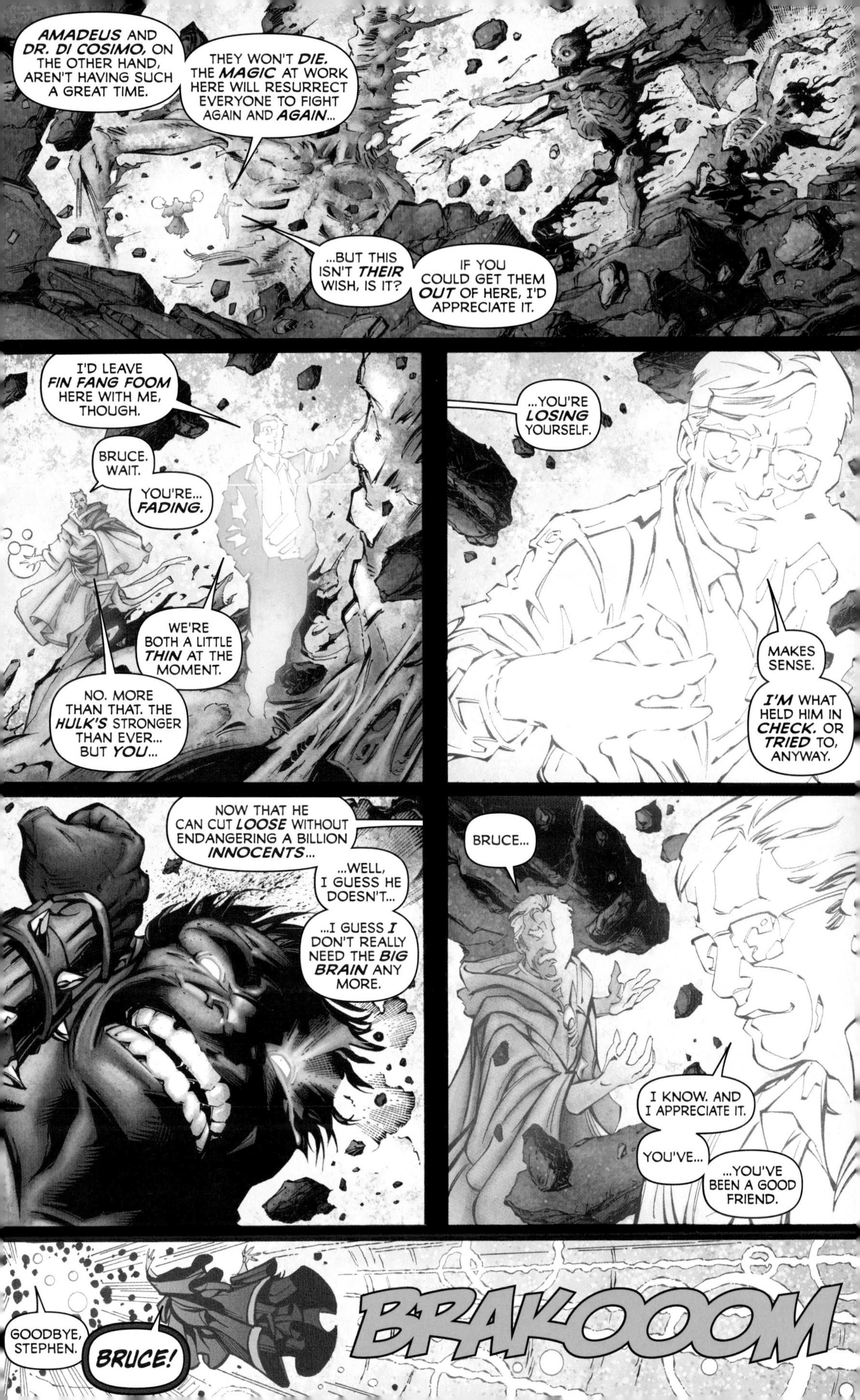
AMADEUS AND DR. DI COSIMO, ON THE OTHER HAND, AREN'T HAVING SUCH A GREAT TIME.
THEY WON'T DIE. THE MAGIC AT WORK HERE WILL RESURRECT EVERYONE TO FIGHT AGAIN AND AGAIN...
...BUT THIS ISN'T THEIR WISH, IS IT?
IF YOU COULD GET THEM OUT OF HERE, I'D APPRECIATE IT.
I'D LEAVE FIN FANG FOOM HERE WITH ME, THOUGH.
BRUCE. WAIT.
YOU'RE... FADING.
WE'RE BOTH A LITTLE THIN AT THE MOMENT.
NO. MORE THAN THAT. THE HULK'S STRONGER THAN EVER... BUT YOU...
...YOU'RE LOSING YOURSELF.
MAKES SENSE.
I'M WHAT HELD HIM IN CHECK. OR TRIED TO, ANYWAY.
NOW THAT HE CAN CUT LOOSE WITHOUT ENDANGERING A BILLION INNOCENTS...
...WELL, I GUESS HE DOESN'T...
...I GUESS I DON'T REALLY NEED THE BIG BRAIN ANY MORE.
BRUCE...
I KNOW. AND I APPRECIATE IT.
YOU'VE...
...YOU'VE BEEN A GOOD FRIEND.
GOODBYE, STEPHEN.
BRUCE!
BRAKOOOM

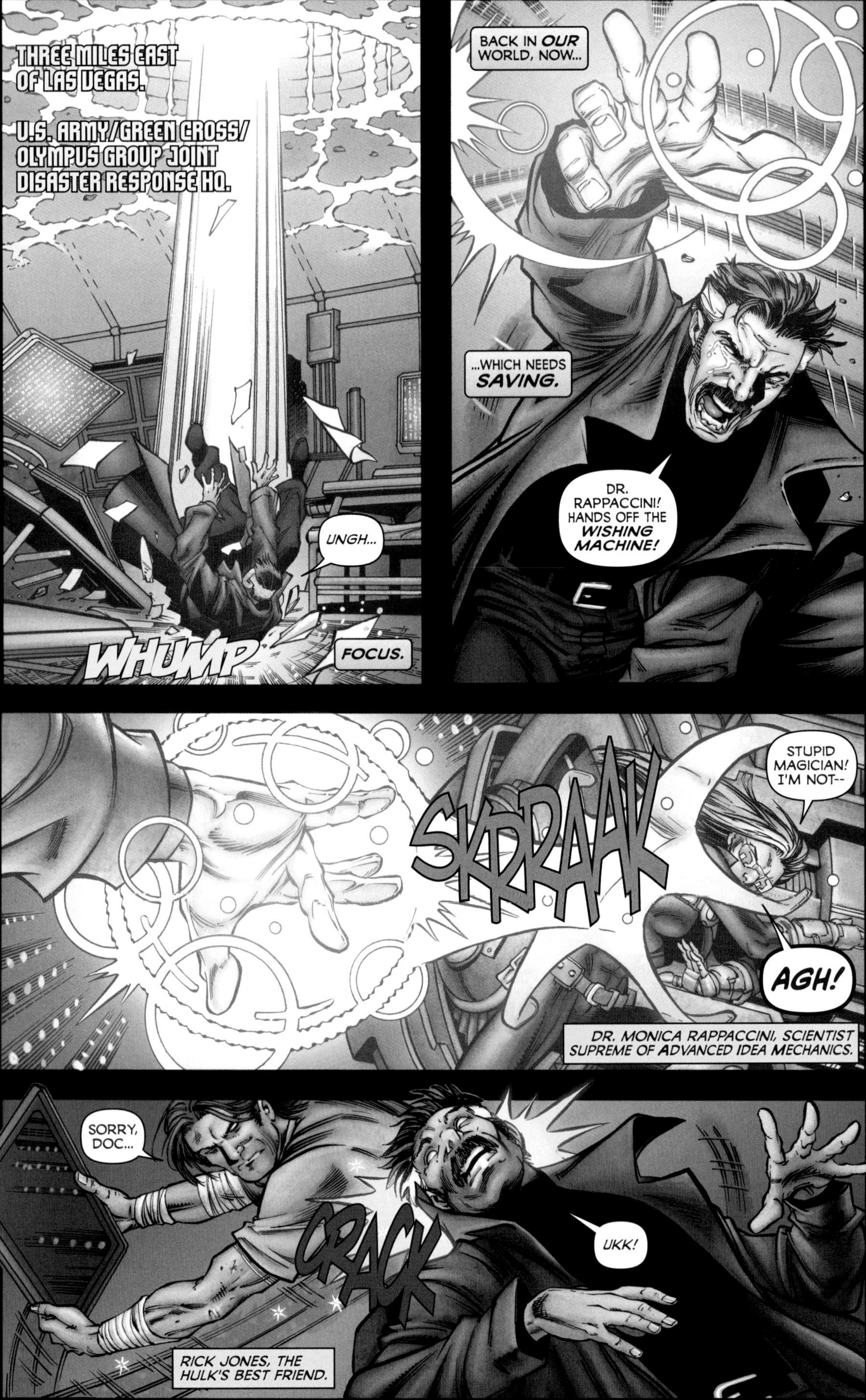
THREE MILES EAST OF LAS VEGAS.
U.S. ARMY/GREEN CROSS/ OLYMPUS GROUP JOINT DISASTER RESPONSE HQ.
UNGH...
WHUMP
FOCUS.
BACK IN OUR WORLD, NOW...
...WHICH NEEDS SAVING.
DR. RAPPACCINI! HANDS OFF THE WISHING MACHINE!
SKRAAK
STUPID MAGICIAN! I'M NOT--
AGH!
DR. MONICA RAPPACCINI, SCIENTIST SUPREME OF ADVANCED IDEA MECHANICS.
SORRY, DOC...
CRACK
UKK!
RICK JONES, THE HULK'S BEST FRIEND.

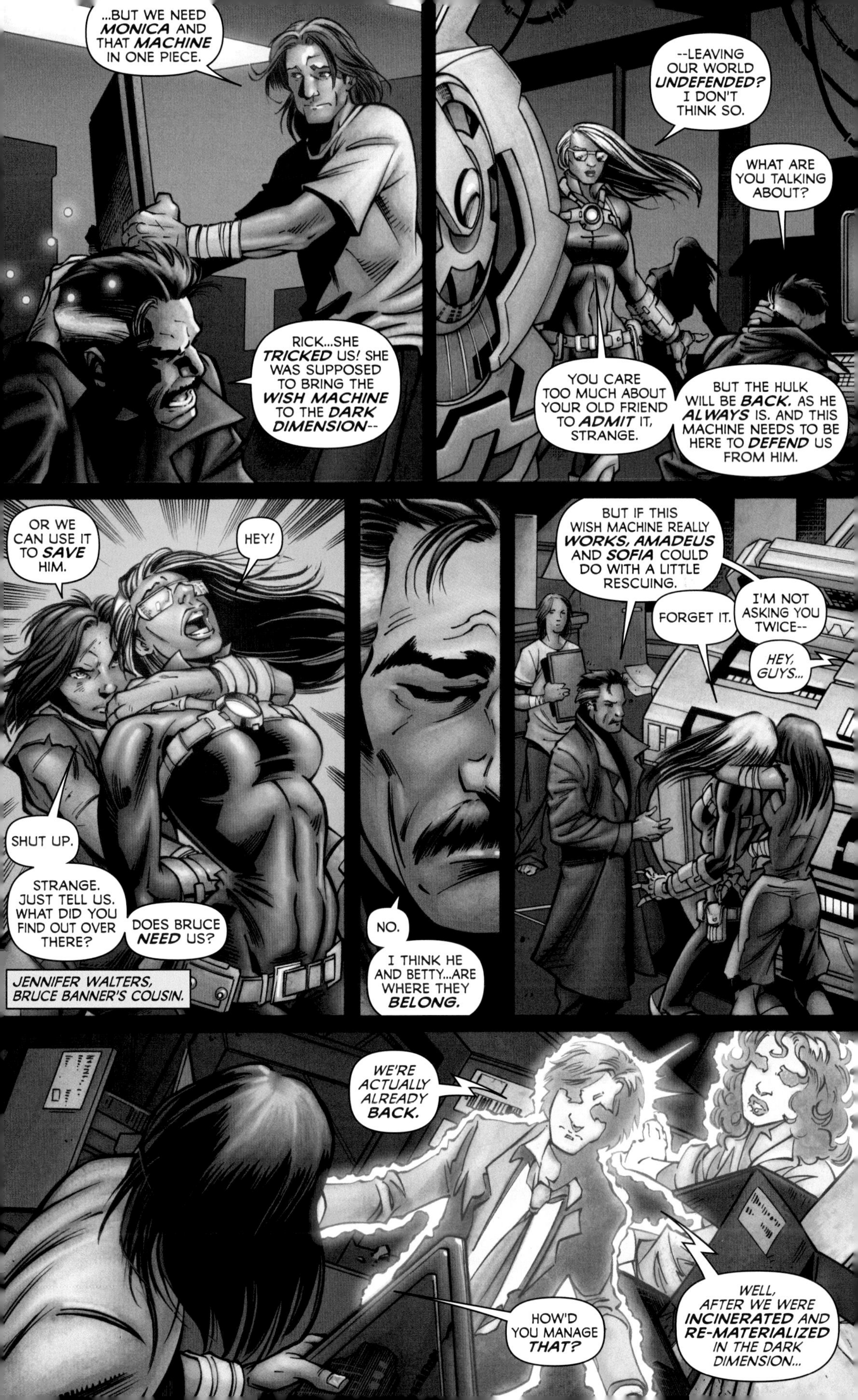
...BUT WE NEED MONICA AND THAT MACHINE IN ONE PIECE.
RICK...SHE TRICKED US! SHE WAS SUPPOSED TO BRING THE WISH MACHINE TO THE DARK DIMENSION--
--LEAVING OUR WORLD UNDEFENDED? I DON'T THINK SO.
WHAT ARE YOU TALKING ABOUT?
YOU CARE TOO MUCH ABOUT YOUR OLD FRIEND TO ADMIT IT, STRANGE.
BUT THE HULK WILL BE BACK. AS HE ALWAYS IS. AND THIS MACHINE NEEDS TO BE HERE TO DEFEND US FROM HIM.
OR WE CAN USE IT TO SAVE HIM.
HEY!
SHUT UP.
STRANGE. JUST TELL US. WHAT DID YOU FIND OUT OVER THERE?
DOES BRUCE NEED US?
JENNIFER WALTERS, BRUCE BANNER'S COUSIN.
NO.
I THINK HE AND BETTY...ARE WHERE THEY BELONG.
BUT IF THIS WISH MACHINE REALLY WORKS, AMADEUS AND SOFIA COULD DO WITH A LITTLE RESCUING.
FORGET IT.
I'M NOT ASKING YOU TWICE--
HEY, GUYS...
WE'RE ACTUALLY ALREADY BACK.
HOW'D YOU MANAGE THAT?
WELL, AFTER WE WERE INCINERATED AND RE-MATERIALIZED IN THE DARK DIMENSION...

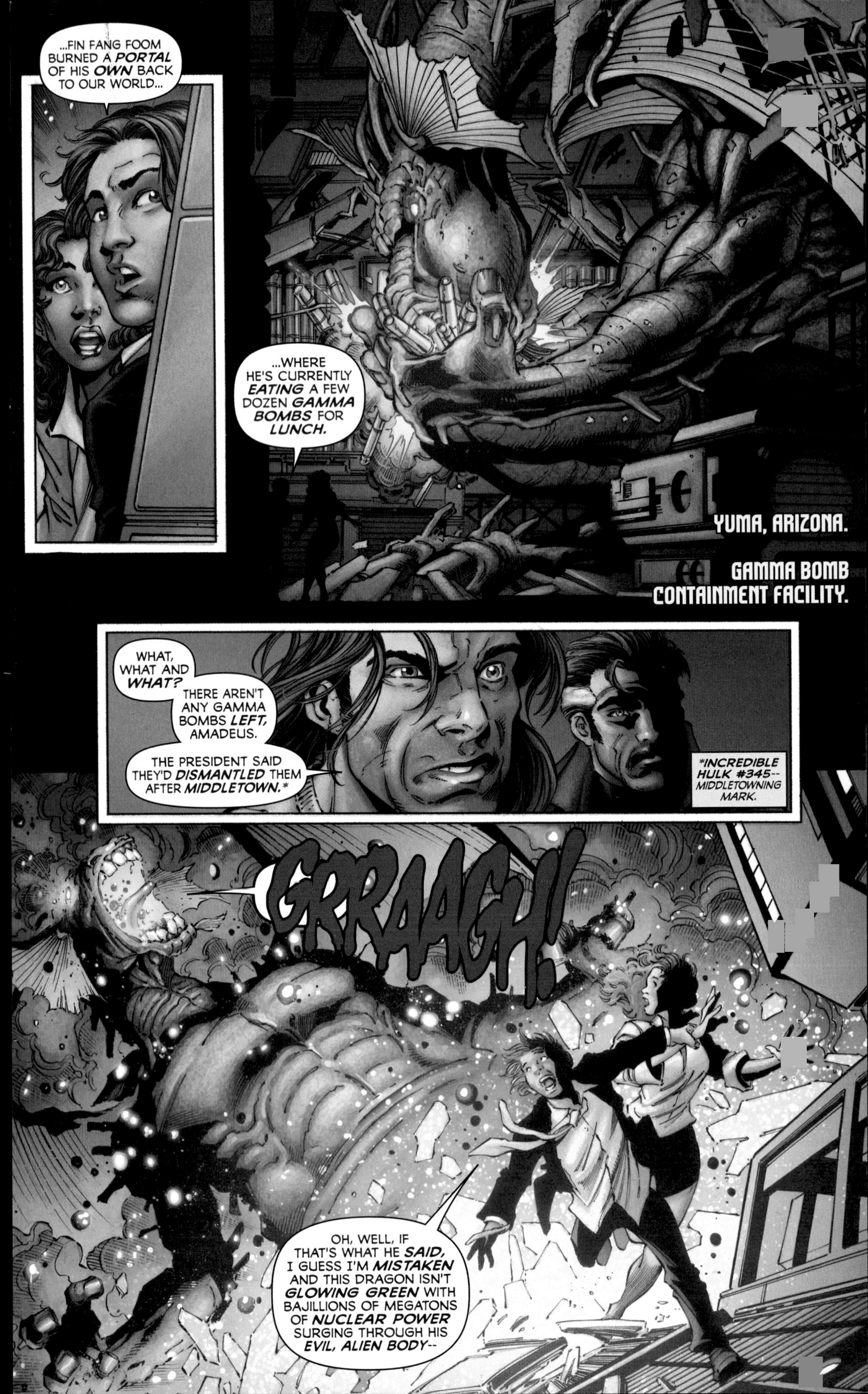
...FIN FANG FOOM BURNED A PORTAL OF HIS OWN BACK TO OUR WORLD...
...WHERE HE'S CURRENTLY EATING A FEW DOZEN GAMMA BOMBS FOR LUNCH.
YUMA, ARIZONA.
GAMMA BOMB CONTAINMENT FACILITY.
WHAT, WHAT AND WHAT?
THERE AREN'T ANY GAMMA BOMBS LEFT, AMADEUS.
THE PRESIDENT SAID THEY'D DISMANTLED THEM AFTER MIDDLETOWN.*
*INCREDIBLE HULK #345--MIDDLETOWNING MARK.
GRRAAGH!
OH, WELL, IF THAT'S WHAT HE SAID, I GUESS I'M MISTAKEN AND THIS DRAGON ISN'T GLOWING GREEN WITH BAJILLIONS OF MEGATONS OF NUCLEAR POWER SURGING THROUGH HIS EVIL, ALIEN BODY--

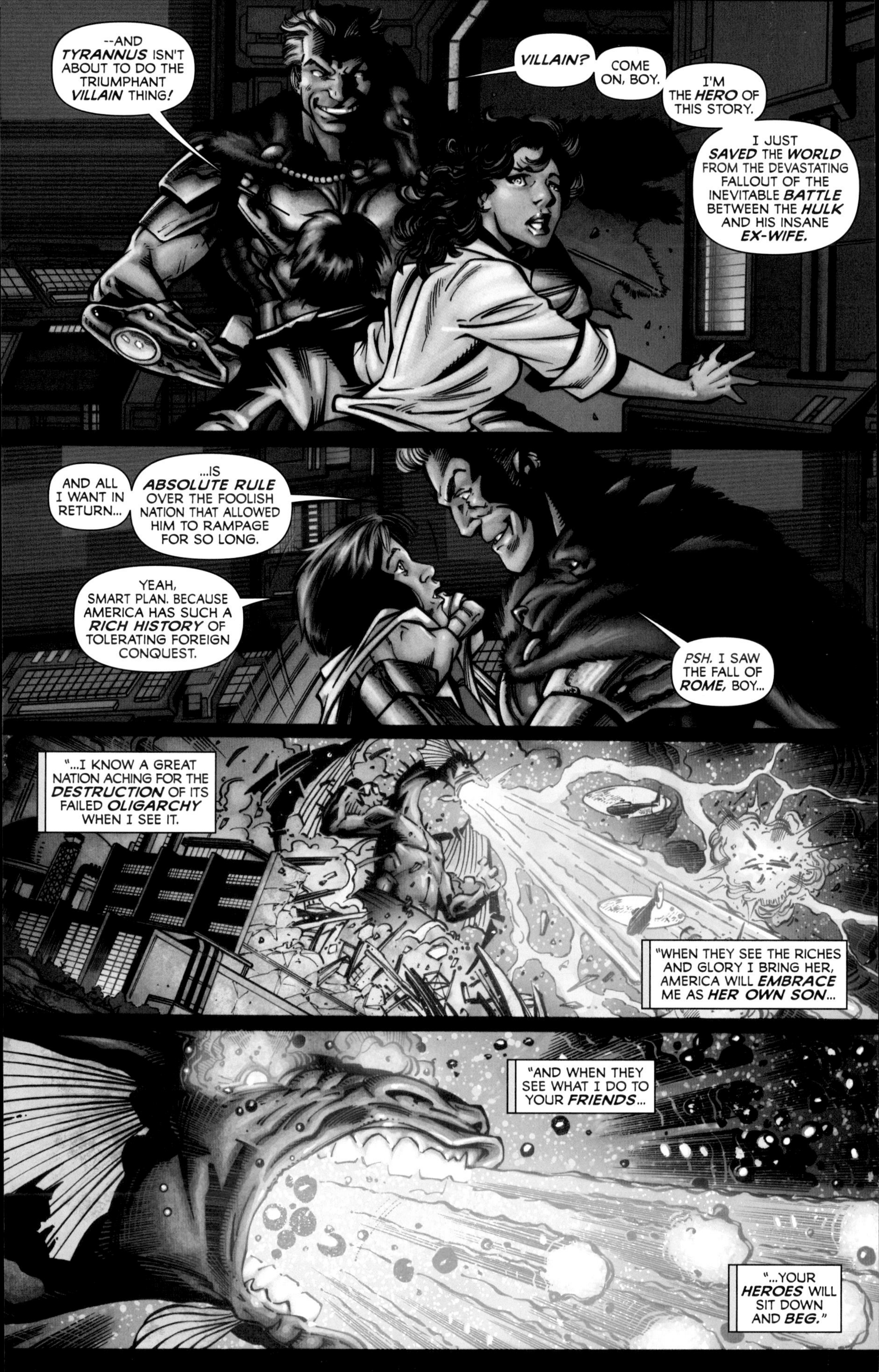
--AND TYRANNUS ISN'T ABOUT TO DO THE TRIUMPHANT VILLAIN THING!
VILLAIN?
COME ON, BOY.
I'M THE HERO OF THIS STORY.
I JUST SAVED THE WORLD FROM THE DEVASTATING FALLOUT OF THE INEVITABLE BATTLE BETWEEN THE HULK AND HIS INSANE EX-WIFE.
AND ALL I WANT IN RETURN...
...IS ABSOLUTE RULE OVER THE FOOLISH NATION THAT ALLOWED HIM TO RAMPAGE FOR SO LONG.
YEAH, SMART PLAN. BECAUSE AMERICA HAS SUCH A RICH HISTORY OF TOLERATING FOREIGN CONQUEST.
PSH. I SAW THE FALL OF ROME, BOY...
"...I KNOW A GREAT NATION ACHING FOR THE DESTRUCTION OF ITS FAILED OLIGARCHY WHEN I SEE IT.
"WHEN THEY SEE THE RICHES AND GLORY I BRING HER, AMERICA WILL EMBRACE ME AS HER OWN SON...
"AND WHEN THEY SEE WHAT I DO TO YOUR FRIENDS...
"...YOUR HEROES WILL SIT DOWN AND BEG."

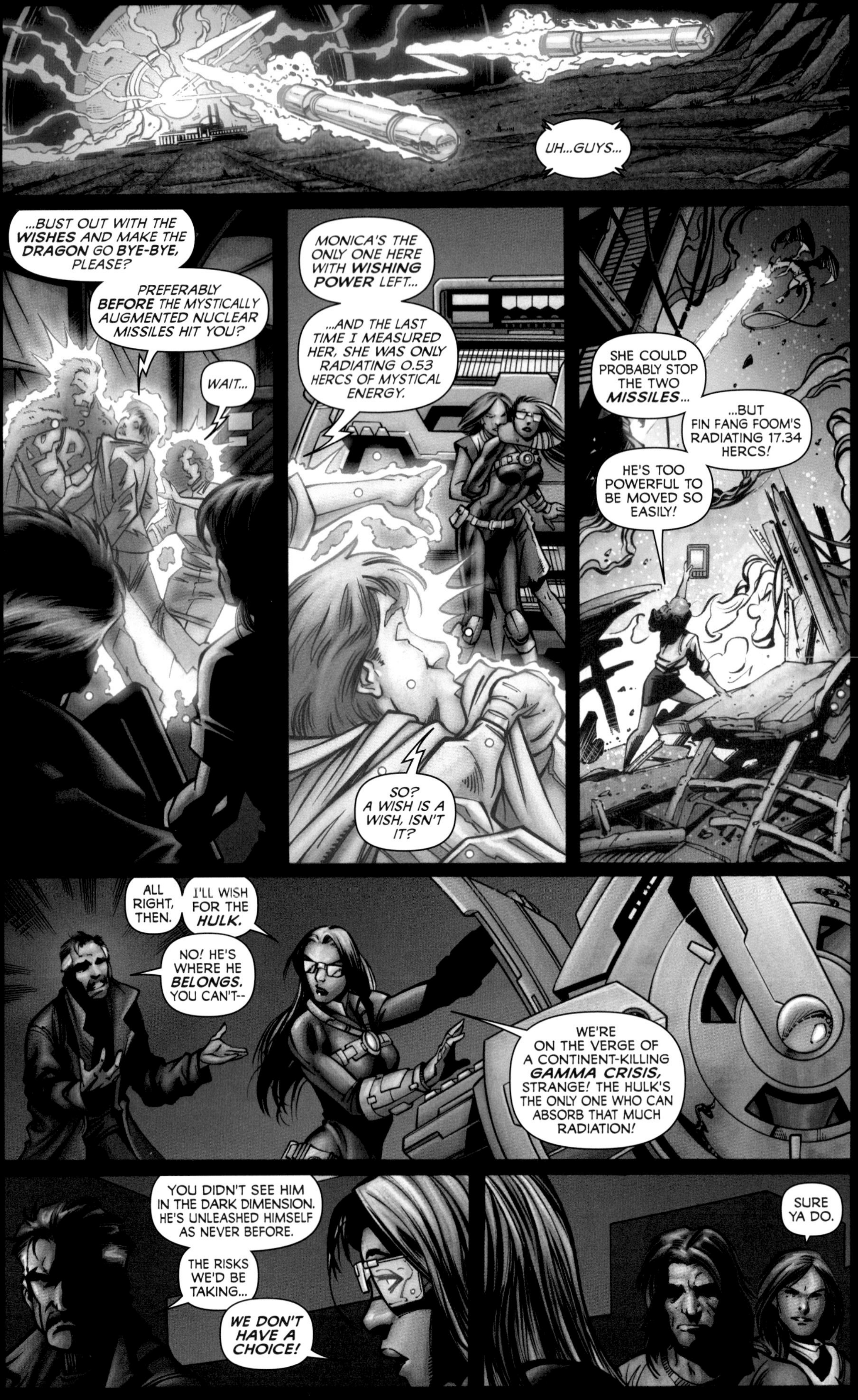
UH...GUYS...
...BUST OUT WITH THE WISHES AND MAKE THE DRAGON GO BYE-BYE, PLEASE?
PREFERABLY BEFORE THE MYSTICALLY AUGMENTED NUCLEAR MISSILES HIT YOU?
WAIT...
MONICA'S THE ONLY ONE HERE WITH WISHING POWER LEFT...
...AND THE LAST TIME I MEASURED HER, SHE WAS ONLY RADIATING 0.53 HERCS OF MYSTICAL ENERGY.
SO? A WISH IS A WISH, ISN'T IT?
SHE COULD PROBABLY STOP THE TWO MISSILES...
...BUT FIN FANG FOOM'S RADIATING 17.34 HERCS!
HE'S TOO POWERFUL TO BE MOVED SO EASILY!
ALL RIGHT, THEN.
I'LL WISH FOR THE HULK.
NO! HE'S WHERE HE BELONGS. YOU CAN'T--
WE'RE ON THE VERGE OF A CONTINENT-KILLING GAMMA CRISIS, STRANGE! THE HULK'S THE ONLY ONE WHO CAN ABSORB THAT MUCH RADIATION!
YOU DIDN'T SEE HIM IN THE DARK DIMENSION. HE'S UNLEASHED HIMSELF AS NEVER BEFORE.
THE RISKS WE'D BE TAKING...
WE DON'T HAVE A CHOICE!
SURE YA DO.

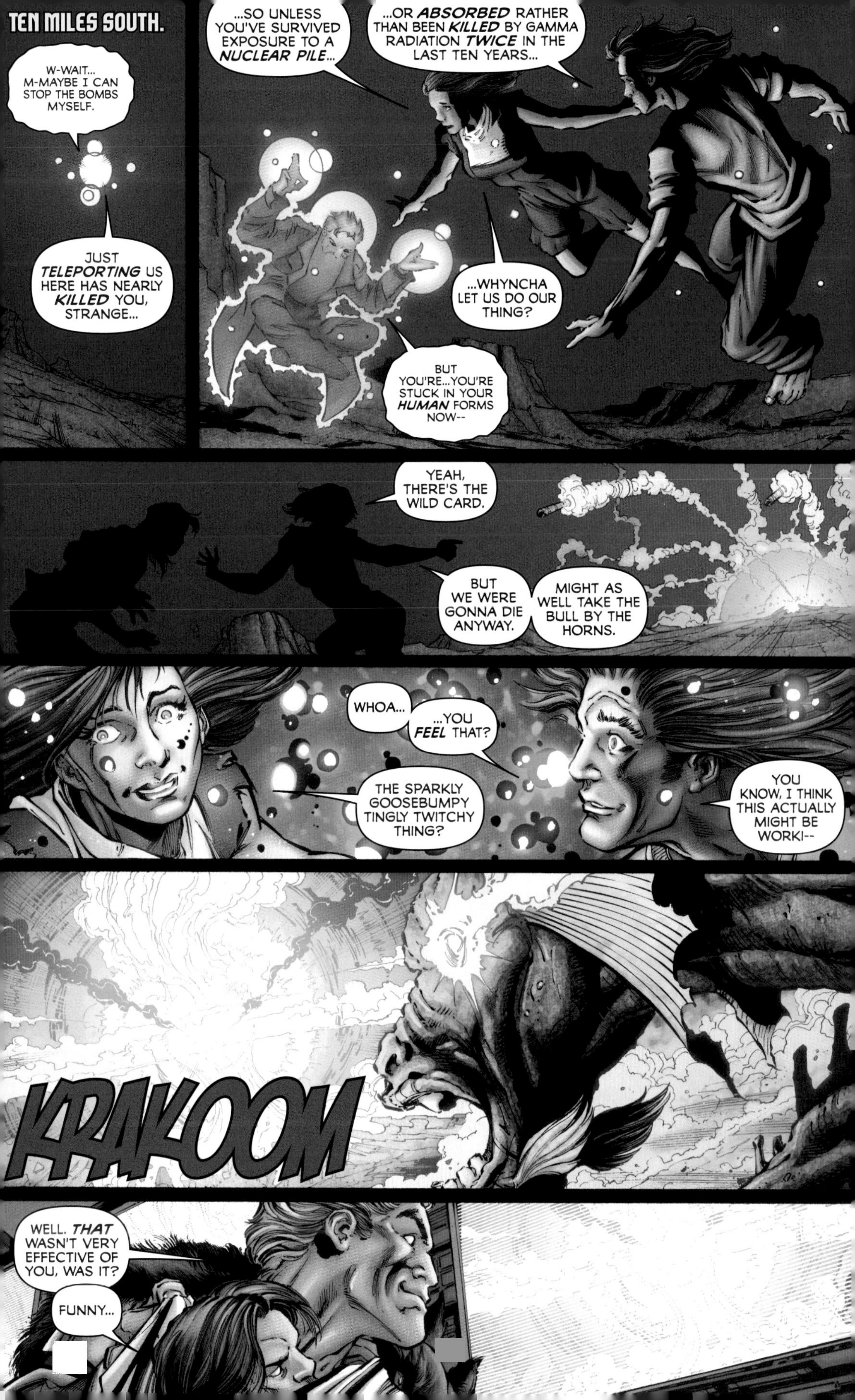
TEN MILES SOUTH.
W-WAIT... M-MAYBE I CAN STOP THE BOMBS MYSELF.
JUST TELEPORTING US HERE HAS NEARLY KILLED YOU, STRANGE...
...SO UNLESS YOU'VE SURVIVED EXPOSURE TO A NUCLEAR PILE...
...OR ABSORBED RATHER THAN BEEN KILLED BY GAMMA RADIATION TWICE IN THE LAST TEN YEARS...
...WHYNCHA LET US DO OUR THING?
BUT YOU'RE...YOU'RE STUCK IN YOUR HUMAN FORMS NOW--
YEAH, THERE'S THE WILD CARD.
BUT WE WERE GONNA DIE ANYWAY.
MIGHT AS WELL TAKE THE BULL BY THE HORNS.
WHOA...
...YOU FEEL THAT?
THE SPARKLY GOOSEBUMPY TINGLY TWITCHY THING?
YOU KNOW, I THINK THIS ACTUALLY MIGHT BE WORKI--
KRAKOOM
WELL. THAT WASN'T VERY EFFECTIVE OF YOU, WAS IT?
FUNNY...

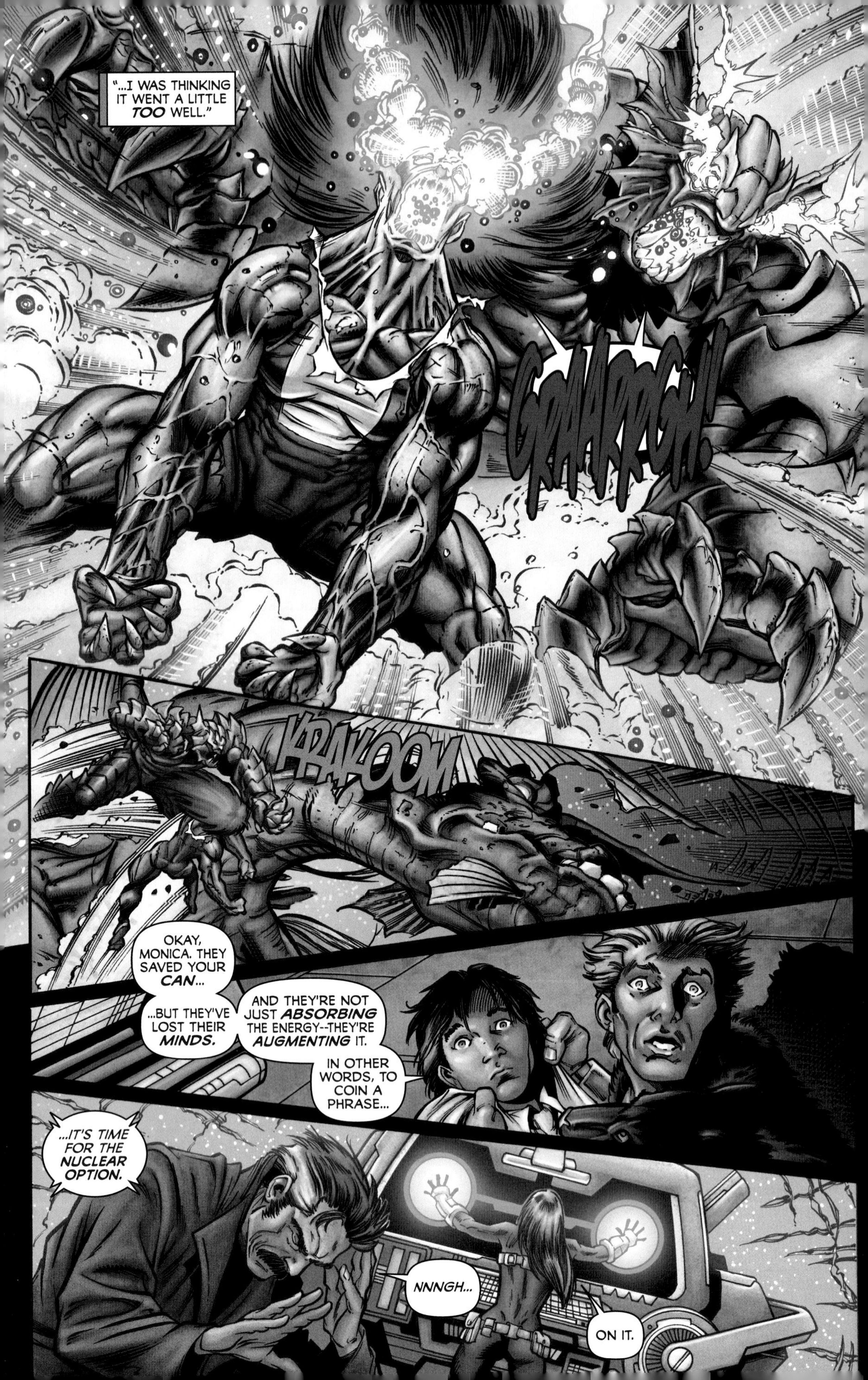
"...I WAS THINKING IT WENT A LITTLE TOO WELL."
GRAARRGH!
KRAKOOM
OKAY, MONICA. THEY SAVED YOUR CAN...
...BUT THEY'VE LOST THEIR MINDS.
AND THEY'RE NOT JUST ABSORBING THE ENERGY--THEY'RE AUGMENTING IT.
IN OTHER WORDS, TO COIN A PHRASE...
...IT'S TIME FOR THE NUCLEAR OPTION.
NNNGH...
ON IT.

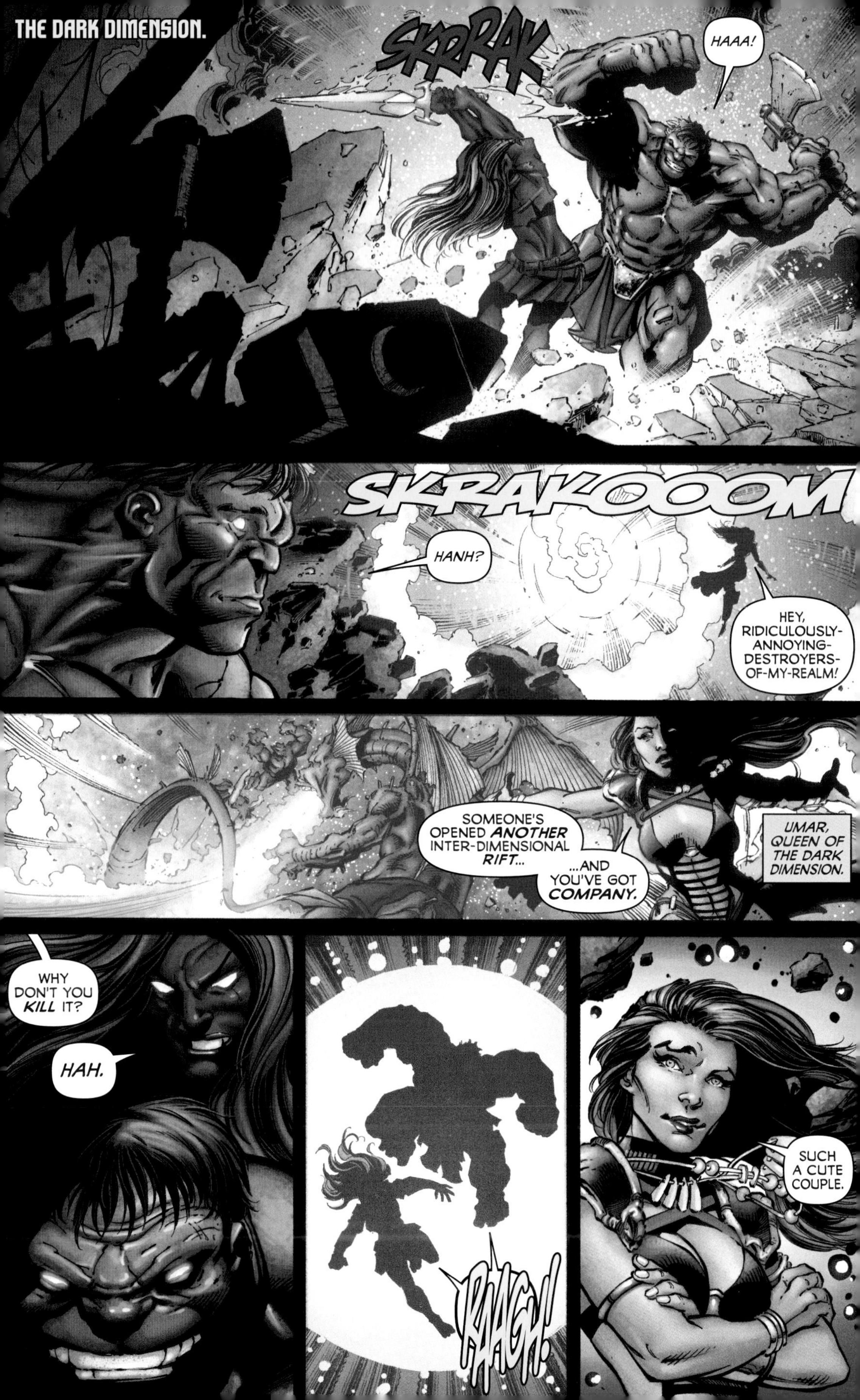
THE DARK DIMENSION.
SKRRAK
HAAA!
SKRAKOOOM
HANH?
HEY, RIDICULOUSLY-ANNOYING-DESTROYERS-OF-MY-REALM!
SOMEONE'S OPENED ANOTHER INTER-DIMENSIONAL RIFT...
...AND YOU'VE GOT COMPANY.
UMAR, QUEEN OF THE DARK DIMENSION.
WHY DON'T YOU KILL IT?
HAH.
RAAGH!
SUCH A CUTE COUPLE.

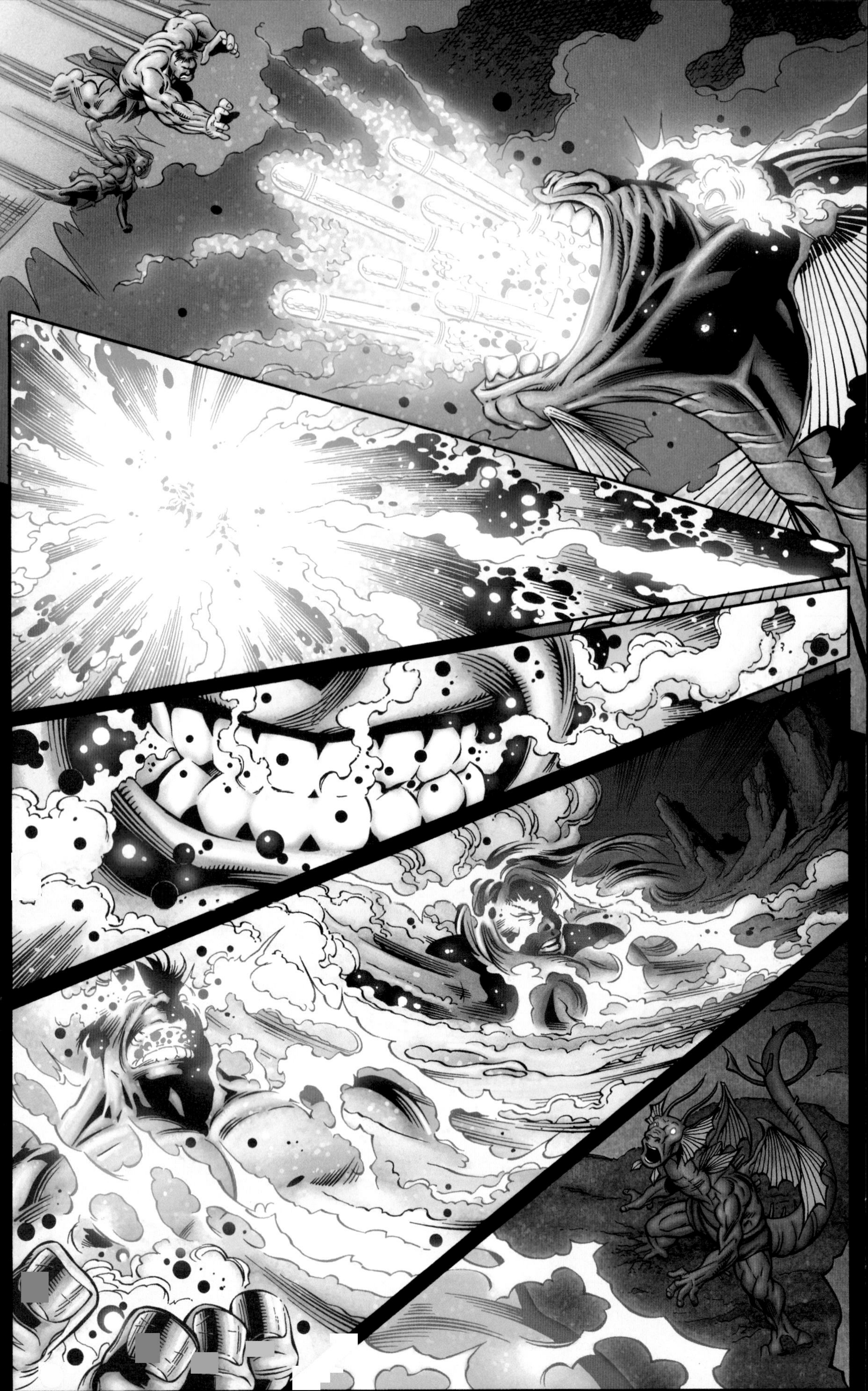

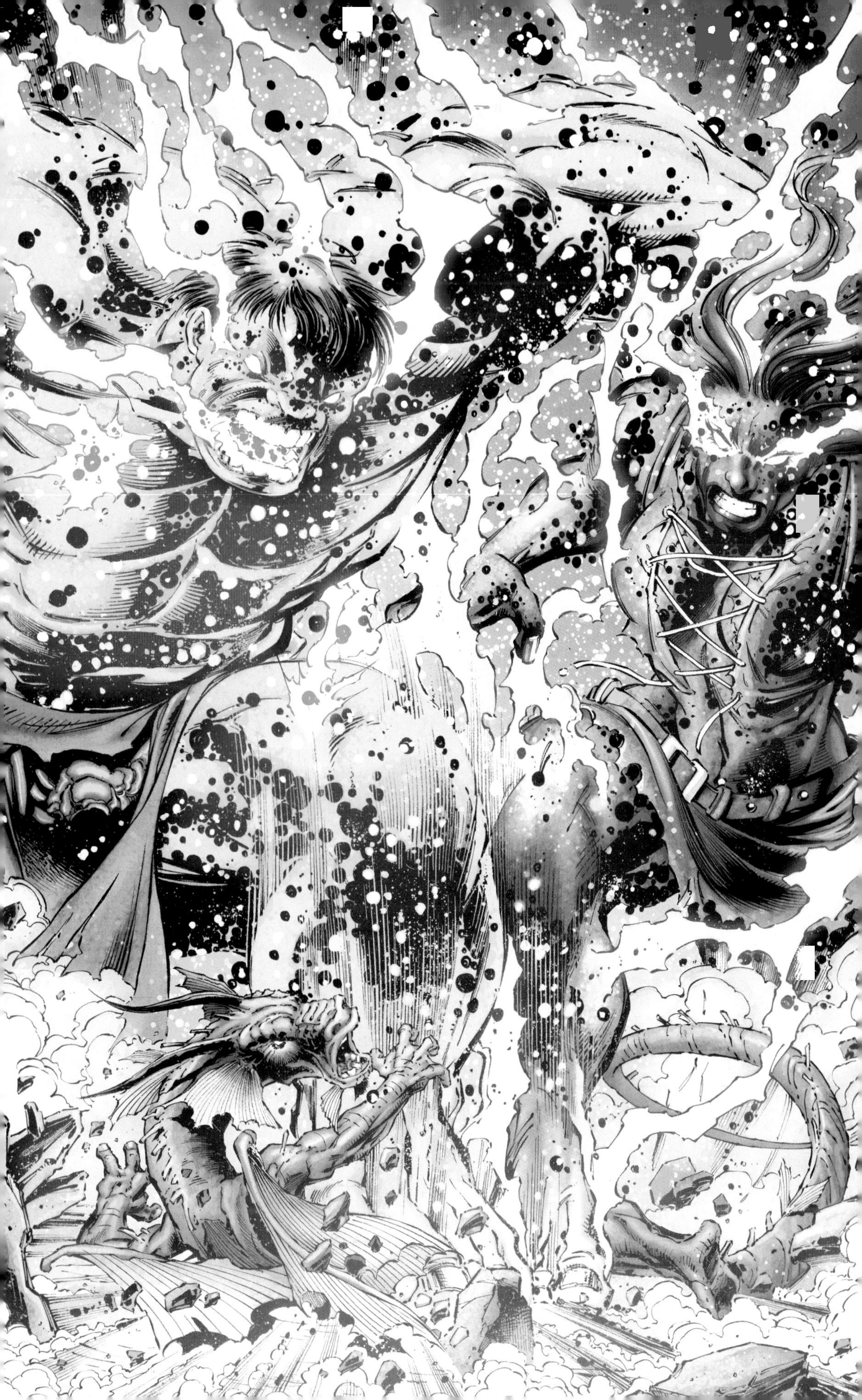

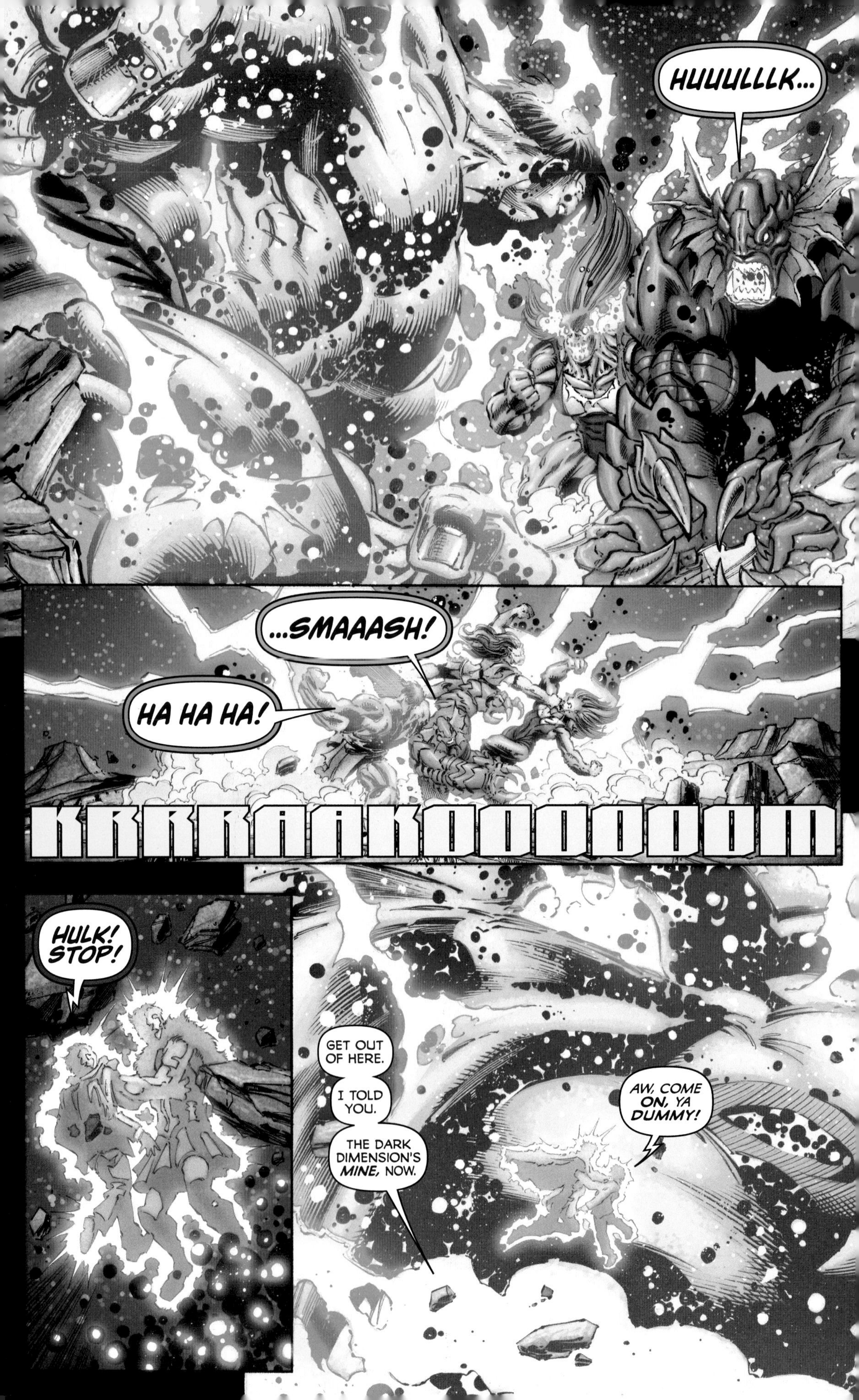
HUUUULLLK...
...SMAAASH!
HA HA HA!
KRRRAAKOOOOOOOM
HULK! STOP!
GET OUT OF HERE.
I TOLD YOU.
THE DARK DIMENSION'S MINE, NOW.
AW, COME ON, YA DUMMY!

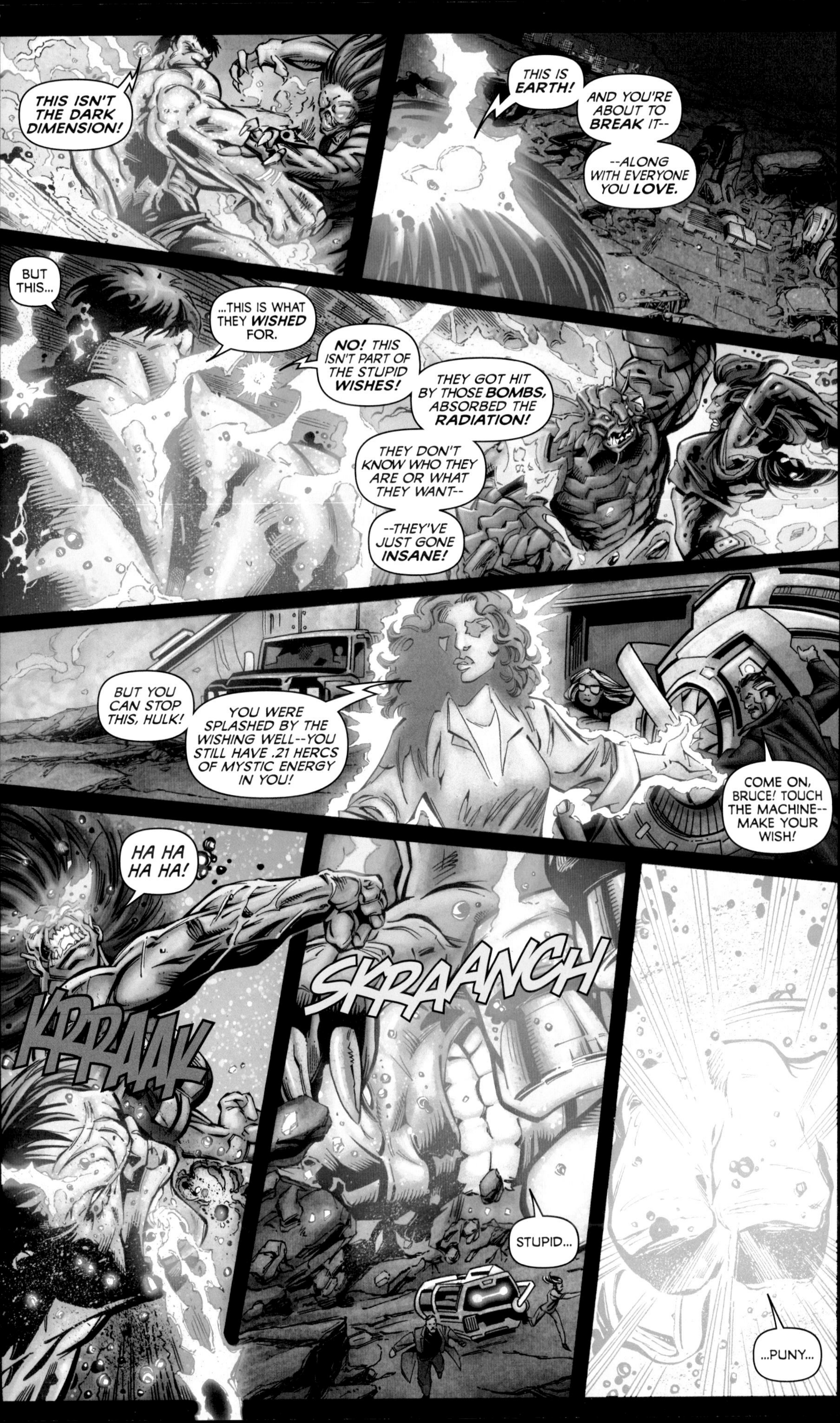
THIS ISN'T THE DARK DIMENSION!
THIS IS EARTH!
AND YOU'RE ABOUT TO BREAK IT--
--ALONG WITH EVERYONE YOU LOVE.
BUT THIS...
...THIS IS WHAT THEY WISHED FOR.
NO! THIS ISN'T PART OF THE STUPID WISHES!
THEY GOT HIT BY THOSE BOMBS, ABSORBED THE RADIATION!
THEY DON'T KNOW WHO THEY ARE OR WHAT THEY WANT--
--THEY'VE JUST GONE INSANE!
BUT YOU CAN STOP THIS, HULK!
YOU WERE SPLASHED BY THE WISHING WELL--YOU STILL HAVE .21 HERCS OF MYSTIC ENERGY IN YOU!
COME ON, BRUCE! TOUCH THE MACHINE--MAKE YOUR WISH!
HA HA HA HA!
KRRAAK
SKRAANCH
STUPID...
...PUNY...

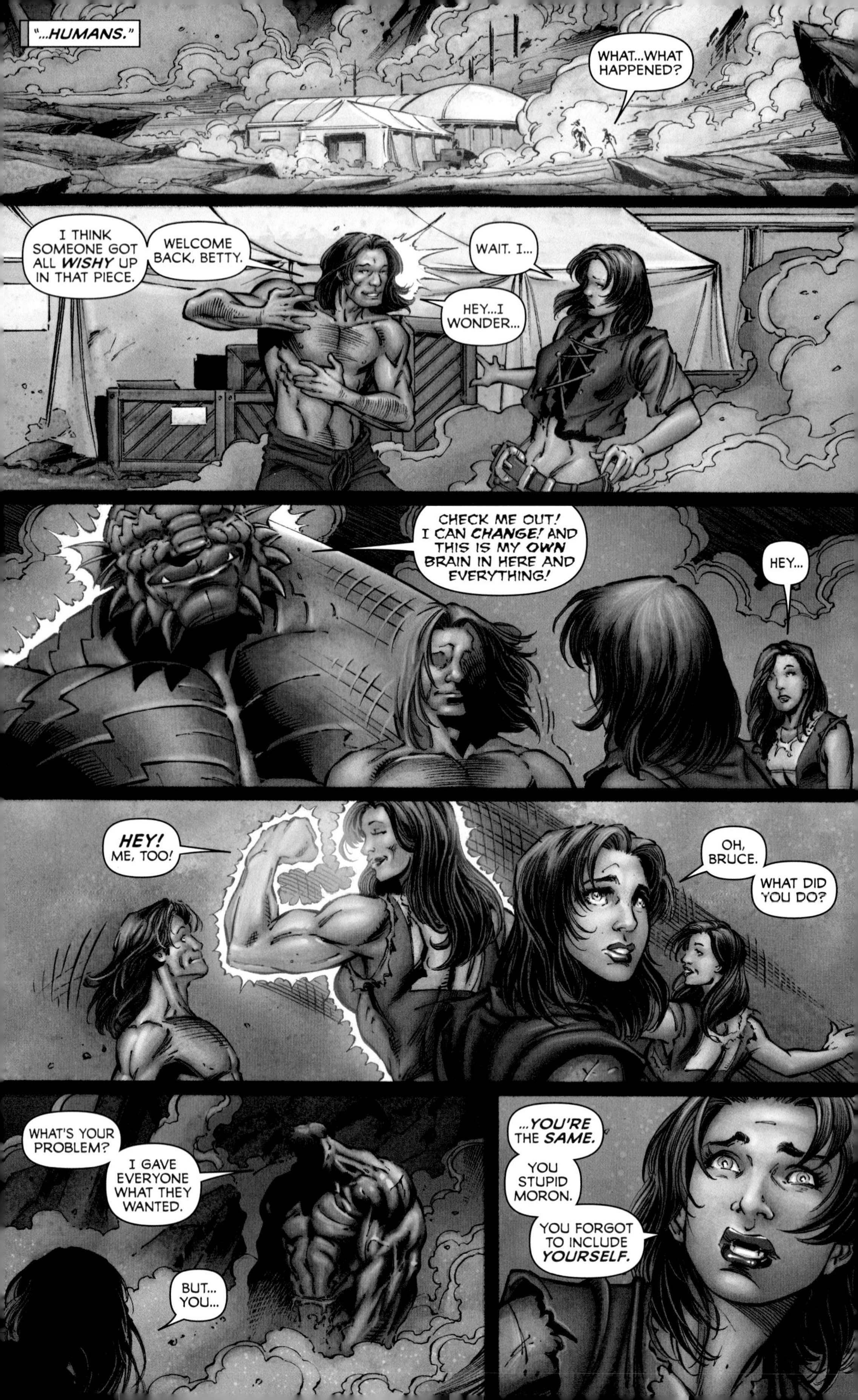
"...HUMANS."
WHAT...WHAT HAPPENED?
I THINK SOMEONE GOT ALL *WISHY* UP IN THAT PIECE.
WELCOME BACK, BETTY.
WAIT. I...
HEY...I WONDER...
CHECK ME OUT! I CAN *CHANGE!* AND THIS IS MY *OWN* BRAIN IN HERE AND EVERYTHING!
HEY...
HEY! ME, TOO!
OH, BRUCE.
WHAT DID YOU DO?
WHAT'S YOUR PROBLEM?
I GAVE EVERYONE WHAT THEY WANTED.
BUT... YOU...
...YOU'RE THE *SAME.*
YOU STUPID MORON.
YOU FORGOT TO INCLUDE *YOURSELF.*

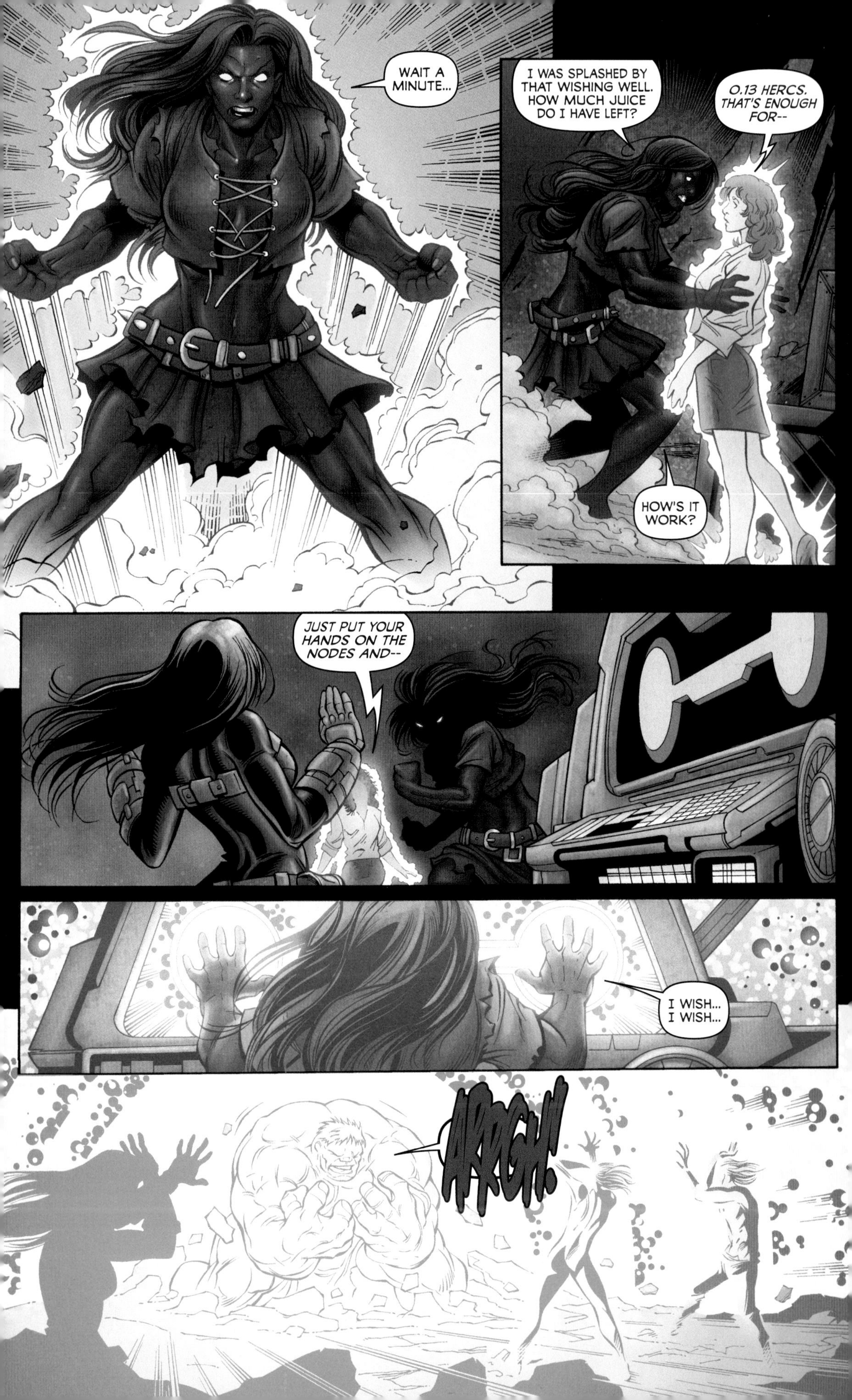

WAIT A MINUTE...
I WAS SPLASHED BY THAT WISHING WELL. HOW MUCH JUICE DO I HAVE LEFT?
O.13 HERCS. THAT'S ENOUGH FOR--
HOW'S IT WORK?
JUST PUT YOUR HANDS ON THE NODES AND--
I WISH... I WISH...
ARRGH!

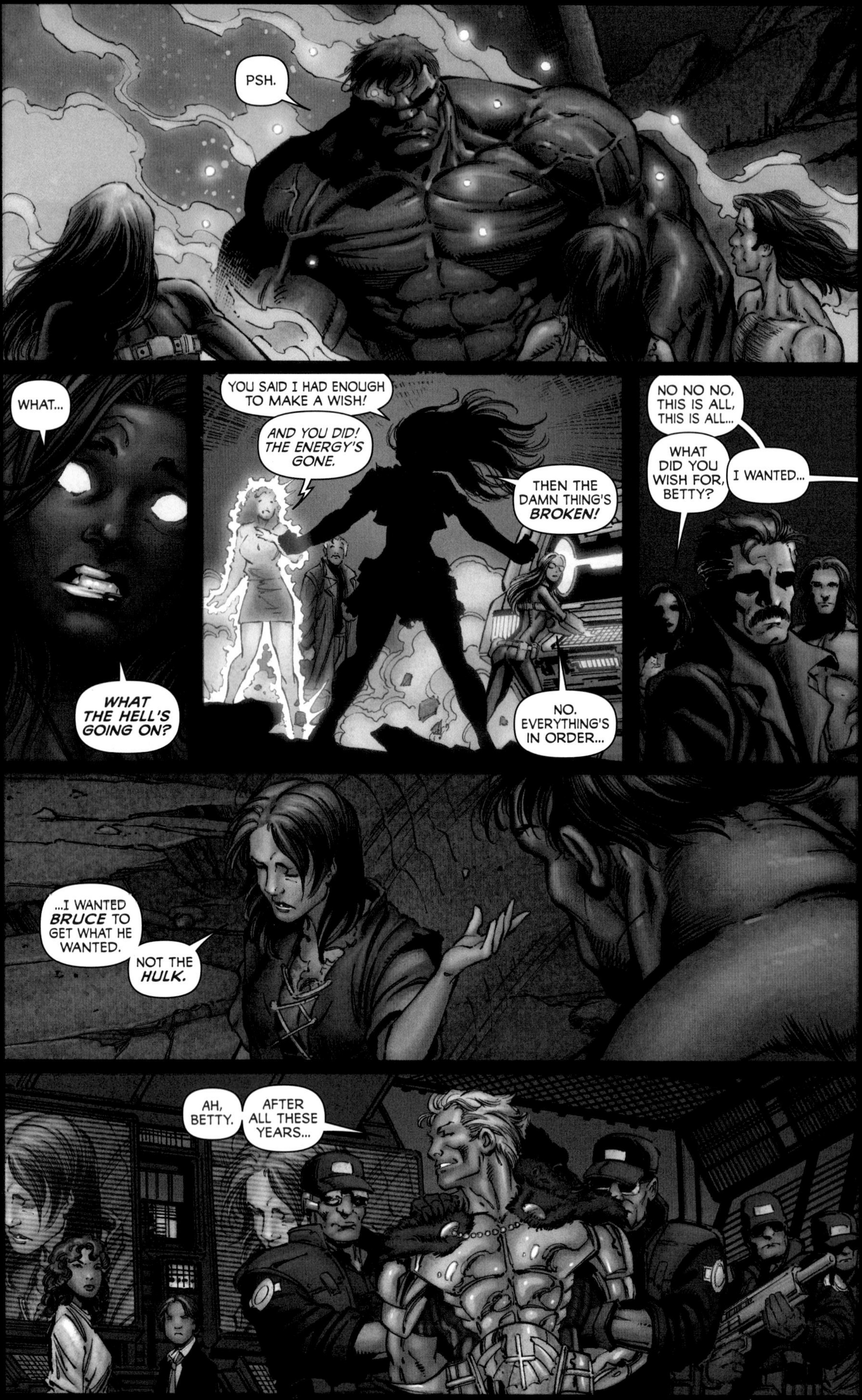
PSH.
WHAT...
WHAT THE HELL'S GOING ON?
YOU SAID I HAD ENOUGH TO MAKE A WISH!
AND YOU DID! THE ENERGY'S GONE.
THEN THE DAMN THING'S BROKEN!
NO. EVERYTHING'S IN ORDER...
NO NO NO, THIS IS ALL, THIS IS ALL...
WHAT DID YOU WISH FOR, BETTY?
I WANTED...
...I WANTED BRUCE TO GET WHAT HE WANTED.
NOT THE HULK.
AH, BETTY.
AFTER ALL THESE YEARS...

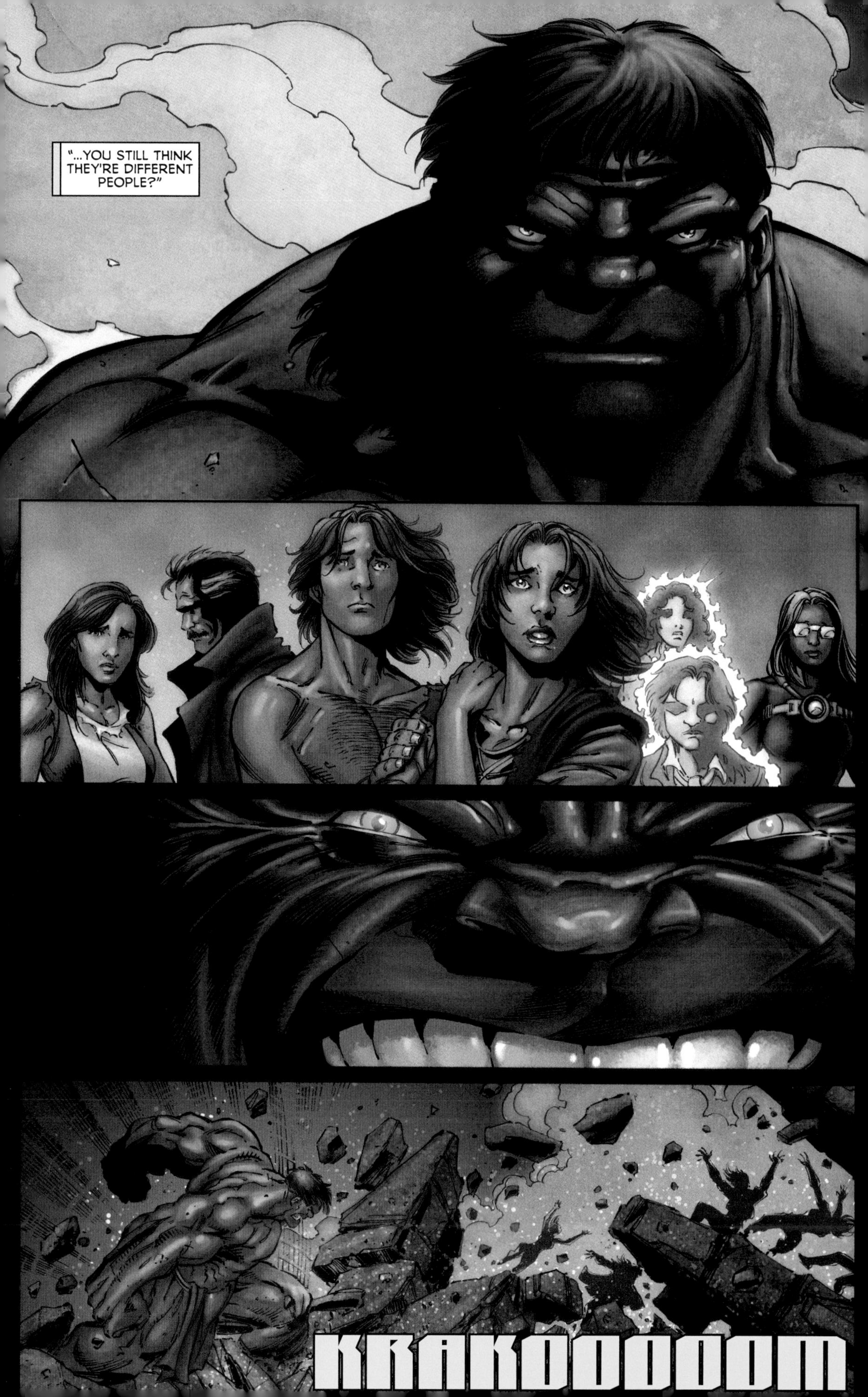
"...YOU STILL THINK THEY'RE DIFFERENT PEOPLE?"
KRAKOOOOOOM

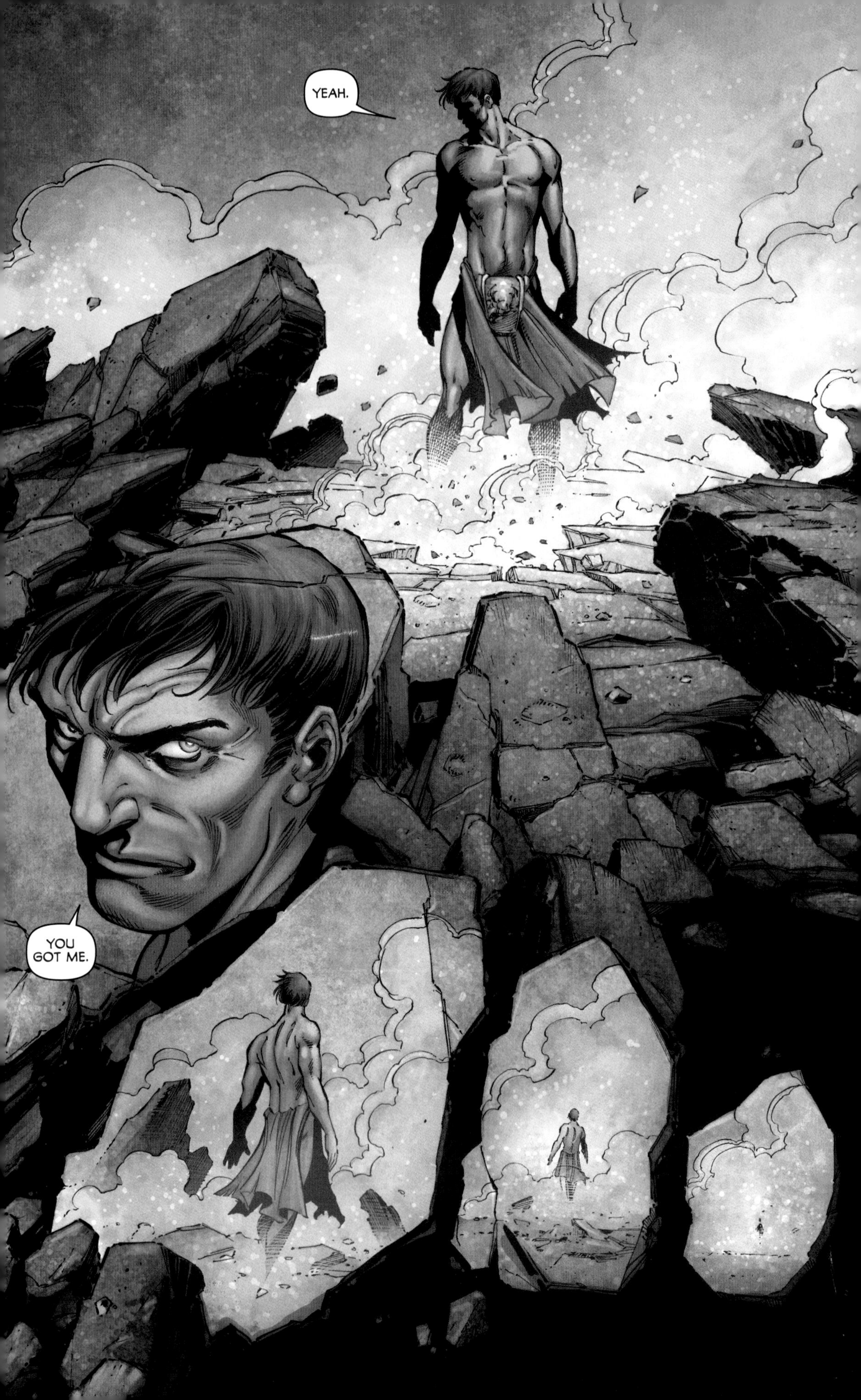
YEAH.
YOU GOT ME.

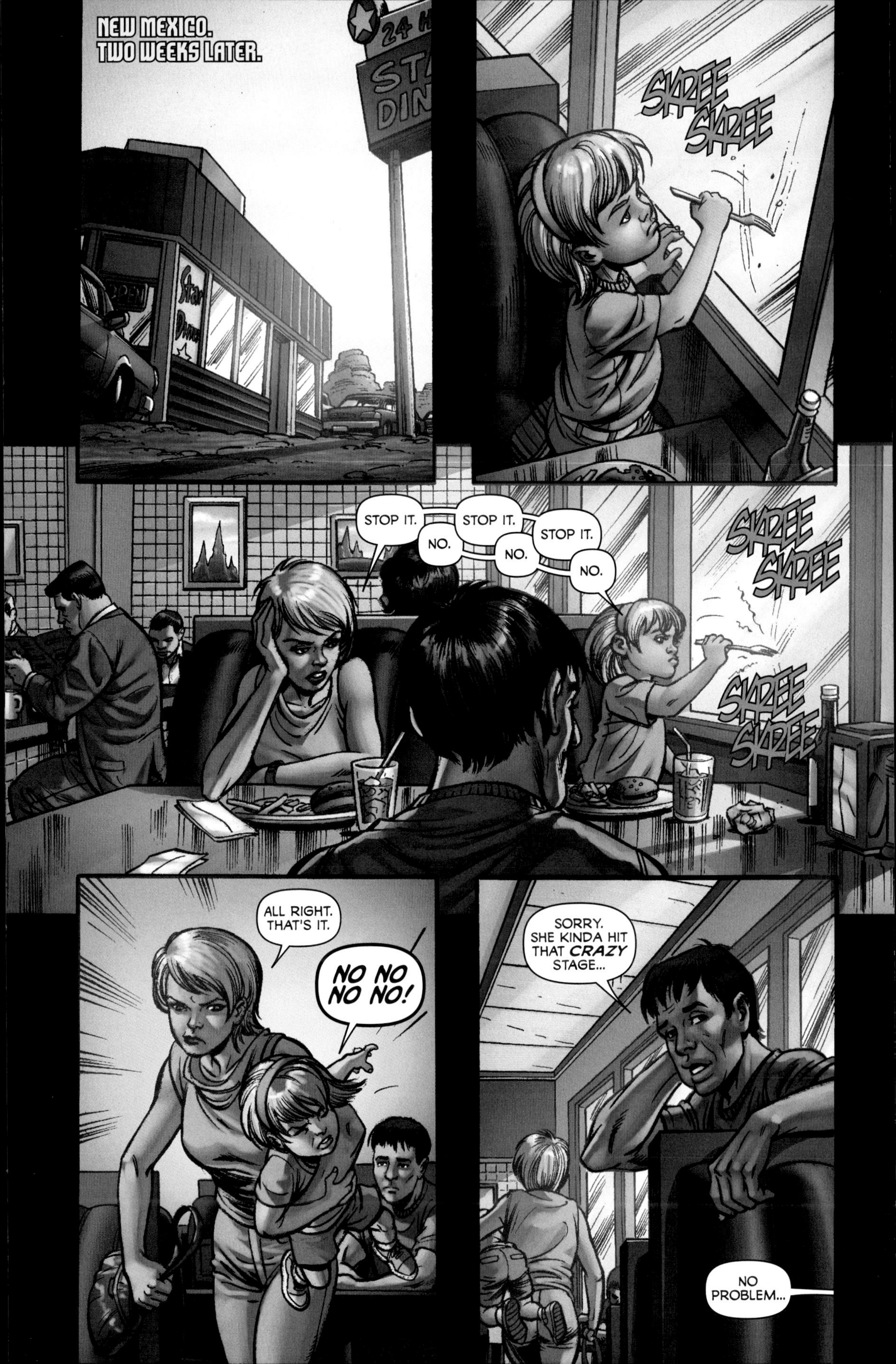
NEW MEXICO.
TWO WEEKS LATER.
SKREE SKREE
STOP IT.
NO.
STOP IT.
NO.
STOP IT.
NO.
SKREE SKREE
SKREE SKREE
ALL RIGHT. THAT'S IT.
NO NO NO NO!
SORRY. SHE KINDA HIT THAT CRAZY STAGE...
NO PROBLEM...

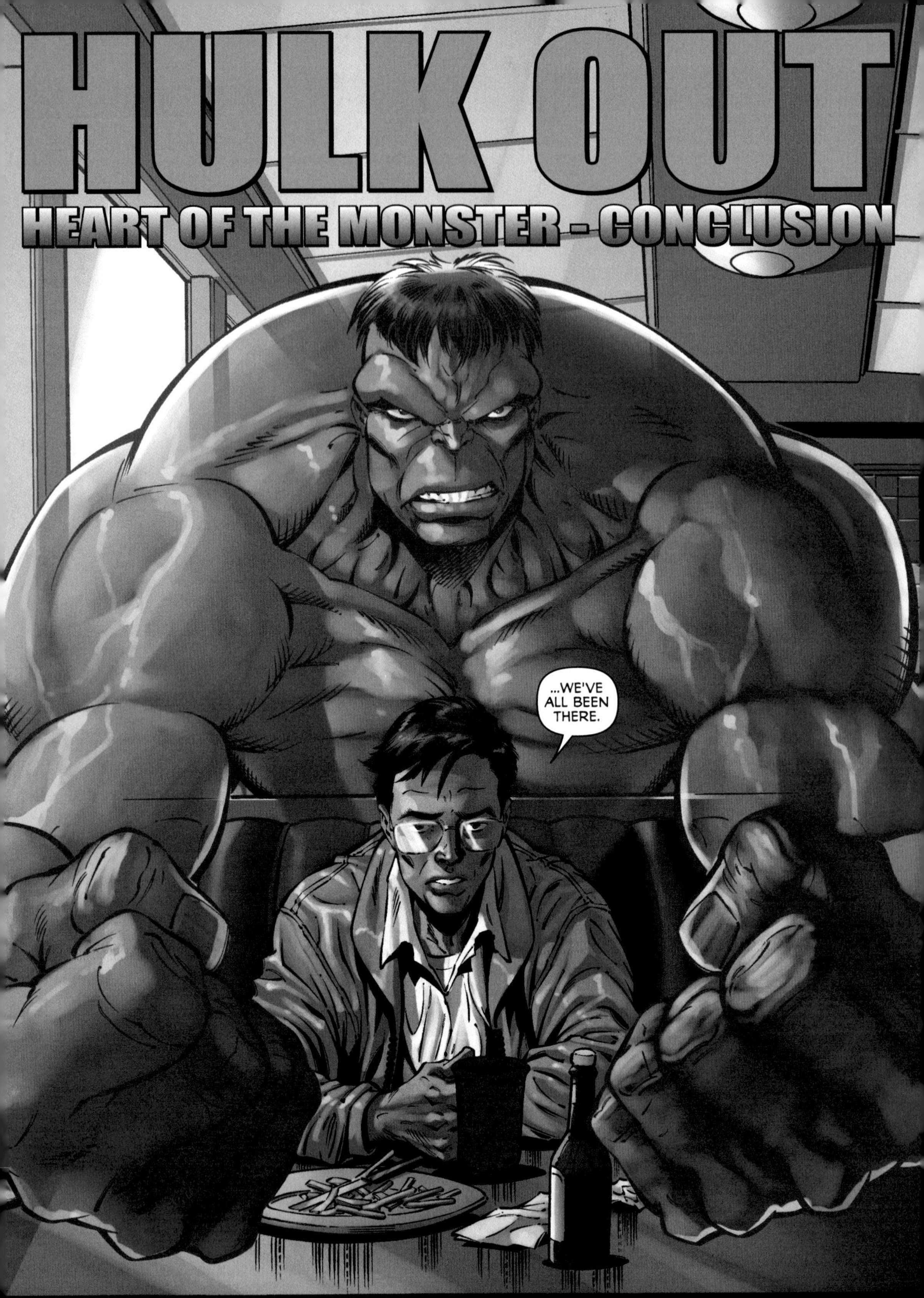
HULK OUT
HEART OF THE MONSTER - CONCLUSION
...WE'VE ALL BEEN THERE.

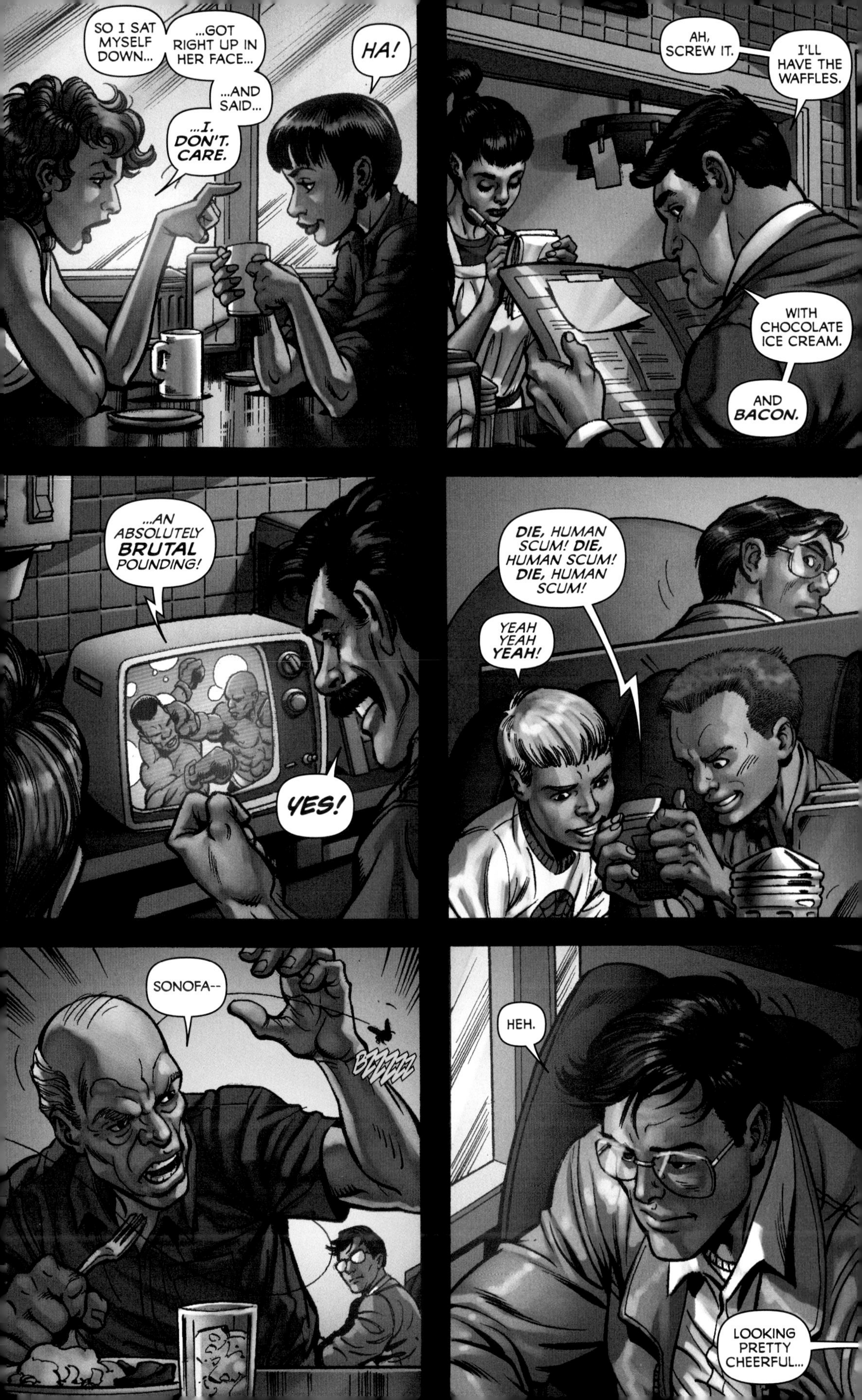
SO I SAT MYSELF DOWN...
...GOT RIGHT UP IN HER FACE...
...AND SAID...
...I. DON'T. CARE.
HA!
AH, SCREW IT.
I'LL HAVE THE WAFFLES.
WITH CHOCOLATE ICE CREAM.
AND BACON.
...AN ABSOLUTELY BRUTAL POUNDING!
YES!
DIE, HUMAN SCUM! DIE, HUMAN SCUM! DIE, HUMAN SCUM!
YEAH YEAH YEAH!
SONOFA--
BZZZZ
HEH.
LOOKING PRETTY CHEERFUL...

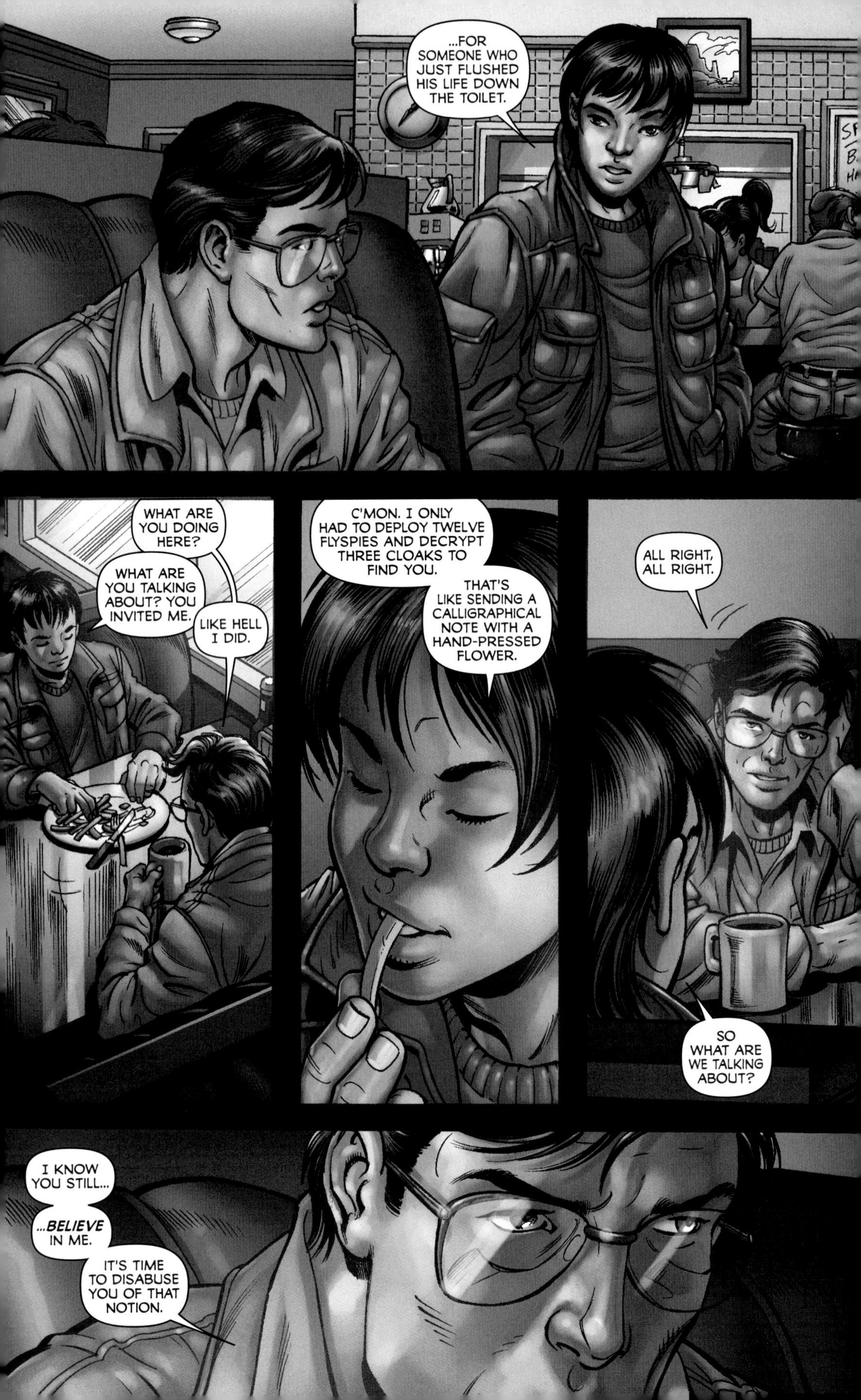
...FOR SOMEONE WHO JUST FLUSHED HIS LIFE DOWN THE TOILET.
WHAT ARE YOU DOING HERE?
WHAT ARE YOU TALKING ABOUT? YOU INVITED ME.
LIKE HELL I DID.
C'MON. I ONLY HAD TO DEPLOY TWELVE FLYSPIES AND DECRYPT THREE CLOAKS TO FIND YOU.
THAT'S LIKE SENDING A CALLIGRAPHICAL NOTE WITH A HAND-PRESSED FLOWER.
ALL RIGHT, ALL RIGHT.
SO WHAT ARE WE TALKING ABOUT?
I KNOW YOU STILL...
...*BELIEVE* IN ME.
IT'S TIME TO DISABUSE YOU OF THAT NOTION.

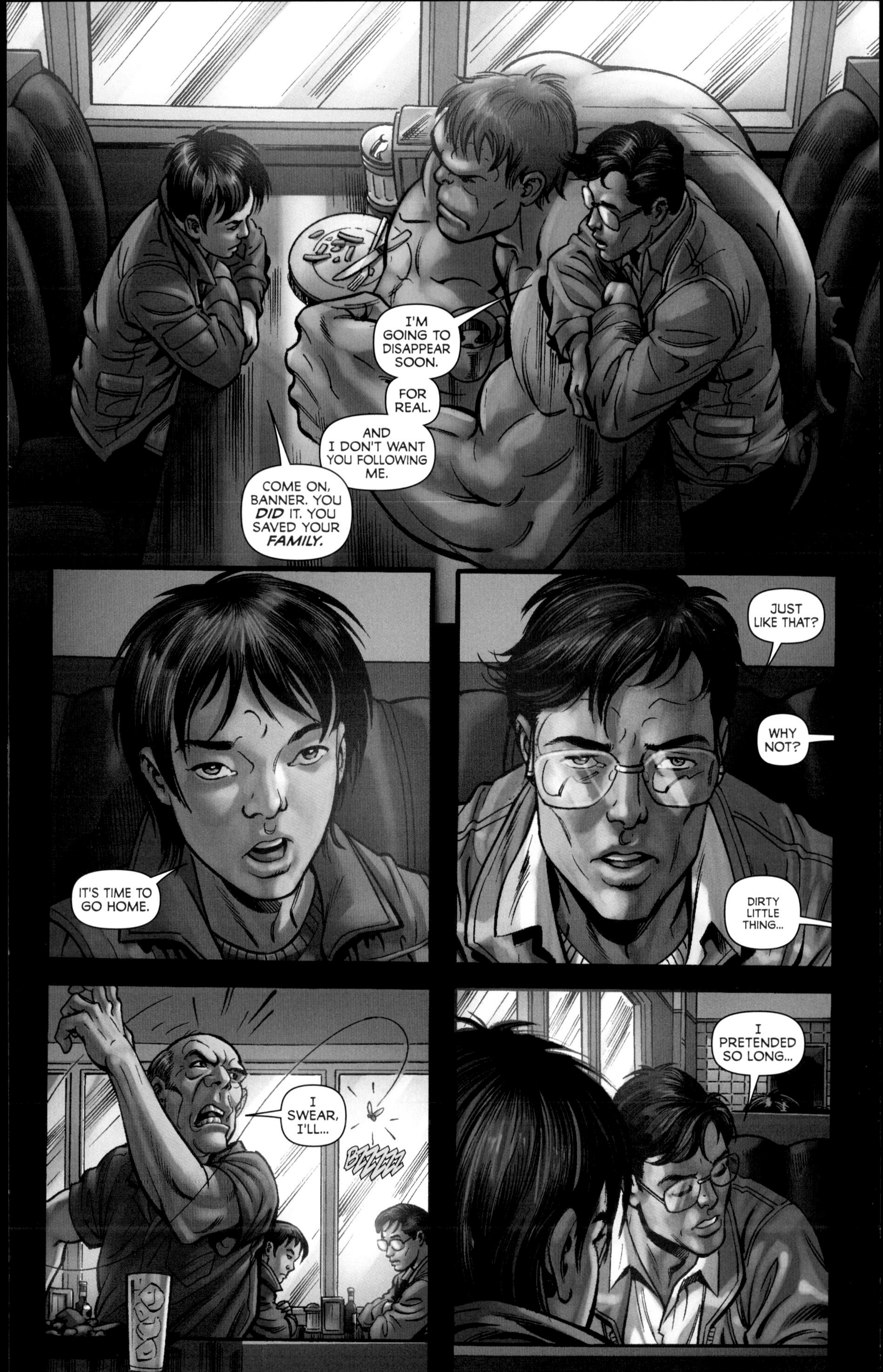
I'M GOING TO DISAPPEAR SOON.
FOR REAL.
AND I DON'T WANT YOU FOLLOWING ME.
COME ON, BANNER. YOU *DID* IT. YOU SAVED YOUR *FAMILY.*
IT'S TIME TO GO HOME.
JUST LIKE THAT?
WHY NOT?
DIRTY LITTLE THING...
I SWEAR, I'LL...
BZZZZ
I PRETENDED SO LONG...

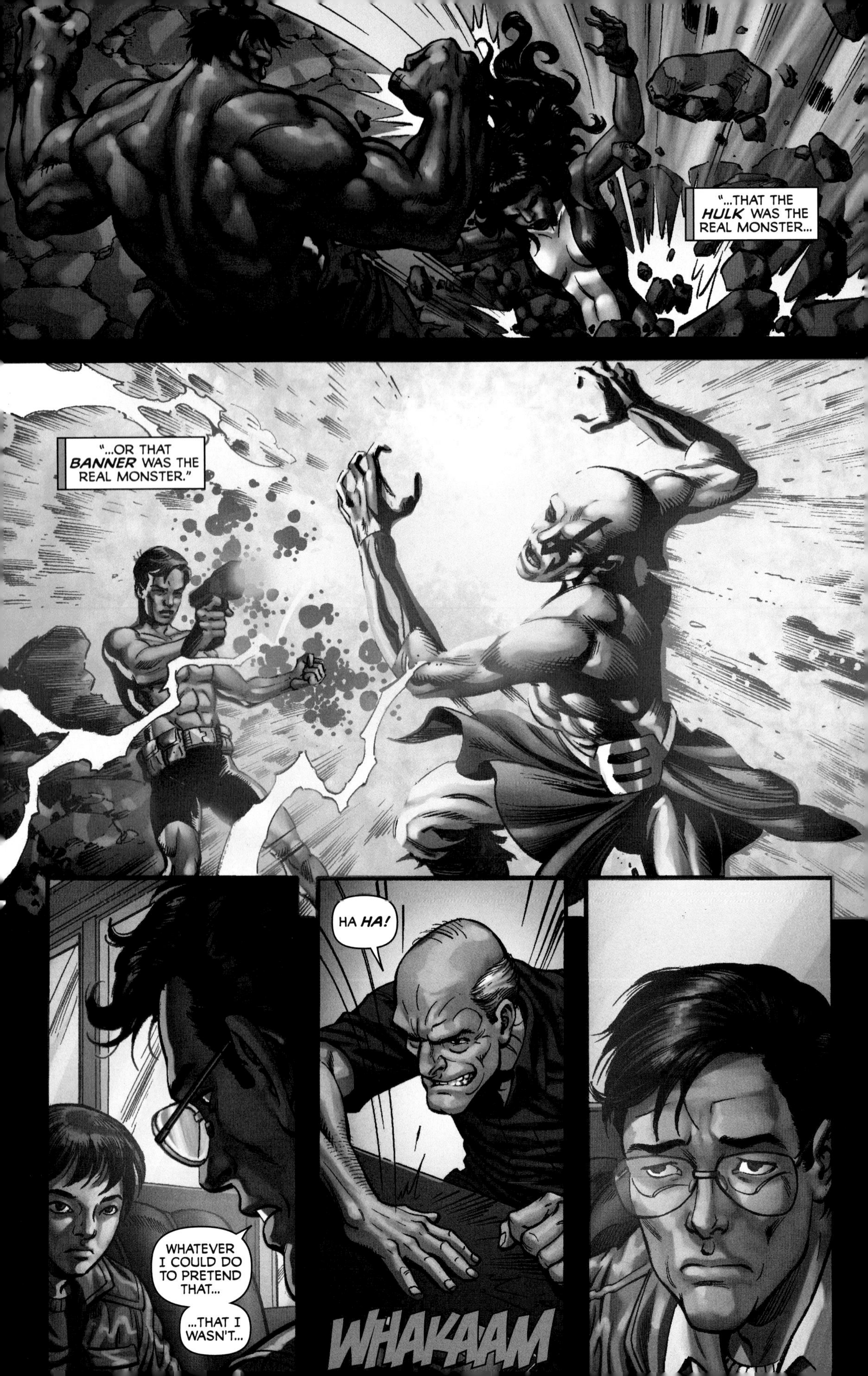
"...THAT THE HULK WAS THE REAL MONSTER...
"...OR THAT BANNER WAS THE REAL MONSTER."
WHATEVER I COULD DO TO PRETEND THAT...
...THAT I WASN'T...
HA HA!
WHAKAAM

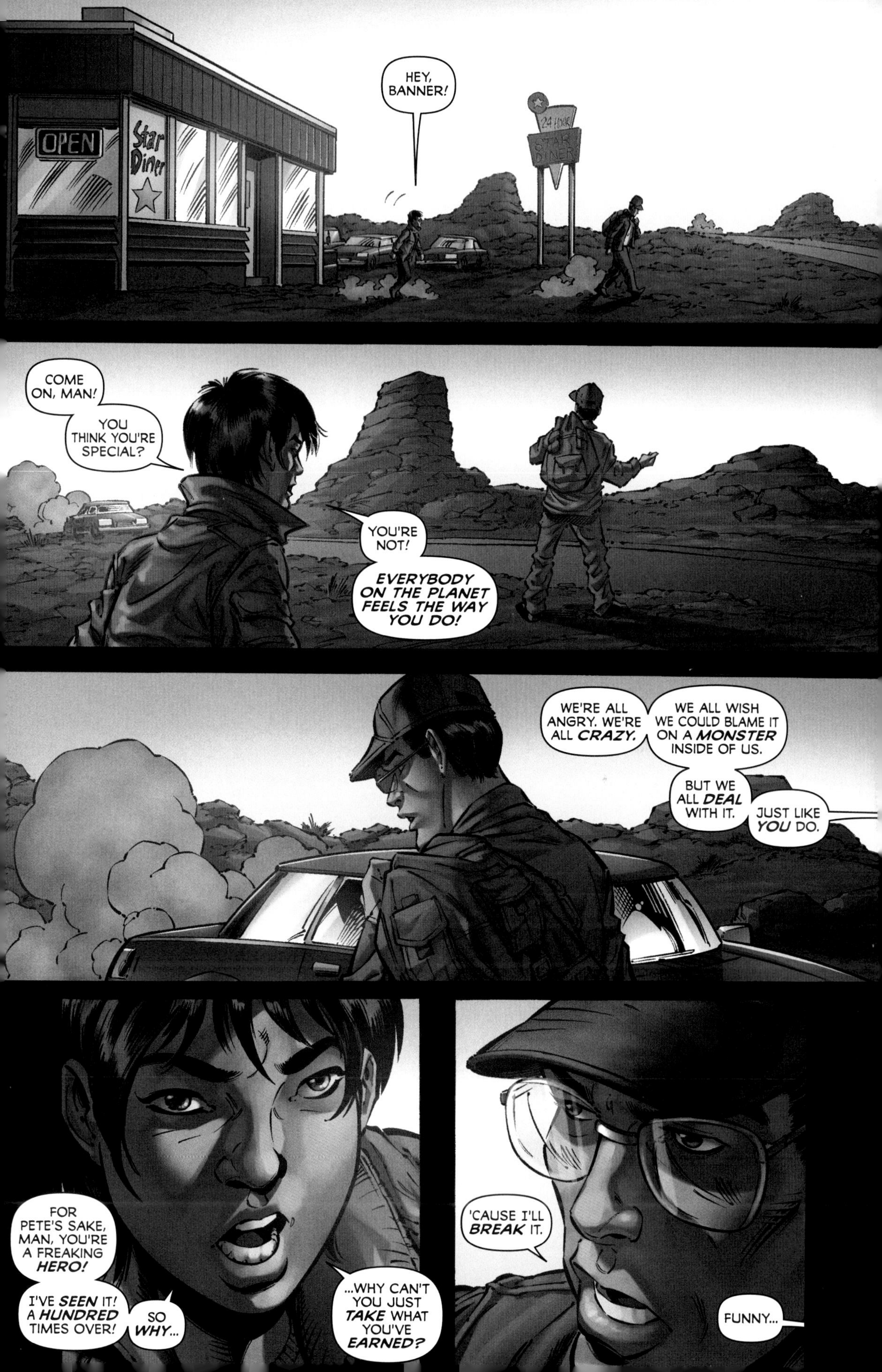
HEY, BANNER!
COME ON, MAN!
YOU THINK YOU'RE SPECIAL?
YOU'RE NOT!
EVERYBODY ON THE PLANET FEELS THE WAY YOU DO!
WE'RE ALL ANGRY. WE'RE ALL CRAZY.
WE ALL WISH WE COULD BLAME IT ON A MONSTER INSIDE OF US.
BUT WE ALL DEAL WITH IT.
JUST LIKE YOU DO.
FOR PETE'S SAKE, MAN, YOU'RE A FREAKING HERO!
I'VE SEEN IT! A HUNDRED TIMES OVER!
SO WHY...
...WHY CAN'T YOU JUST TAKE WHAT YOU'VE EARNED?
FUNNY...
'CAUSE I'LL BREAK IT.

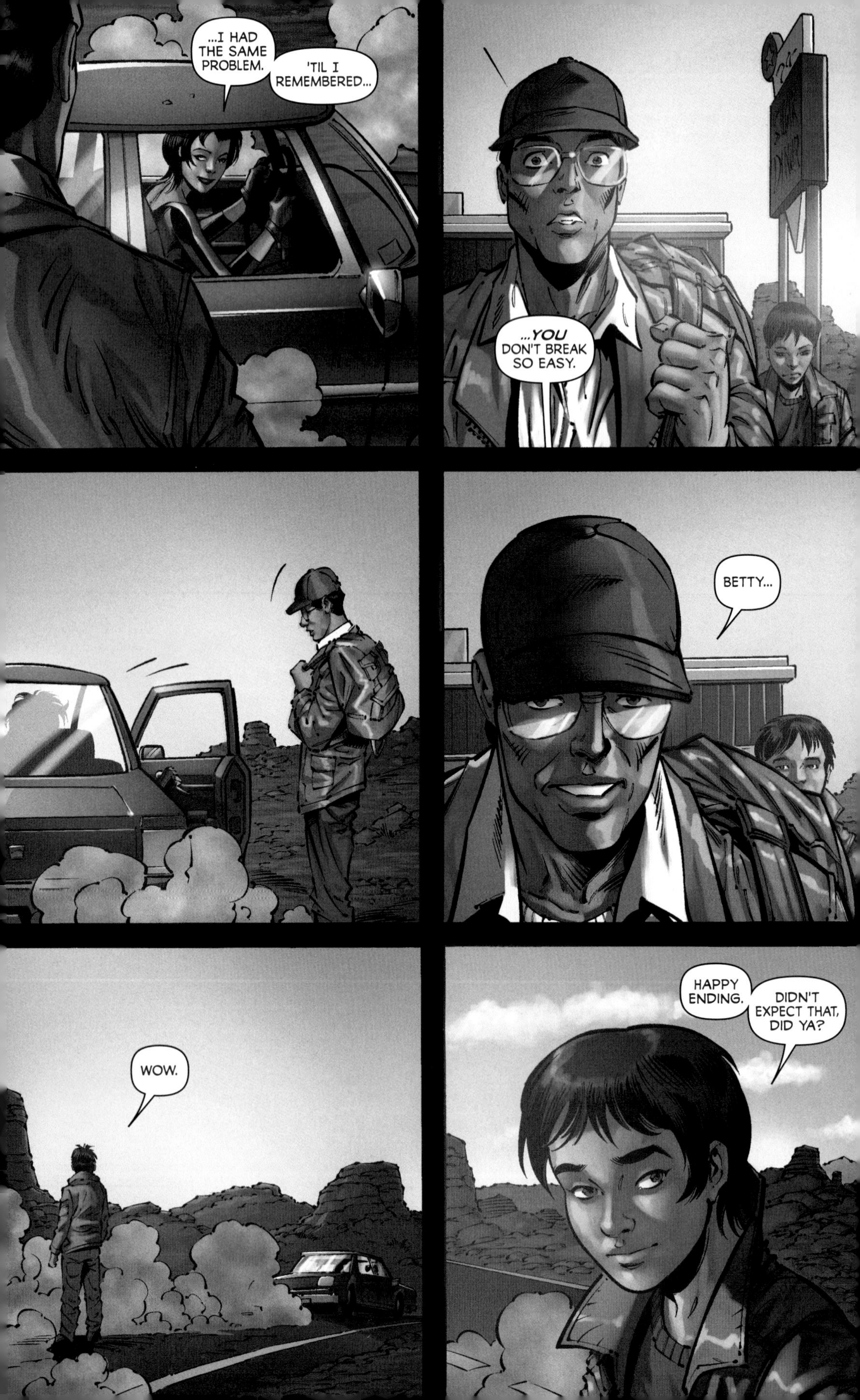
...I HAD THE SAME PROBLEM.
'TIL I REMEMBERED...
...YOU DON'T BREAK SO EASY.
BETTY...
WOW.
HAPPY ENDING.
DIDN'T EXPECT THAT, DID YA?

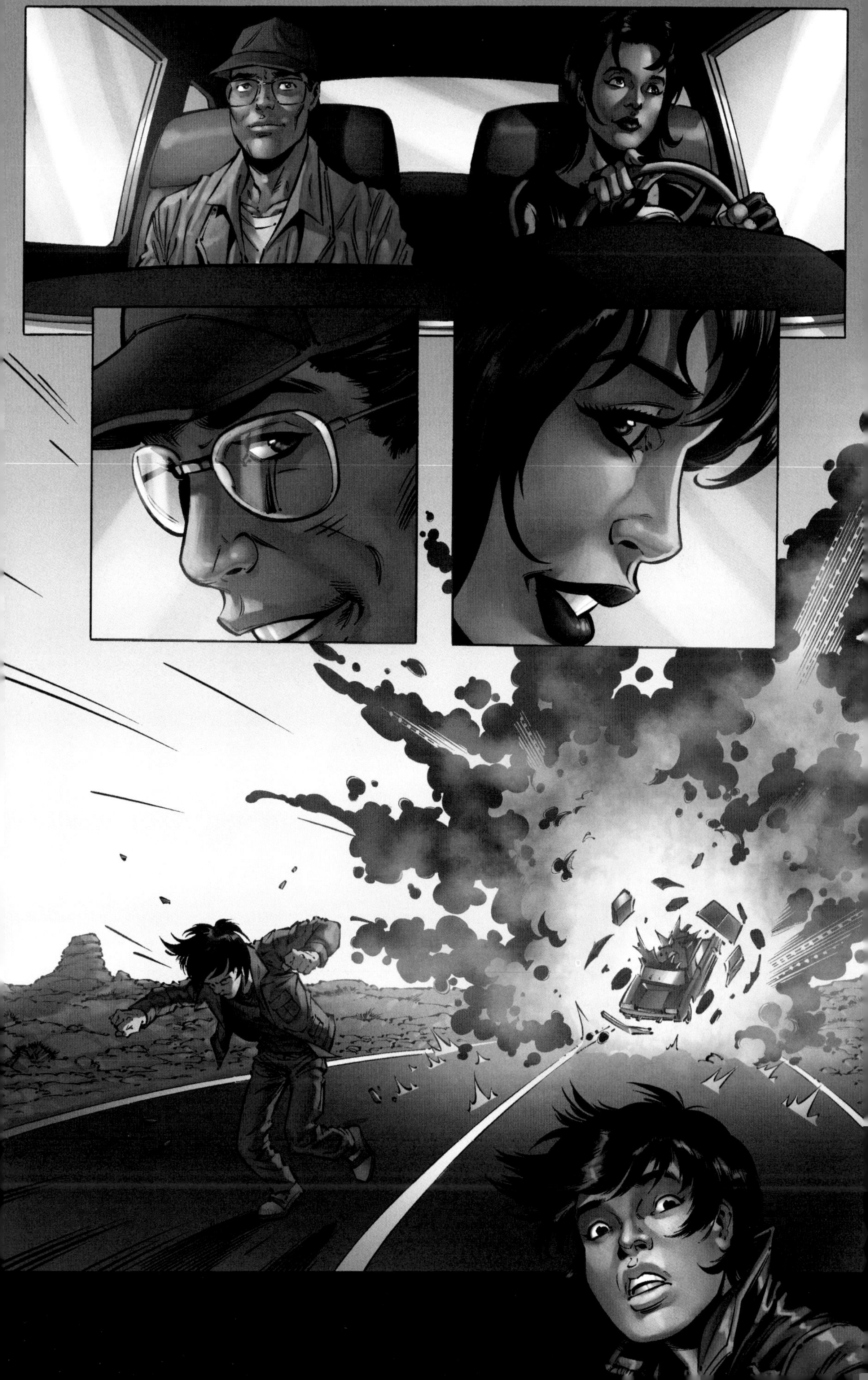

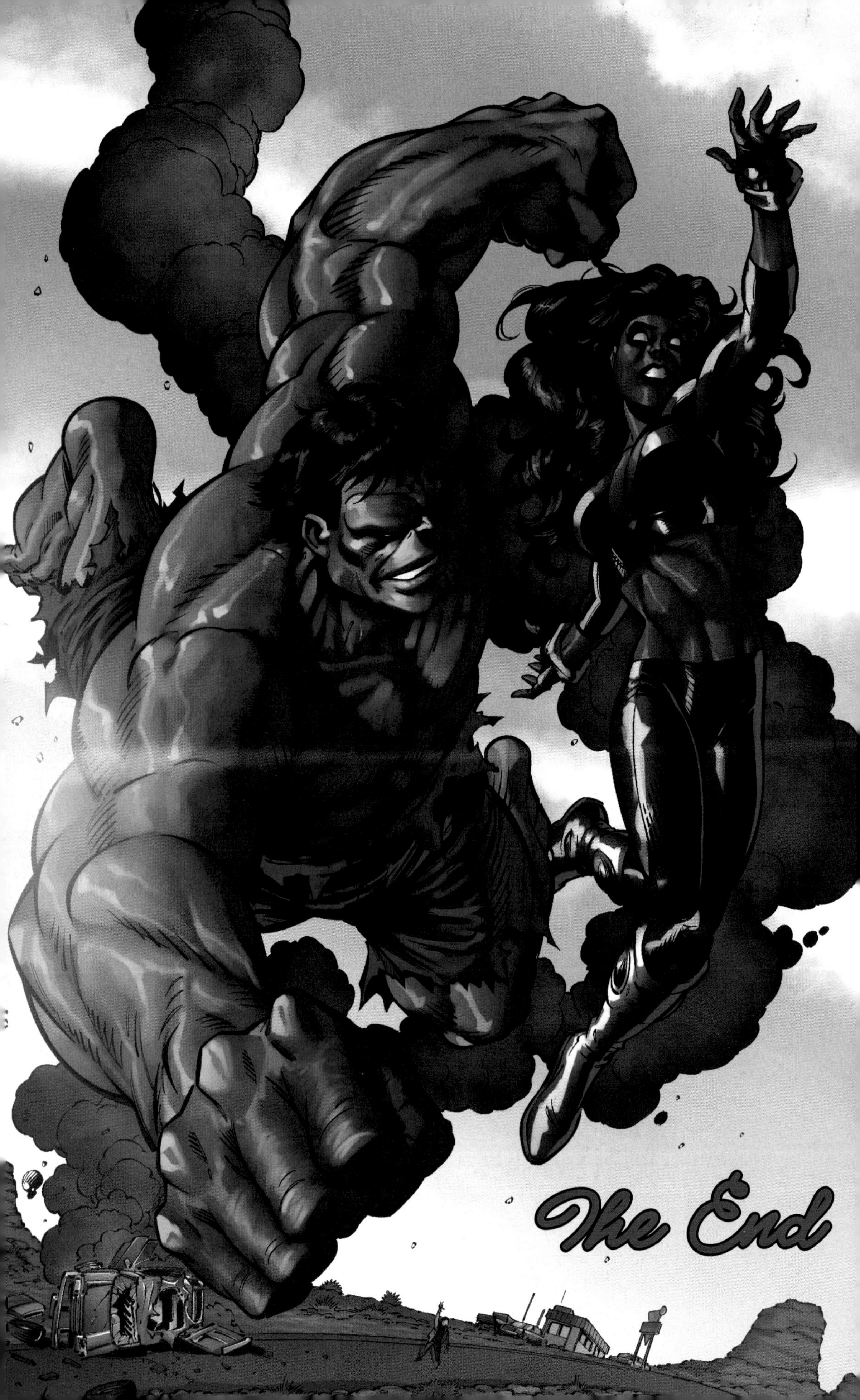
The End

When I started at Marvel seven years ago, the Hulk was the character I most desperately wanted to write. I'd read and reread his origin story as a kid and absolutely loved the Bixby/Ferrigno television show, which I jokingly but truthfully refer to as my introduction to the literary concept of tragedy. Even though (or maybe because!) I'm about as physically non-confrontational as you can get, I was completely enthralled by this furious hero who always paid the price, no matter how justified his rage might be.

So many thanks to all of the editors and assistant editors at Marvel who have let me and helped me take the Hulk on such a huge journey over the past five and a half years, especially Mark Paniccia, my number one partner in smash; to all the readers and retailers who have been so amazingly supportive; to all of my artistic collaborators who have brought so much passion, emotion, and power to each and every page; to all of the letterers who have put up with all my tweaking; to the Loeb/Parker braintrust; to the Hulk's creators, Stan Lee and Jack Kirby; and to all of the Hulk writers who over the years have created the history that's immeasurably enriched the stories I've been able to tell.

I'd like to especially sing the praises of Bill Mantlo, who wrote so many of my favorite Hulk stories and so movingly explored Bruce Banner's relationship with his father and mother, critical emotional storytelling that the great Peter David expanded on and that played a huge role in the climactic Skaar/Hulk confrontation in my own run.

Tragically, Bill Mantlo suffered traumatic brain injury in a hit-and-run car accident in the 1990s. I encourage anyone who has enjoyed my run on these books to look into Mantlo and his work on the Hulk. Joy and inspiration await you.

All the best and see you in the funnybooks,

Greg Pak
New York, 2011

FOR BILL MANTLO

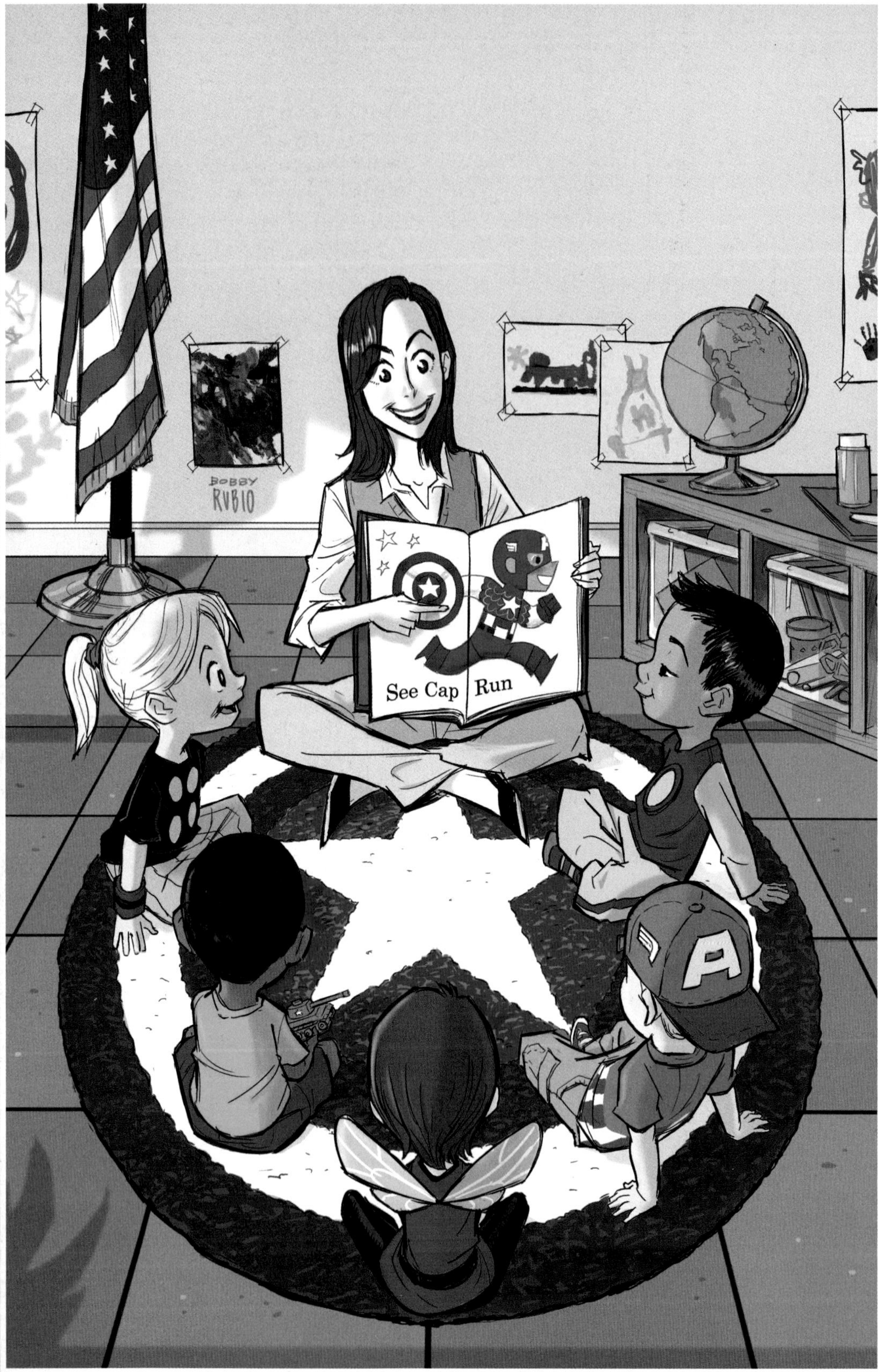
BOBBY RUBIO
See Cap
Run

(632 I AM CAPTAIN AMERICA VARIANT)
BY BOBBY RUBIO

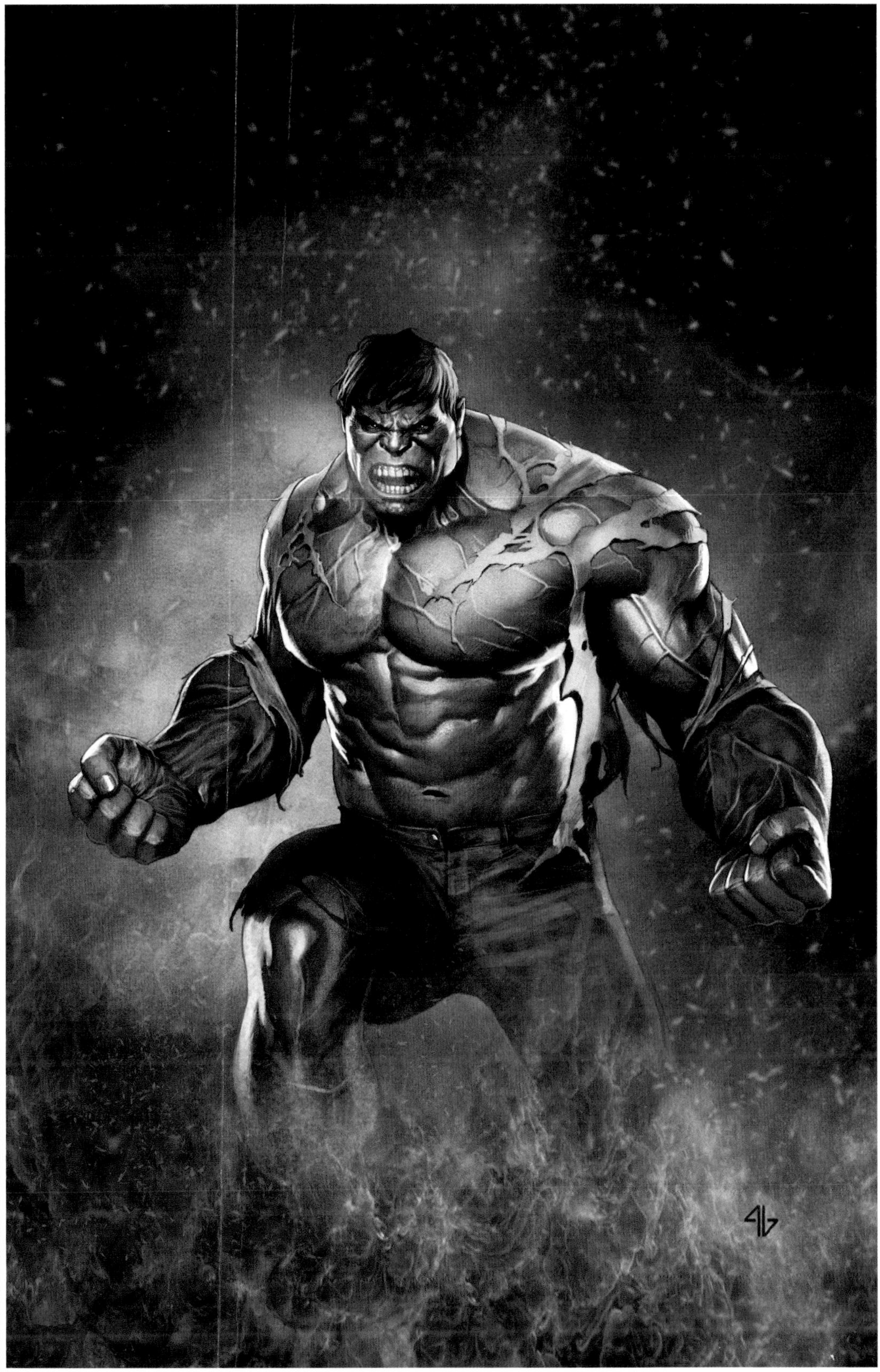

(635 VARIANT)
BY ADI GRANOV

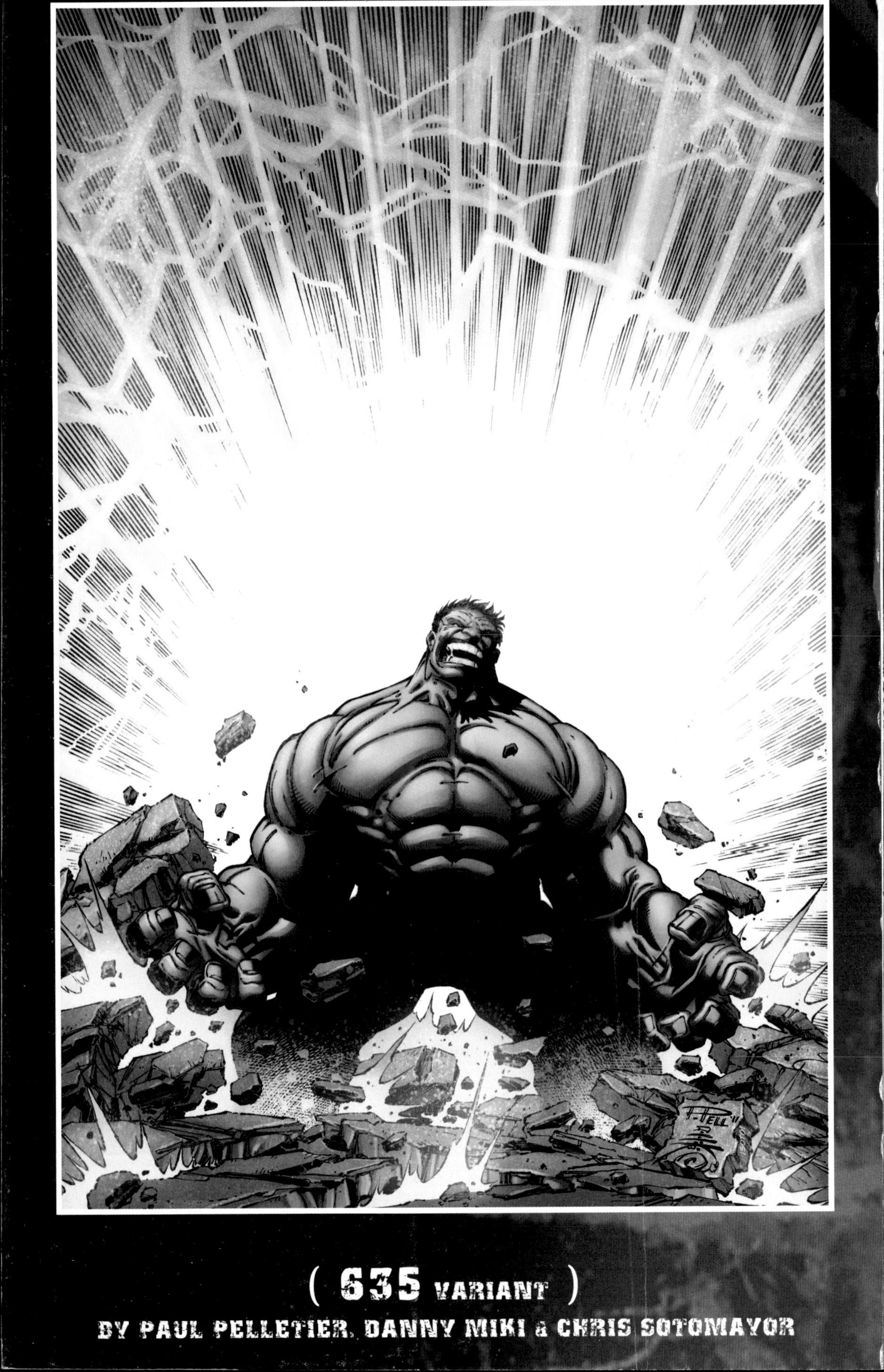

(635 VARIANT)

BY PAUL PELLETIER, DANNY MIKI & CHRIS SOTOMAYOR